Too Many Heroes, Volume 1

Allan D. Lougheed

Too Many Heroes, Volume 1

The Translated War Diaries
of the
1er and 3e Bataillons de Marche d'Infanterie Légère d'Afrique,
From Mobilization to 2nd Ypres

To Alan Holmes

Translation and Introduction by Allan Lougheed

With all my thanks!
Allan Lougheed

Published by Allan Lougheed

ISBN-13: 978-1477467626

Book design by Kathryn Paulin-Lougheed

Front Cover Photo Credit: Allan Lougheed
Back Cover Photo Credit: Musée de l'Armée/Dist. RMN-Grand Palais / Art Resource, NY

For Flora

Contents

Notes on Translation

The reader should take note of some editorial decisions that were made in the preparation of this series. The original documents were journal entries made during the stress of battlefield conditions and there are instances of incomplete sentences and other grammatical or spelling errors. In an effort to remain faithful to the character of the original journals I have limited correcting or anglicizing the grammar and sentence structure. Despite my best efforts, the orthography of proper names cannot be guaranteed. There is no consistency in the spelling of proper names in the original diaries and I have maintained spellings as they appear in the original. It is customary to use [sic] to indicate a known spelling error but I have not done so in order to be as unobtrusive as possible.Occasionally, the diarists refer to documents or sketches that were unavailable in the online journal, and unfortunately I was unable to include those.

It is also customary to italicise foreign words, but where these appear within quotations they are not italicized unless they appear that way in the original. I frequently chose not to translate French words or phrases that are also used in English, such as *sang-froid*. The proper names of French units have been left in French. French ordinal numbers have been retained for French unit designations, for example, *3ᵉ Bataillon*. Those of other nations have been anglicized. No italics have been used for foreign words within the translated war diaries unless they appear that way in the original. As most journals were hand-written (some presented in future volumes were originally type-written), that will rarely be the case.

In this series, I have used square brackets to indicate any text that is not found in the original diary. On occasions where a word from the original text could not be deciphered, I have inserted the word [illegible] in square brackets. Readers should be aware that occasionally the original diarist was forced to transcribe a word as illegible, normally because of an illegible signature. In those cases the word illegible will appear without square brackets. On rarer occasions where an entire passage was illegible or could not be translated, I have inserted ellipses in square brackets like this: [...]. Once again, ellipses are occasionally found in the original diary and those will appear without square brackets. Square brackets have also been used to differentiate between footnotes inserted by myself and those inserted by the original diarist.

Forward

On 22 April 1915, near the Belgian town of Ypres, French soldiers fighting an already terrible war faced an entirely new horror. At 5:00 o'clock in the evening, an enormous cloud of chlorine gas – six kilometres wide – issued from the German trenches across No Man's Land. When the gas cloud swept through the French lines, two French divisions – the *87ᵉ Division Territoriale* and the *45ᵉ Division d'Infanterie* – retreated precipitously, with advancing Germans following closely. Within minutes, French soldiers were seen staggering back from the front lines, clutching their throats, gasping for air, blood streaming from their noses. Canadian soldiers holding trenches to the right of the French lines looked on in disbelief and it fell initially to the 1st Canadian Division to plug the breach in the front line. The Second Battle of Ypres raged on for several weeks afterward, as soldiers from Britain, Canada, France and India desperately sought to eject the Germans from the ground they had taken. Canadian and British eye-witnesses to the French retreat have left numerous written accounts and, consequently, historians have tended to tell the story from a Canadian point of view. Yet, it was the French soldiers who bore the initial brunt of the attack, and they too were called upon to counter-attack and stave off what looked like the collapse of the front line and the possibility of total defeat. This series, which presents the war diaries of French battalions and regiments at the Second Battle of Ypres in translation, came from my own efforts to understand those men. It is my contention that the two French divisions holding the north face of the Ypres salient have been misunderstood by historians and unnecessarily maligned for retreating.

What are the war diaries? Each diary translated in this series is an official unit record kept during the war, called a *Journal de Marche et Operations* (JMO). Each JMO was kept by an officer of that unit and the contents vary considerably from unit to unit. Along with the translated diaries, I will provide an introduction to the historical background for each of the battalions or regiments to be covered. The diaries in this series are those of units present at the Second Battle of Ypres and they cover the period from mobilization at the start of the First World War to the Second Battle of Ypres and its aftermath. The *45ᵉ Division* was an active division of the French army colloquially known as the *45ᵉ Division Algérienne* and its troops were drawn from the garrisons of the French North African colonies. The *87ᵉ Division Territoriale* was drawn from older men, aged 34 to 41, who were recalled into active service from civilian life upon mobilization in 1914. My examination of the French soldiers at the Second Battle of Ypres will touch upon a number of themes that will be developed as this series progresses.

One theme will consider the human factor. The individual soldier of the First World War recedes quickly against the industrial scale of the forces involved. The soldiers of the North African regiments wore an elaborate uniform, intended to help instill the *élan* needed for the fanatical bayonet charge. Yet there was an ordinary human being beneath each those uniforms, with his own fears and motivations. Official records do tend to dwell on the contributions of officers rather than the ordinary soldier. Yet, the diaries of the *Infanterie légère d'Afrique* are exceptional for the vignettes of individual soldiers that they sometimes provide. Indeed, I think the diaries reflect a profound respect that the officers and men of the *Infanterie Légère d'Afrique* held towards each other. It is not easy to recapture the personal experience of the ordinary soldier of the French army, but it is hoped that this series will leave readers with a better ability to appreciate them for the human beings they were.

The question of how proficient these soldiers were must inevitably come up, because it is a subject that has been raised since the first books to be published about the Second Battle of Ypres. Many historians have asserted that the Ypres Salient was being defended by second-rate soldiers when the chlorine gas cloud struck. Yet, the French themselves held the soldiers of the *45e Division* to be among their very best. The soldiers of the *Infanterie Légère d'Afrique* were acknowledged to be brave even if, as ex-convicts, they were sometimes viewed with suspicion by the rest of the army. The *Zouaves* and *Tirailleurs* were held to be the very embodiment of *élan*; they were called the bravest of the brave. Were they? What about the *87e Division Territoriale*, men well past the best years of their life? They really were meant to be the army's second line of defense, so how should they be regarded? These are questions best answered by their own combat record, which includes the months of fighting prior to Second Ypres.

Moreover, in a war of industrial scale, a soldier was really only as good as the doctrine he was trained to follow. The battle doctrine of both the German and French armies in August 1914 led to a human disaster. Within 48 hours, roughly from 20 to 22 August 1914, close to a million soldiers on each side and the generals who led them had their first (and many cases their last) experience of real battle. Things did not go as planned for anyone, and over the next four years theoretical doctrine would be adapted to meet reality. While the popular image of the French army of the First World War is that of reckless and futile bayonet charges – and these certainly did occur in the opening battles of the war – it is amazing how quickly tactics evolved, which is not to say that battlefield experiments were always successful. The war diaries chronicle some superb examples of the tactical changes that took place in the first nine months of the war; they also reveal how some out-dated notions were stubbornly adhered to.

The use of poison gas was an extreme development of tactical experimentation that must have shattered any lingering illusions of chivalry. The shock of its first battlefield use threw the defenders of the Ypres salient into disorder and allowed the Germans to seize several kilometres of ground in a few hours. But war is chaos, and how defenders respond to catastrophe is just as important as the planning that goes into an attack. The war diaries reveal that the *45e Division* had previously inflicted similar defeats on the Germans by other means that were arguably just as cruel, and that they knew the dangers of unplanned counter-attacks. What then should we make of the hasty and fruitless attempts by French forces to take back the lost ground? Did the inability to push the Germans back represent a failure on the part of the troops, or did the generals make a bad situation even worse? General Quiquandon, who commanded the French divisions at Ypres, was an experienced veteran and should have known better than to counter-attack without sound preparation. His actions at Second Ypres deserve to be examined. On occasion, there will be opportunity to include British generals in this discussion of course, but this series will focus on the role of the French.

While General Quiquandon made decisions based on reports coming into his command post behind the lines, officers on the front lines dealt with the immediate realities of the situations they found themselves in. Despite the vast scale of the war, the talents of a junior officer could still make a crucial contribution to success and to the odds of survival for the men they led. The war diaries translated in this series provide a view of the war at the small unit level; the section, platoon, company and battalion. A lieutenant of the French Army had as many as 125 men in the platoon under his command. Casualties among officers were high and units were frequently commanded by officers of lower rank than what the position called for, with lieutenants leading companies and captains commanding battalions when necessary. The junior officer bore a tremendous burden of responsibility. The story that emerges in the war diaries from the day-to-day chronicle of events and after-action reports is told from the perspective of junior officers and it is a compelling one. For these reasons, the role of junior officers will also figure prominently.

Ultimately, it is also hoped that this series will encourage historians to take a fresh approach to the way the story of the Second Battle of Ypres is told. The French sources available for Second Ypres deserve attention, and I hope that English translations will furnish historians with a useful research tool. Some readers will be disappointed that these volumes do not provide a more coherent narrative. I do intend to provide such a narrative as a concluding volume to this series. In the meantime, I want to make these sources available to historians and casual readers alike.

Introduction

"There are only a few books written on the Joyeux in existence," wrote Pierre Mac Orlan in 1933. "It is only with great difficulty that one finds documents on the origin and history of the five battalions of light infantry... Zéphyrs, Légères, Agiles and Joyeux disappear year by year without leaving a trace."[1] I can attest to that. When I set out to research the French soldiers who bore the brunt of the first chlorine gas attack on 22 April 1915, I found very little written in English and obtaining French sources can be challenging in North America. On 22 April 1915, the *1er Bataillon de Marche d'Infanterie Légère d'Afrique* (1st Field Battalion African Light Infantry) was swallowed up in the chlorine gas cloud and the rapid German breakthrough; few eyewitnesses to their final moments survived. There have been no memoirs left from private soldiers of the *Infanterie Légère d'Afrique* from prior to the 1950s. For the most part, their story has been told by outside observers. While the translated *Journaux de Marche et Operations* (JMO) of the *1er* and *3e Bataillons de Marche*, which are presented in this volume, are a window into the combat service of these men, we need a better understanding of their history to place it in context. In the *Journaux*, we read about two battalions with a spectacular combat record, yet when we read all of the secondary literature surrounding those battalions, we read of street hooligans and delinquents. In order to understand those men we need to reconcile two divergent pictures of them, but how? With only the accounts of outside observers to go on, the question is a difficult one, and one that is likely impossible to answer with certainty. The volumes in this series set out to demonstrate that the French soldiers at the Second Battle of Ypres were not second-rate troops, as they are they are often characterized in historical accounts. The men of the *1er* and *3e Bataillons de Marche* were easy to underestimate because of their criminal past, but they were an effective corps that had earned a reputation for bravery. The battalions sent to the front in 1914 were comprised of hand-picked men determined to carry on a heroic tradition, but the Great War would make far too many heroes.

The *Bataillons d'Infanterie Légère d'Afrique* were a corps comprised almost entirely of men who had spent time in prison, and a hard existence in North Africa was intended to reform them and make them worthy to be reintegrated into the French army and the rest of society. The soldiers who served in the *Infanterie Légère d'Afrique* were officially known as *chasseurs d'Infanterie Légère d'Afrique*. Perhaps because the official title was a mouthful, both the battalions and the men themselves acquired a plethora of nicknames. The battalions were often referred to as the *Bataillons d'Afrique*, which was shortened to the *Bat' d'Af* or even simply the *Bataillons*. The *1er* and *2e Bataillons d'Afrique* were raised in 1832, with the *3e* formed in 1833. For much of their early history, the men of the *1er Bataillon* were known as *Flore*, those of the *2e* were called *Zéphyrs*, and men of the *3e* were called *Chardonnerets*.[2] By the time the *4e* and *5e Bataillons* were created in 1889, nicknames for the individual battalions seem to have fallen out of fashion, as the new battalions do not seem to have acquired nicknames of their own. The names *Flore* and *Chardonnerets* had fallen out of use towards the twentieth century, and the *chasseurs* of the *Bat' d'Af* were being called *Zéphyrs*, *Bataillonnaires*, *Légères*, and *Joyeux*. By 1914, *Joyeux* – the happy ones - was the most prominent nickname, and the one that found resonance in French popular culture. "We called ourselves calots violets,* (the colour of discipline it seems) and paradoxically, we also called ourselves 'les Joyeux,'" wrote Paul Deschaume, who served in the 1950s. "It's bizarre. I didn't feel like laughing."[3]

The date of origin is not known, but the name *Joyeux* was used in print as early as 1863, in an essay on the *Bat' d'Af* by Antoine Camus entitled *Les Bohêmes du Drapeau*.[4] The name *Joyeux* is believed to have originated in the words sung to the bugle call of the *Bat' d'Af*, which I will leave in the original French as there is no direct English translation:[5]

Joyeux fais ton fourbi
Pas vu, pas pris,
Mais vu, rousti
Bat' d'Af![6]

The song conveys some complicated ideas with some very short words. *Fourbi* is a double entendre; it can mean a soldier's kit (everything that needs to be polished), or it can mean a scam or theft. *Pas vu, pas pris* can be translated as "not seen, not caught" – or in other words, they only catch him if they see him. *Mais vu, rousti* means "but seen, busted"; since he was seen, he did get caught, and he is going to end up in the *Bat' d'Af* ! There was, perhaps, both irony and an element of gallows humour in calling ex-convicts *Joyeux*. According to Louis Garros:

> From those long and exhausting columns in the desert, the "bataillons" returned dead-beat, clothing in scraps, feet bare or nearly. But one saw them passing hearty jokes between their lips. Joyeux in those tattered rags, and their chums in the barracks, named them "naked zephyrs."[7]

The *Joyeux* had a reputation for pranks, but probably no more so than any other group of young soldiers thrown together under trying circumstances. Albert Londres, a prominent French journalist of the early 20th century, related the story of a near mutiny in the years following World War One by a platoon of *Joyeux* who were armed and on their way to their Captain to complain about their Sergeant. On their way, they discovered the wine-ration casks had been left out in the sun. Well, they couldn't let it spoil… and in the process of drinking themselves into a stupor the original intent of their visit to the Captain

---

* *Calots violets* translates as "purple caps." After the Second World War the uniform of the *Bat' d'Af* featured a purple cap.

was evidently forgotten.[8] But not everyone found their devil-may-care attitude amusing. "The one called 'the Joyeux' is the least cheerful companion one can meet in the military," wrote Dr. Louis Combe, a psychologist who studied the Joyeux in 1912.[9] It must be said however, the *Joyeux* probably did not always respond pleasantly to inquisitive outsiders. Combe admitted the difficulties he had in studying them. "To penetrate the psychology of a chasseur," wrote Combe, "it is not enough to question and observe him; when he feels he is under examination he plays a role, because he is by nature a liar and a poser."[10] With an attitude like that, it is little wonder that Combe had a difficult time gaining the trust of the *Joyeux*. While we have to expect that the existence of the *Joyeux* was brutal at times, we should not assume that their spirit was entirely broken. One wonders if they ever revealed their true side to outsiders, and we are left with only fragmentary glimpses into their world.

Life in the disciplinary system of the French army was compared to the three volumes of Dante's *Divine Comedy*: the *Inferno*, *Purgatorio* and *Paradisio*. A grim *esprit de corps* was vital to cope with the hell on earth in which the *Joyeux* found themselves. The *Infanterie Légère d'Afrique* was the purgatory they had to pass through before returning to the paradise of France. Discipline was often harsh in the *Bat' d'Af*, but the *Joyeux* had as much, or more, to fear from their environment. The *Joyeux* garrisoned the remote Saharan outposts of French North Africa. On the punishing marches alluded to by Garros in the previous paragraph, *Joyeux* faced heat stroke and dehydration, but the next outpost had to be reached; there was no choice but to push through exhaustion and thirst. Joseph Dimier, who served as a corporal in the *Bat d'Af* in 1920, recalled one *Joyeux* who tattooed *Marche ou Crève* (march or perish) on his feet.[11] Even when not actively on campaign, there was the ever-present danger that fighting could erupt at any moment, the caravan they were escorting could be ambushed, the outpost they held could be attacked. The *Joyeux* were perpetually fighting insurrections against French rule in North Africa. But there is no single experience that can define life in the *Bat d'Af*. Some would have described it as a nightmare, others found a surrogate family. There were harsh and dangerous postings on the edge of the Sahara, and there were reasonably comfortable ones in the coastal towns like Tunis.

♦ ♦ ♦

The *Infanterie Légère d'Afrique* formed part of a larger disciplinary system of the French army; this in turn was part of the larger *Armée d'Afrique* that garrisoned North Africa.[12] It is no accident that the disciplinary corps served in North Africa. After the French Revolution, and the defeat of Napoleon, France eagerly sought to regain its former position as a European power by expanding overseas colonies.[13] Renewed imperialism witnessed expeditions into North Africa in 1830, with the conquest of Algeria. French forces achieved some initial success, but would be faced with several decades of effort consolidating their gains. In truth, dissent was always just below the surface of French rule, and military campaigns were a constant feature of French North Africa.

The French regiments which had conquered Algeria could not be kept there indefinitely, but creating *forces de remplacement* to provide the North African possessions with permanent garrisons proved difficult. There was no lack of manpower, since a system of conscription was already in place. Nevertheless, Republican principles and the requirements of continental defense resulted in laws that forbade deploying soldiers overseas without their consent or special act of legislation.[14] Among the solutions found for this conundrum was conscription of former convicts into special battalions to serve as a garrison force for North Africa (with additional deployments to Asia later on, especially Indo-China). In addition to civilian convicts, the battalions would include solders who had been punished for disciplinary infractions and had not yet finished their term of service, as well as any volunteers who wished to join. They would be easy to keep under guard, since there were few places to which they could escape. They were doing duty that most Frenchmen would have avoided and, moreover, they were not wanted in France. "Which town of France," wrote Deputy Pierre Richard to the Minister of War in 1899 "would be flattered to receive a disciplinary company as a garrison?"[15] Nor did middle-class families want their sons sharing a mess with criminals.[16]

The *Infanterie Légère d'Afrique* was thus one of the oldest elements of a very diverse *Armée d'Afrique*. To meet the military needs of colonial empire, France turned to a mixed force of volunteers, foreigners, and local mercenaries as well as ex-convicts.[17] There were the *Zouave* Regiments, recruited in 1830 from North African mercenaries (which evolved into regiments of conscripted Frenchmen by 1914) who wore an elaborate uniform reminiscent of their North African heritage. There were regiments of *Tirailleurs*, locally recruited African troops with a cadre of French Officers and Non-Commissioned Officers (NCOs). Senegalese, Algerian, Tunisian and Moroccan men were recruited into such regiments of indigenous *Tirailleurs* (the *Zouaves* and *Tiraileurs* will be the focus of future volumes in this series). The *Légion Étrangère*, or Foreign Legion, was first raised from men recruited from outside France in 1832; often they were deserters from other European armies. France also took full advantage of the horse cultures of North Africa, employing some superb cavalry formations composed of North African horsemen: the *Spahis* Regiments, and camel-mounted *Méharistes* of the *Compagnies Sahariennes*. Consequently, the *Armée d'Afrique* was a substantial force; on the eve of the First World War, an ongoing campaign in Morocco alone employed 70,000 troops, mostly African despite nine battalions of *Zouaves*.[18] The contribution of African troops was not only important in scale, the troops themselves were generally well-regarded; they had an outstanding service record, and operational experience that soldiers in France had no way of acquiring at home. Locally raised troops were often valuable on campaign for their knowledge of the ground and local languages.

Always hungry for manpower, the recruitment of North and Black Africans into the French army permitted the *Armée d'Afrique* to do its job with a comparatively small contingent of European troops. With a war against

Germany looming in 1914, the *Zouaves, Légion Étrangère* and the *Infanterie Légère d'Afrique* represented the largest contingents of French troops in Africa. Indeed, the threat of war with Germany was reversing the flow of soldiers between the two continents. In the latter half of the 19th century, France found itself unable to compete with the superior resources of a united Germany. The Franco-Prussian War of 1870-71 was a disaster for France. The French defeat exposed their military vulnerability and highlighted the need to put every available man in uniform simply to keep pace with the growth of the German army. *Zouaves*, Algerian *Tirailleurs*, and 3 battalions of the *Infanterie Légère d'Afrique* had fought in France during the Franco-Prussian War and had acquitted themselves well. France began to see Africa as a potential source of soldiers to fight in European conflicts, not just in African ones. There was certainly an element of exploitation in the employment of African soldiers. West African men were thought to be naturally warlike according to racial theories of the time.[19] Moslem recruits of North Africa were considered particularly desirable, as many French officers believed that Moslems were unafraid of death, which sometimes may have led French officers to behave callously when commanding *Tirailleurs* in battle.[20] A more complete discussion of this aspect of African recruitment is beyond the scope of this volume, but the subject will be examined further in the volume on the *Tirailleurs*.

In the process of recovering from the turmoil that followed the French defeat in 1871, a number of changes were made which impacted the *Armée d'Afrique*. In 1870 Algeria was declared to be an extension of metropolitan France, which permitted conscripted soldiers to be stationed there without legally being considered to be "overseas." Inhabitants of Algeria could freely adopt French citizenship which, in turn, made them eligible for conscription. Conscription became truly universal in France for the first time. The *Zouaves*, who owed their fierce reputation to being recruited from carefully selected French volunteers, became regiments of conscripts and lost something in the process. The *Zouaves* were expanded to four regiments with a total of twenty-four active battalions by 1914. The *Tirailleurs* were also expanded, from twenty-four battalions to thirty-eight battalions in nine regiments. Regiments of *Zouaves* and *Tirailleurs* were organized into the *37e* and *38e Divisions*, and the *19e Corps d'Armée* was created to facilitate their logistical needs in 1873. Sixteen of the *Tirailleurs* battalions were committed to the *37e* and *38e Divisions*, which would deploy rapidly to France on the outbreak of war with Germany.

North African colonies thus retained their military importance to France, which renewed efforts to expand its authority into the hinterlands. By 1873, France had regained control of the populous coast of Algeria, but the grip on the more remote desert regions to the south remained tenuous. The Sahara Desert and the Atlas Mountains provided a refuge for opponents to French rule. Highly mobile mounted raiders could readily evade French columns by escaping into the desert, to re-emerge and attack somewhere else. Denying this refuge to its enemies required France to gain control of the oases and caravan routes. In addition to expanding southward, France began looking east to Tunisia and west to Morocco, once again because these regions were becoming a refuge for dissidents and to provide a buffer from the encroachment of other European powers. Battalions of the *Infanterie Légère d'Afrique* were integral to the forces involved in those operations, yet they were noticeably absent from mobilization plans in the event of war with Germany. From a strictly military point of view, the *Bat d'Af* in Africa permitted tens of thousands of North African men to be recruited by the army, while tying up only a few thousand undesirables. It is just as interesting to note that the French army actually preferred North African soldiers to their battalions of ex-convicts in the defence of France. Nonetheless, their role in garrisoning North Africa was indispensable and they were actively involved in operations that continued almost unabated from 1832 and up to Algerian independence in 1962.

From 1881 through to the turn of the Twentieth Century, the garrisons of the *Bat' d'Af* shifted deeper into the Sahara Desert from the coastal cities of Alger, Oran, Constantine, Tunis and Gabès. Garrisons occupied villages on the boundaries between the Atlas mountains and the Sahara, such as Kreider (modern El-Quarante), Laghouat, Batna, Biskra, El-Kef, and Gafsa. Detachments pushed even further into the desert. An example of one such operation in 1900 at El-Goléah was described by a French journalist:

> Between Ghardaïa and El-Goléah the first dunes of the erg appear for about eighty square kilometres. They are the route forced upon caravans and military convoys, and they will be more than ever, the latest events at Touat obliging France to undertake an important garrison at El-Goléah. That garrison is composed of about sixty Méharistes and a detachment of Spahis. In addition, some Joyeux are detached there for drilling wells.[21]

Working during the day in blazing 56° heat, the *Joyeux* constructed enough wells to make pools of water available for soldiers and caravans. Barracks went up to house the additional detachments of *Tirailleurs* who would now have enough water to drink. A small European community even settled around the existing inhabitants, with a hotel, bistros, bakeries, a general store and, of course, a brothel. It is interesting to note that the *Joyeux* were being employed for construction, while the *Spahis* and *Tirailleurs* were the principle fighting component at El-Goléah, but it would be a mistake to conclude that the *Joyeux* were regarded as a labour force rather than fighting soldiers. The *Joyeux* fought or laboured, whatever circumstances demanded, but it has to be said that if there was back-breaking work to be done, the *Joyeux* would get the duty before anyone else. The *Joyeux* were, of course, kept busy when they weren't fighting and they could both defend and consolidate French claims. With a handful of *Joyeux* to establish some basic infrastructure and a larger force of locally raised soldiers, France was pushing the boundaries of its empire.

On the outbreak of the First World War, the *4e* and *5e Bataillons d'Afrique* were at El-Kef and Gabès in Tunisia respectively, and the *1er*, *2e* and *3e* were actively engaged in Morocco.[22] Operations in Morocco took on many modern elements in the decade prior to the Great War. Aircraft were used for reconnaissance and radio communications were used on some occasions.[23] It was routine to dig defensive ditches around encampments on campaign. The defensive value of machine guns was readily recognized by isolated detachments that could find themselves outnumbered at any moment. There were sizable battles, but also small unit skirmishes and patrolling. In short, some aspects of campaigning in Morocco had lessons applicable to the Western Front. The *Joyeux* were employed in road building as well as convoy escort and patrolling. In consequence, some of the *Joyeux* who went to France in 1914 were combat veterans with recent fighting experience.

♦ ♦ ♦

The men who served in the *Infanterie Légère d'Afrique* were French citizens, and nearly all of them had done time in prison. As of 1914, all French men spent three years in the active army, beginning at the age of twenty, as long as they were not physically unfit. To end up in the *Bat' d'Af*, a man had to spend a minimum amount of time in jail; how much time depended on the nature of the crime. For assault, a man would go to the *Bat' d'Af* if he had spent at least six months in jail. More than one conviction for assault meant service in the *Bat' d'Af* regardless of time served. For crimes such as public indecency, theft, fraud, breach of trust and corruption of a minor, a one month jail term was enough. *Any* conviction for pimping was sufficient, no matter what the length of time served. Those were certainly serious convictions, but note that those were minimum jail terms; a lighter sentence meant that a young man would still serve his period of active service in a regular regiment in France. Men condemned to more than two years in prison served in a *Section d'Exclus*, and those men were ineligible even for the *Bat' d'Af*. The *Joyeux* were not murderers, and they ranged from those with a laundry list of convictions to basically decent young men who had made a mistake. Others might hardly be termed criminals at all by today's standards; more than one conviction for vagrancy, begging, or stealing food was also grounds for being sent to the *Bat d'Af* if at least three months was served in jail. In October of each year, the annual class of recruits destined for the *Infanterie Légère d'Afrique* was dispatched from France to North Africa. If they happened to be in jail when their class was called, they went the following year. The new *Joyeux* would be paraded through their home town to the railway station, escorted by *gendarmes* as wives and girlfriends bade farewell. Not all of the *Joyeux* came directly from civilian life. Men who committed an act of "grave misconduct during their presence under the colours," such as desertion or disobeying an order, could be transferred to the *Bat' d'Af* by judgement of their Commanding Officer. Dr. Louis Combe reported 94 such men serving in the 1er battalion in 1907.[24] If a soldier was convicted by a court-marshal and spent time in a military penitentiary, he would serve out the remainder of his active term of service in the *Bat d'Af* once his sentence was finished.

Those were the criteria in force in 1914 (See appendix A). The recruitment laws were frequently adjusted and updated over the years, and minimum sentences normally varied from three to six months. Terms of conscription changed frequently too, and these changes caused the overall size of the *Bat' d'Af* to vary considerably over time. Since the supply of recruits was dependent on men coming out of the correctional system, there was no fixed establishment for strength of a battalion. The battalions were as large or small as they needed to be to accommodate the influx of recruits, but could range between 750 and 1,500 men. Their organization was roughly modeled on *Chasseurs à pied* battalions of the metropolitan army, having six companies of infantry instead of the usual four found in line battalions. In 1903, when the term of conscription was three years and men were sent to the *Infanterie Légère d'Afrique* after serving only three months in jail, the *Journal des Sciences Militaires* reported a strength of 6,000 men. In 1905, changes to the law reduced the term of conscription to two years and the requisite time in prison increased to six months. Consequently, Dr. Louis Combe reported that the overall strength of the battalions had fallen to 3,820 men by 1907. The term of conscription was raised again to three years in 1913, and given the short minimum sentences indicated in the preceding paragraph, the intelligence branch of the British army estimated the five battalions of the *Infanterie Légère d'Afrique* to number 7,500 men.[25] The extension of the term of conscription service from two years to three years would certainly have swelled their ranks and on the eve of the First World War the *Bat d'Af* was probably larger than it had ever been at any point in the past. There would also have been an additional pool of reservists serving in units called *Groupes Spéciaux,* numbering approximately 25,000 men.[26]

While it was also possible to volunteer for service in the *Bat' d'Af*, why would anyone wish to do so? Generally, a young man was not permitted to choose the unit in which he wanted to serve. Service away from home was one of the guiding principles of the recruitment laws - a recruit would typically be sent to a regiment away from his home town - though to reiterate a point made earlier, a soldier could not be compelled to serve overseas. Most opportunities for a soldier to choose the unit in which he served were calculated to encourage a man to enlist in the colonial services. It was possible to volunteer for the *Infanterie Coloniale*, which was a highly respected corps, but even then the recruit could not be sent overseas without his consent (24 of the 32 battalions of the *Coloniale* were stationed in France).[27] The only others who could choose the corps in which they wanted to serve were young men who had acquired a *Brevet d'Aptitude Militaire* (Certificate of Military Aptitude, hereafter referred to as a BAM) during their adolescence. A young man who had acquired a BAM could voluntarily engage with a regiment in his home town (a popular choice) or a prestigious unit elsewhere if he wanted to be a career soldier.[28] Would an aspiring career soldier choose the *Infanterie Légère* over a more prestigious post? According to Dr. Combe, the *1er Bataillon d'Afrique* had 94 voluntarily engaged men from a total of 749 in 1905.[29] It may seem counter-intuitive, but the desert held an exotic allure for many young men at the turn of the 20th century. The *Bat' d'Af* may have had an appeal for young men wanting to test themselves against the rigours of a harsh environment. Veterans of the *Infanterie Légère d'Afrique* were also permitted to re-enlist in the *Bat' d'Af* for one-year terms (they would have been ineligible to re-enlist in other corps due to their criminal record). In the absence of firm statistics, it can be estimated that fewer than ten percent of the *Joyeux* were volunteers, but that is not an insignificant number and it shows that at least some were highly motivated soldiers.

♦ ♦ ♦

The *Infanterie Légère d'Afrique* was not, strictly speaking, a penal corps, yet it was closely connected to the disciplinary system of the French army. French commentators often took great pains to differentiate the *Bat' d'Af* from actual disciplinary formations, but it could be argued that the distinction was a blurry one. Most of the Joyeux had already "done their time" on arriving at the Bat' d'Af, but as article 93 of the recruiting laws indicated, a commanding officer could transfer a man to the *Bat' d'Af* without a court martial. In that sense, the *Bat' d'Af* could certainly be used to punish, though it was regarded as an attempt to rehabilitate. Because convicted men were being segregated from other soldiers of the army, it must also be said that service in the *Bat' d'Af* amounted to a *de facto* extension of civilian and military punishment. French commentators referred to the *Bat' d'Af* as "*bataillons d'épreuve*." In this context, *épreuve* can be translated as "ordeal;" the *Joyeux* were being tested through hardship, which was intended to be rehabilitative. The *Bat' d'Af* performed the role of "probationary battalions" in which soldiers transitioned from punishment to re-integration with the regular army.

The *Joyeux* had a chance to prove that he was worthy of re-entering French society through acts of bravery or proficiency and good conduct as a soldier. Good conduct for eight to twelve months (the amount of time varied according to changes to the term of conscription) resulted in transfer to an ordinary numbered regiment in France. If they failed to prove themselves worthy, and ended their active service with the *Infanterie Légère d'Afrique*, they would continue to be regarded as members of *la pègre* – the criminal class. Such men were not enlisted in their local reserve regiment when they got back home, since it was feared they would create disciplinary problems. Alternatively, the French army created a *Groupe Spécial* for every army corps, to segregate undesirable men from the front line units. The *Groupes Spéciaux* included not only the reservists of the *Infanterie Légère d'Afrique*, but reservists of other units who had been convicted of crimes after their term of conscription was complete. Continually rotating the best men out the battalions was not ideal from an organizational point of view, but the possibility of transfer was an important motivation to good behavior. When every other man he knew and worked with went to his hometown reserve regiment for periodic training, the former *Joyeux* went to a *Groupe Spécial*; there would be no escaping the stigma. Transfer to a line regiment meant normalcy, as well as escape from the desert. Of 204 men that Dr. Louis Combe followed from one battalion during his study, 33 had transferred to regiments in France within a year.[30] Overall, Combe calculated that no more than a quarter of men transferred back to France before the end of their service; it was not an easy privilege to earn.

If a soldier of the active army was convicted of a disciplinary offense, his commanding officer also had the option of sending the offender to a *Compagnie Disciplinaire*. If convicted by court-martial, punishments could include time in a military prison, penitentiary, or hard labour in *Ateliers de Travaux Publics*. Collectively, the units of the disciplinary system, including the penitentiaries, hard labour companies and the *Compagnies Disciplinaires* were nicknamed *Biribi*, in reference to a game of chance. Time served in punishment did not count towards the obligations of active service, and after completing a sentence in a *Compagnie Disciplinaire* (there were also opportunities to be released early for good conduct) a soldier would be sent to the *Bat' d'Af* to finish the remainder his military term. It was possible for a soldier to go repeatedly between the *Infanterie Légère d'Afrique* and the *Compagnies Disciplinaires*, and in that respect they could be regarded as extensions of each other. Yet the *Compagnies Disciplinaires* were independent formations with their own North African town to garrison. They are important to the story of the *Joyeux* because even though *Disciplinaires* were not meant to serve as fighting combat units the army ultimately turned to them to replace the high number of *Joyeux* who became casualties on the Western Front.

Unlike the *Bat' d'Af*, sections of the *Compagnies Disciplinaires* were most definitely intended to be punitive. Even in the *Disciplinaires* there were degrees of punishment and sections of the companies were divided into two distinct groups: *Sections de Fusil* (rifle sections) and *Sections de Pionniers* (pioneer sections). Men who had committed a military offense but were deemed capable of reform were sent to a *Section de Fusil*. For the rifle sections, military training continued, including live-fire practice, albeit under supervision of armed *Tirailleurs*. *Disciplinaires* of the *Sections de Fusil* were not ordinarily deployed on campaign, though they did fight on some occasions. In 1881, for example, soldiers of the *3ᵉ Compagnie Disciplinaire* were offered a transfer in exchange for fighting alongside *Légionnaires* during an emergency. It is telling that it was deemed necessary to bargain with them in order to take to the field. Soldiers with multiple convictions for disobedience, or those thought to be malingerers, were sent to pioneer sections employed exclusively as forced labour within the army, performing work such as building roads and earthworks. Men in the pioneer sections were not permitted to bear arms and no further military instruction was given. The rifle sections did also do some manual labour, but not usually major construction projects. Most of the work carried out by rifle sections served more mundane needs such as replacing straw for mattresses or maintenance of the camp. In one case, jobs given to the rifle sections included gathering all the stones around a camp and arranging them by size. In another case, a section near the Tunisian town of Gafsa was instructed to carry oil lamps at street corners on nights when there was too little moonlight.[31]

Prisoners in disciplinary sections were not locked up during the day, and were not normally shackled, but they were under the constant supervision of their Officers and NCOs supported by armed *Tirailleurs*. Nevertheless, *Disciplinaires* were forbidden from singing, playing games, or visiting the sleeping quarters of another inmate.[32] Acts of disobedience or refusal to work were punished severely. Regulations stipulated a range of available punishments, such as detention in the *Salon de Police* (guardhouse), imprisonment on half rations or rations without meat and assignment to a punishment platoon. [33] Most of these punishments were simply varying degrees of imprisonment, but it is clear that actual punishments went well beyond those allowed by regulation. Corporal punishment, including physical beatings, was routine. A frequently employed punishment called the *crapaudine* involved stripping the man from the waist up and tying him prone and exposed to the desert sun. The term actually comes from a French cooking method of roasting a chicken. The *tombeau* involved keeping the offender in a dirt pit. Alternatively, the offender might be forced to remain prone in his cell, with hands and feet hogtied behind his back; a man might even be suspended from the ceiling this way. Food would have to be eaten by lapping it up from a bowl.

Albert Londres, a well-known journalist in France during the early twentieth century, published an *exposé* on the disciplinary corps in 1924, entitled *Dante N'Avait Rien Vu.** Londres, touring the disciplinary camps and the public works details of North Africa after the First World War, was able to interview the detainees. The stories he heard were shocking. He related an interview with one such inmate working on a road-building project:

> - On my entry to Sidi-Moussah, I fell sick and was found guilty [of malingering], they left me four days under the Marabout, without eating, that I could understand, but [also] without drinking. I drank only one time, a comrade having risked punishment for bringing me water. So, when I protested, I was attached with a chain to the top of the Marabout and hung from the waist. I remained like that all afternoon. In the evening, the sergeant took pity on me and let me down and gave me a quart of water. That was good, because what I had drunk during those four days is not proper to say. That was Sergeant P... In the morning, Sergeant L... dragged me to the work detail.
>
> - Why did you refuse to work?
>
> - I was sick.
>
> There is no doctor in the camps. Is a man sick or not? Is he faking? The consultation is replaced by an invariable dialogue: "Sick, the man says. – I will make him work bessif (by force)," responds the sergeant.
>
> - I was then dragged 200 metres on my back by Tirailleurs; then a revolver under my nose:
>
> "Work, bastard!" I refused. They brought me back under the Marabout, beat me around the arms, hogtied and suspended me all day.[34]

Men could, and did, die from this treatment; those who died were said to have gone to the 5th Company (there were four Disciplinary Companies).

It was the isolation of North African outposts that made this kind of sadism possible and universal conscription that made it seem necessary. Unlike Germany, which could comfortably enlist and train fewer than half of eligible men, France felt compelled to muster everyone available. Some of the men in the *Compagnies Disciplinaires* were conscientious objectors,

---

* Dante Ain't Seen Nothing

having been sentenced to military prison for refusal to serve, such as pacifists, anti-militarists, international socialists, and others who refused to bear arms and obey orders for moral or intellectual reasons. Other inmates may have been suffering from mental illness. Francis Doré, who served as an Officer in the *Compagnies Disciplinaires* and wrote a rebuttal to Londres entitled, *Albert Londres N'a Rien Vu*,* argued in support of the system while tacitly acknowledging the abuse. He argued:

> Biribi cannot and must not disappear.
> Do we abolish the police because an agent strikes a delinquent?
> Is it necessary to abolish the army because of the injustices it produces?[35]

Brutality was, for Doré, an unavoidable by-product of a necessary system. There was no concession for anyone who objected to being in the army. Partly from the lingering humiliation of 1870, France refused to permit any recourse enabling men termed shirkers and malingerers to avoid military service. Military obligations were onerous and the harsh treatment in *Compagnies Disciplinaires* was calculated, in part, to make military service preferable to shirking one's duty.

♦ ♦ ♦

An unintended consequence of collecting petty criminals from urban slums was the introduction of street gangs from civilian life into the rank and file of the *Bat' d'Af.* Dr. Jude, who studied the psychology of the *Joyeux* while he was posted to a hospital in Tunisia, observed that there were two predominant gangs among the *Joyeux*, one from Paris and another from Marseilles.[43] The leaders of these gangs, called *caïds*, were the more physically powerful of the *Joyeux*, capable of exercising authority by force. The existence of gangs continued to be a problem after the First World War and was frequently remarked upon by post-war authors. The *caïds* were a law unto themselves; they enforced gang rules and a strict code of silence that protected their own members and those of other gangs as well. The *Joyeux* feared the *caïds* more than their own sergeants and with good reason: the sergeant would be out of his life in three years, but the *caïd* would still be there when he returned to civilian life. The *caïd* could bully his gang members into providing extra luxuries like tobacco and a share of parcels from home. Francis Doré described one of the precautions that had to be taken because of the existence of gangs:

> After soup, the wine ration: one quart per man. Each one must drink in front of the Sergeant, to prove that the "caïds" are not forcing the weaker ones to give them their share. [44]

These patterns of behaviour were often established in juvenile detention, where an older boy could easily dominate a younger and smaller inmate. It

* Albert Londres Ain't Seen Nothing

also seems likely that some *Disciplinaires* and *Joyeux* experienced repeated sexual assault. "Twenty years old, blond and timid," was Doré's description of one *Disciplinaire* on the day he arrived:

> He asked me... "to lodge [him] in a separate room."
> ...He slept that first night in a cell, and the next he was put with the others in the common dorm...
> On inspection the next morning, he presented himself, stupefied, red and ashamed, ignominiously dirtied by the most cowardly attack that one can imagine.
> - Who did that to you? Demanded the Major.
> - I don't know! There were several who held me.
> Because he knew the least denunciation would cost him his life.[45]

The code of silence left *Disciplinaires* with little choice but to endure abuse. The grim reality of bullying by gangs was arguably the most terrifying aspect of life in the *Compagnies Disciplinaires* and the *Bataillons*.

The consensus of recent scholarship has been that homosexuality was commonplace, though this needs some qualification.[46] The disciplinary corps of the French army had staunch opponents and ardent defenders. What both sides had in common was the marshalling of homosexual practice in support of their arguments. Doré pointed to homosexuality as proof that very bad men in the disciplinary corps were being justifiably punished. Between the turn of the 20th Century and the First World War, the *Joyeux* were the subject of intense study by medical professionals and senior officers who sought to reorganize the corps. Dr. Louis Combe,. Doctor Raoul Jude, and Commandant Ordioni all wrote on the subject of the *Joyeux* within a decade of each other and built upon each other's arguments. From the mid-19th Century, theories of degeneracy became a prominent topic of debate within medical science. The theories of those such as Bénédict Morel of France and Max Nordau of Germany proposed that society and individuals could become degenerate, resulting in physical and mental defects, as well as criminal behaviour. Degeneracy theories gave rise to the advocation of eugenics and were an important contributing factor to the rise of Adolf Hitler and National Socialism in Germany. Because the supposed degeneracy was thought to lead to physical defects, traits such as the shape of a person's ear, a sloping forehead or an asymmetrical face were believed to be indications of a degenerate character. For example, in discussing the psychology of the *Joyeux*, Combe remarked that there was something about the *Joyeux* that was "not quite right." After some deliberation he put his finger on it: "they're all ugly!"[36] Combe's conclusion was well in line with contemporary theories of degeneracy. Could hard work and discipline reverse degeneracy? That was the question theorists and supporters of the disciplinary corps were seeking to answer. Including convictions such as vagrancy and stealing food in the recruitment regulations of the *Bat' d'Af* certainly suggested an attempt at transforming the destitute into hardworking, loyal citizens.

"We [were] the dregs of society," recalled Paul Deschaume. "Repeat offenders, hooligans, gangsters, insubordinates, even homos."[48] When Deschaume did his military service in the 1950s, gay men were still very much associated with the "dregs." Both Combe and Jude studied the *Joyeux* as a test case in degenerate psychology, using criminal behaviour, homosexuality, tattoos and even epilepsy to make a case for degeneracy. Satirical cartoons like those in the *Assiette au Beurre* used homosexuality to illustrate the inhumanity of the disciplinary corps (See illustration by Bernard Naudin, page 43).[47] Was homosexuality commonplace, or was it alluded to so often because it was an easy target for those on both sides of the debate? Since the intense controversy aroused by homosexuality made it a convenient rhetorical device, it is difficult to get an objective point of view on how prevalent it really was. Combe admitted that he had no way of knowing for sure, yet he implied that all *Joyeux* were gay. Jude placed his estimate at two-thirds. Since they were unable to supply any evidence for such stark conclusions, I suspect both were overstating their case.[49] Combe based his assertion on the principle that degeneracy could spread like a contagion. Once exposed, the seed had been planted, or so the theory went. "If the seed does not manifest itself, it is an exceptional thing," wrote Combe. "It subsists in a latent state: ... a glass of wine, a stormy sky... anything can make it flower."[50] Such a dubious argument mainly serves to suggest that Combe had little concern that his conclusions would be challenged. The readiness to make assumptions is unfortunate even if it is, perhaps, not surprising. Yet there do appear to have been genuine relationships, as evidenced by a letter Combe intercepted from one *Joyeux* to another, urging him to leave his new partner in the battalion. "Although you have offended our love, I still love you and I await your response," wrote the unidentified *Joyeux*.[51]

Joyeux and *Disciplinaires* were young men, living in common dorms far from home, contending with an all-male environment not dissimilar to a frontier town of the Wild West. Some were married. Many had left sweethearts behind as they marched out of their hometown to start their military life. "The Joyeux always think of the dear girl they have left in France," wrote Mac Orlan.[52] The isolation of the desert added to the homesickness; some succumbed to the *cafard*, a depression brought on after months of life in the expanses of desert. The young recruit had only limited life experience to deal with these surroundings, and had to find ways to cope. Taking tattoos as a case in point, the *Joyeux* engaged in a number of coping mechanisms that violated expected norms. Jude found that 80% of *Joyeux* had at least one tattoo after six months of service, which is, at least, a claim that could be objectively demonstrated if the data were available (which, regrettably, it is not). Tattoos included the usual portraits: men, women, and other scenes, as well as personal mantras or anti-militarist statements such as "Down with the Army" or "Victim of Militarism." While Combe and Jude argued that tattoos were proof of degeneracy, at least one contemporary scholar disagreed. Alexandre Lacassagne (1843-1924), a professor of medical law, collected 1,300 images of tattoos worn by *Joyeux*.[53] According to Lacassagne's interpretation, tattoos represented a means of expression for men who had been silenced in all other respects. The *Joyeux* could salute and fall into line, while under his uniform his tattoos spoke words his mouth could not. *Joyeux* and *Disciplinaires* had faced all the horrors that a 19th century prison could dish out. They had to stand up for themselves in an intensely aggressive masculine milieu, where any weakness could lead to victimization and where the only women in their lives were in the brothels outside the garrison. Perhaps it is best to acknowledge that they were doing the best they could under circumstances we will never really understand. "All Joyeux are not alike," warned Mac Orlan, "it is an extremely difficult milieu to study and for that reason one must guard against overly definitive conclusions."[54]

Joyeux, unlike *Disciplinaires*, were not prisoners and could leave camp and go into town when possible. "The chasseur of the bataillons d'Afrique is a soldier, a fighting soldier, placed under the same regulations as the infantryman of the Metropole," wrote Combe, "... he can go into town, obtain furlough, leave for France, he can aspire to rank, to re-engage."[55] Garrisons were not always on the edge of the Sahara and the larger towns near battalion depots offered many of the same amenities as a European town. European colonial settlement became quite substantial, even at outposts such as El-Goléah, as we have seen. Taverns and brothels went just about everywhere soldiers did. The facilities were understandably spartan in many cases, as Mac Orlan observed:

> At Gabès, the Joyeux live peacefully in the shadow of their own barracks and their preferred bistros. In the evening they can drink a glass at the Maison Blanche or at the Maison Rose, the two "joints" placed facing the other, like two forts in front of the desert where the angular stones contribute to the desolation of the scorched countryside... It would suffice to place a machine gun or a 37mm cannon in front of their door for a completely engaging aspect.[56]

They were expected to be on their best behaviour, with kit polished and well turned-out before leaving camp. Mac Orlan recalled a conversation he had with a waiter at the Hôtel du Sahara:

> The waiter, an amiable Bônoise, spoke to me of the Joyeux. "They are very kind," he said to me. "They are reasonable when one knows how to talk to them. When I came to Tataouine, I did not dare say a word to them. Since, I have found that the Joyeux are not bad kids. Would you care for some cheese?[57]

They were a long way from Paris, but even in Tataouine there were bistros and amiable waiters to serve gruyère. It was as close to Paris as they could manage, perhaps better, since they were paid by the army and had money to spend.

Because of their preoccupation with degeneracy, the writings of Jude, Combe and Ordioni are deeply problematic sources, but the statistics they have left give us some glimpses into the background of the rank-and-file men. Ordioni found that of 300 recruits, 91 came from single-parent households and another 45 were orphans.[37] From another survey of 1,000 *Joyeux*, Ordioni found that 348 had worked at a variety of unskilled and semi-skilled trades; they were journeymen, manual labourers, domestic servants, and others who claimed no profession at all.[38] The remainder of the sample group of 1,000 came from diverse but unfortunately unspecified professions. Dr. Jude reported that the *Joyeux* had often been neglected children even in cases where the mother or father had been available.[39] Examining the *5e Compagnie* of the *3e Bataillon* stationed at Ain-Draham, Tunisia, in 1907, Jude found that of 125 men, 72 were in the *Bat' d'Af* due to civil convictions, 42 were convicted soldiers, and 11 had transferred from disciplinary sections.[40] Among 52 men serving in a detachment at Tabarka, there were 15 day-labourers and 5 farmers. Even where men claimed to know a trade, Jude asserted that it was often pursued itinerantly. Two men had 12 convictions each for theft, fraud and vagrancy. Moreover, Jude recorded an illiteracy rate of 10% among men he interviewed in the *Bat' d'Af*, and 25% in the *Comapgnies Disciplinaires*.[41] This is, perhaps, not surprising as Combe found that only 10 to 15% had achieved a primary school certificate, and most had left school by the age of 12.[42] Some had been imprisoned for vagrancy, and a hard life on the streets had left many of them in poor health.

♦ ♦ ♦

As noted earlier, the disciplinary regime of the *Bat' d'Af* has often been called harsh, and we have seen how bad it could be in the *Compagnies Disciplinaires*, but it is very difficult to get into specifics with respect to the *Joyeux*. Ordioni cited an interesting quotation: "Good for the good subjects, hard for the bad, such must be the line of conduct of the ranking men of the *Bataillons d'Afrique*."[58] He doesn't say "bad" for the bad, just hard. Mac Orlan observed that the NCOs placed an emphasis on making life as close as possible to that of a metropolitan battalion. "The effort of command insisted on a unique point: to restore the esprit de corps of the chasseurs," wrote Mac Orlan.[59] The disciplinary system of the corps seems to have been designed to separate the wheat from the chaff. If a new recruit was fit and took to his training quickly he was probably treated well. If he was a misfit or a trouble maker, there were ways of getting rid of him. If the *chasseur* committed an act of indiscipline, he could always be put in front of a disciplinary council and sent to a *Compagnie Disciplinaire*. Combe reported that of 204 men from a group he studied, 44 had been sent to a *Compagnie Disciplinaire* within a year, so this was evidently a tool they had no qualms about using.[60]

"The NCOs we observed were brave guys, dignified and calm, with an admirable sang-froid," wrote Jude, "...in my two-year sojourn with the Battalion, I have never seen an NCO commit the least act of brutality."[61] But perhaps we need to expand the definition of abuse. Certainly, the ability to send men to the *Disciplinaires* had tremendous potential for abuse. A corporal named Joseph Dimier, writing in 1928, revealed that there were indeed NCOs that took perverse pleasure in finding fault or even inventing faults. Dimier called such NCOs "chercheurs d'hommes:"

> That signified that one watched for occasions to punish, that one was on the look out for all that was done or said that could risk discipline; even if the occasion didn't offer itself, one sought to create it in order to seize upon some court-marshal case. In a battalion that was not very difficult. A vast field opened itself to the chercheurs d'hommes.[62]

One of the tools that NCOs use in training new recruits is hyper-attention to details of kit maintenance. Paul Deschaume recalled his experience:

> Astonishing! Incredible! The kit... on four thicknesses of different colours, 7 cm piles, on I don't know how much width. The flannel belt: the blue belt 7 cm, the shirt 7 cm, everything else 7 cm, I don't know why.
>
> 7 cm. 7, not 6.9, not 7.1! No, 7.[63]

If the *Joyeux* failed to meet this standard, the first step might be punishment drill, which could involve hefting a full sand bag and running around the parade square. When the struggling soldier still could not cope, he could end up in the *Disciplinaires*. Deschaume was sent to the *Disciplinaires* after swatting a fly from his eye while on parade, a harsh punishment for such a minor offense. *Marche ou Crève*: march or perish was the mentality that produced an elite corps from the remnants of those who could make the stark adjustment from civilian life. The Officers and NCOs had no need to be abusive; they could leave that to their counterparts in the *Disciplinaires*.

Yet, the sources I consulted for this work all seem to agree that most Officers and NCO's were experienced and capable. The Officers were selected from volunteers, and Lieutenants were required to have at least two years in rank before they could transfer to the *Bat' d'Af.* Most of the sergeants were re-engaged NCOs from other French regiments who had already served one term of service. There were no restrictions on the number of NCOs who could re-engage for another term of service in the *Bat' d'Af*, whereas infantry regiments in France were permitted to re-engage only two-thirds (or fewer in some branches of service) of their NCOs.[64] The *Bat' d'Af* had little need to make room for NCOs promoted from the ranks, instead they needed to retain anyone they could. The NCO had to have the confidence that came from long service and time in rank. Casualties recorded in the war diary of the 1er *Bataillon de Marche d'Infanterie Légère d'Afrique* (1er BMILA) tend to confirm the experience of their sergeants. Of the seven sergeants that could be identified among the fatal casualties, six were re-engaged veterans and only one was from the class of 1911.[65] The Officers identified were also long-service veterans. Lieutenant Ernst turned twenty-eight just four days before he was killed on 22 April 1915.

Corporals, by contrast, tended to be rather young. On entering the army, a soldier could attain the rank of corporal after six months, or after as little as four months if he had a *Brevet d'Aptitude Militaire* from a French academy.[66] It was possible for *Joyeux* to earn a promotion but sergeants and corporals promoted from among the *Joyeux* were rare. The *Joyeux* spoke of the *cadre noire* comprised of men promoted from the ranks, and the *cadre blanc* comprised of NCOs from other regiments. According to Ordioni, there were only six or seven sergeants in the battalions who had come from the ranks. Some *Joyeux* had formerly been NCOs in other regiments, before they had been busted down to private and sent to the *bataillons* after punishment, and some of them were good candidates for promotion again. The existence of gangs made it very difficult to promote most *Joyeux*. The code of silence made it impossible for men promoted from the ranks to punish their fellow gang members. Unless they took firm but reasonable control, their former comrades were prone to tease them mercilessly. Yet if they became too harsh, they had to be on their guard against reprisals. Nevertheless, it is evident that many of the corporals killed in the *1er Bataillon de Marche* were members of the class of 1913. Indeed, they were often two years younger than the typical *Joyeux* they were leading. The war diaries do not reveal if those corporals were promoted from the *Joyeux* or transferred from other units. Jude argued that only re-engaged corporals could command the moral authority to get obedience without verbal or physical abuse, noting corporals transferred from other regiments were often too young and inexperienced to command respect.[67] On the other hand, it would be hard to find fault with the combat record we see of corporals in the JMOs. If there was reluctance to promote *Joyeux*, wartime conditions likely necessitated the rapid promotion of men from the ranks. An entry in the war diary of the *1er Bataillon de Marche* for 10 November 1914 reveals that on arriving in France, eight *Joyeux* were promoted to corporal and any reluctance to promote *Joyeux* seems to have vanished almost completely.

♦ ♦ ♦

It is fair to say that outside observers have struggled to explain the battlefield record of the *Bat' d'Af* for almost as long as they had existed. While the *Joyeux* had a bad-boy reputation, they also had a reputation for bravery. Even if calling ex-convicts *Joyeux* was meant to be ironic, the *Joyeux* wore the name like a badge. In the *Journaux de Marche*, the name *Joyeux* is used with reverence. Mac Orlan remarked upon their *esprit de corps*:

> The Joyeux, in spite of themselves, are proud of their uniform, which indicates their doubly exceptional personality, and their civilian past, and the resulting military consecration. They are often animated by the pride of not being soldiers "like the others," and when one knows how to play to that pride one can obtain the best of things from a battalion of Joyeux.[68]

Like many corps, the reputation of the *Joyeux* rested largely on heritage. The most legendary example of the heroism of the *Joyeux* was certainly the battle of Mazagran. On 3 February 1840, a company of 123 *Joyeux* holding the desert fortification at Mazagran were attacked by an Arab column believed to number 8,000 men. The *Joyeux* desperately held off their attackers for four days before a relief column arrived. When the fighting was over, the flag that waved over the fort was found to have been shot through by 120 musket balls and 4 rifle bullets. The *Joyeux* memorized not only how many bullet holes the flag had, but also how many pierced each of the three bands of colour: 53 balls and 2 bullets through the blue band, 35 balls through the white band, 32 balls and 2 bullets through the red band.[69] In 1907, Sergeant-Major Paul Guénin commented on the fact that the *bataillons d'Afrique* had not yet received their colours:

> Our Zéphyrs have a flag however, a flag of which they have the right to be proud, a sacred standard, a pious relic: it is the flag of Mazagran, souvenir of glory, symbol of what courage can do against numbers...[70]

The Flag of Mazagran became an object of veneration for the *Joyeux*; it secured their reputation as an elite force, and was paraded in front of the battalions at all important ceremonies.

The reputation of the *Joyeux* was widely acknowledged, as exemplified in an 1863 essay by Antoine Camus, entitled *Les Bohêmes du Drapeau*:

> There are among those men some passionate hearts, devoted arms, elevated intelligences, and why not say it, veritable heroes, Mazagran proves it. Nevertheless, some singular characters! What astonishing characteristics![71]

Even those who studied them for their alleged degeneracy agreed that there were good soldiers in the *bataillons*. Combe observed:

> Certainly, he has suffered some well-deserved condemnations before being incorporated, and it is precisely because his judicial record is no longer clear that he has been sent to an African battalion.
>
> But he has expunged his fault, paid his debt to society, and since he is allowed to pay what he owes to his country under honourable conditions, it would be just to forget his past. What is more, we have seen him conduct himself bravely in the wars of Africa, Tonkin, and elsewhere; he even has a flag where enemy bullets have left heroic souvenirs.[72]

The *Joyeux* were a paradox: split between a military tradition that built them up to be heroes and societal judgements that branded them either degenerates or a criminal underclass.

♦ ♦ ♦

When the long-expected war with Germany came in August 1914, the *Joyeux* were not initially mobilized. Ongoing campaigns in Morocco and rumours of trouble brewing in Algeria ensured that garrisons needed to remain in place. The *Joyeux* would be called upon when the shocking casualties suffered in the first two months of the war made it necessary to put every available soldier on the Western Front. The opposing armies were still attempting to out-maneouvre each other with repeated outflanking movements, ever further to the north of each other in what has since been called the "race to the sea," when three battalions of the *Bat' d'Af* were ordered to France in October 1914. No individual battalion of the *Infanterie Légère d'Afrique* went to the front intact. Instead, companies from all five battalions were grouped together into three *bataillons de marche*. In the event, only two of these went to France immediately: the 2e *Bataillon de Marche d'Infanterie Légère d'Afrique* was kept on active duty in North Africa until 1918. The *1er* and *3e Bataillons de Marche* were small formations, with only four companies and fewer than 800 men in the 1er *Bataillon*, which is interesting when we consider that there were as many as 7,500 men available to the corps. Why were their numbers so small? The answer seems to be found in the opening entry for the *3e Bataillon de Marche* diary for 26 October 1914, which states that the battalion would be made up of the "best elements... with men trained rigorously, and of a high degree of morale." If we examine those *Joyeux* killed in 1914, we see an overwhelming representation of men from the class of 1911 (See Appendix B). The *Joyeux* seem to have been selected on the basis of seniority, which presumably meant they had the most training. The *1er Bataillon de Marche* diary added that their battalion was raised "under the aegis of the Flag of Mazagran."[73] The *Joyeux* who went to war in October 1914 were highly motivated, well trained and determined soldiers, and it shows in the pages of their war diaries.

Readers will have the opportunity to follow the entries of the war diaries themselves, but there are a few points worth highlighting. Both *bataillons de marche* in France established a hard-fighting reputation for themselves very quickly. The *1er Bataillon de Marche* arrived at the Arras sector near Vimy ridge in November 1914, where it joined the *45e Division d'Infanterie*, often called the 45th Algerian Division by English historians. The *1er Bataillon de Marche* arrived on the front at a time of intense tactical experimentation. The Arras sector was the scene of bloody fighting, but the reckless mass bayonet charges of August 1914 had chiefly given way to quick, violent raids and an underground war of tunnels and mines. Within a day of arriving, the *1er Bataillon de Marche*, along with the other battalions of their Brigade, was ordered to form a *groupe franc* (loosely translated: a raiding party).[74] Rather than committing entire battalions to an attack, small teams of volunteers would seize limited objectives on vulnerable, localized sections of trench. The raiders would do their damage and then withdraw before the enemy could mount an organized counter-attack. These operations fit the immediate needs of the war. They were not intended to break through the trench lines, but rather to gain the upper hand in the battle of attrition, and to "keep the enemy under constant threat of a general attack."[75]

The *1er Bataillon de Marche* diary entry for 21 November 1914 offers an exceptional glimpse into raiding tactics of the time. The target was a section of trench perilously close to the French lines: only 15 metres of ground separated French and German lines at their closest point. The degree of planning and preparation that went into this raid is surprising for November 1914. The raid featured a night artillery shoot illuminated by entrenched searchlights. Close coordination between the raiders and their supporting artillery was ensured by telephones and a forward observer from the batteries who accompanied the raider's commanding officer. Runners were sent to the Brigade headquarters to synchronize time and ensure the precise timing of the raid. The success of the raid brought numerous citations for bravery. One *Joyeux* in particular, a bugler named Maxime Tindy, would earn repeated citations, the *médaille militaire*, as well as a promotion to corporal and then to sergeant. He was wounded at least three times in the period covered by this volume. Fighting on the Arras sector continued at a relentless pace until the *45ᵉ Division* was finally rotated out of the fighting line in March 1915.

The *3ᵉ Bataillon de Marche* arrived at the front in Belgium on 5 November 1914, just as the "race to the sea" was reaching its anti-climax. Having disembarked by rail at Dunkerque, the *3ᵉ Battalion de Marche* was brought by busses right onto the battlefield at Lizerne, just north of Ypres. According to their battalion history, they came under fire even as they were unloading.[76] They relieved a unit in the line on 7 November and after holding that line for two days, launched their first attack on 9 November. The assault on German positions entrenched with barbed wire obstacles at a nearby farm was carried out as the *Joyeux* broke out into singing the *Marseillaise*. The attack became a storied moment for the battalion, which succeeded at a stage in the war when French attacks seldom achieved their objectives. The attack had relied solely on the *élan* of the *Joyeux*, but it must have been apparent soon that *élan* was not enough. Another attack, only days later, also succeeded initially, but none of the neighbouring battalions had left their trenches, and the isolated *Joyeux* were forced to pull back.

The next attack of the *3ᵉ Bataillon de Marche* was conducted with much more careful planning. On 4 December 1914, the *3ᵉ Bataillon de Marche* resumed the offensive towards the *Maison du Passeur*, a fortified house on the west bank of the Yser Canal that was covering the bridge at Drie Grachten. Like the raid conducted by the *1ᵉʳ Bataillon de Marche* at Arras a few days earlier, this attack was carried out by smaller parties of volunteers, with careful coordination of the attacking troops and measures to consolidate the ground afterwards. Again, the attack succeeded and the conquered position was held. The *Maison du Passeur* itself was captured on 6 December 1914. The front remained relatively quiet while the *3ᵉ Bataillon de Marche* held trenches in the Ypres salient until 3 February 1915, when the battalion withdrawn from the line to be transferred to the *45ᵉ Division*. By this time, both *bataillons de marche* had demonstrated their value. By the end of January 1915, six officers from among the two *bataillons de marche* had been named to the Legion of Honour. They had learned how to conduct methodical attacks that succeeded more often than not, and they had held their ground against determined German attacks.

On 10 February 1915, both *bataillons de marche* were at last reunited in the *90ᵉ Brigade* of the *45ᵉ Division*. Unlike the Ypres salient, the fighting in the Arras sector had continued unabated throughout the winter of 1914-15. Order number 45 of the *10ᵉ Armée* for 20 January 1915 sums up the situation well:

> Placed for three months in a particularly difficult sector, exposed to incessant attacks from an aggressive and enterprising enemy, which was cited as a model of the 6ᵗʰ German Army by its Chief the Prince of Bavaria, the 45ᵉ Division held its positions.
>
> It turned each attack of the adversary with remarkable energy.

> Under the impulsion of its Chief, General **Quiquandon**, it clearly retook the moral ascendancy over the enemy at last by attacking in a war of saps and mines without respite.[77]

But it was not over yet. The culmination of the *45e Division's* tour of the Arras sector came on 17 February 1915. It was their biggest operation up to that point. For weeks leading up to 17 February, sappers had been pushing tunnels under the German positions in front of the *45e Division*, with the intent of blowing up whole sections of the front prior to an attack. Then, on the night of 15 to 16 February, one of the tunnels collapsed into a German dugout.[78] The gig was up, and the decision was taken to exploit the remaining tunnels immediately before the Germans could take counter-measures. The attack on 17 February was therefore a much hastier affair than had been planned. The battalion diaries provide a superb narrative of the planning and execution of the attack. The new plan was to detonate six mines under the German front lines. The forces leading the attack, which included both the *1er* and *3e Bataillons de Marche* and elements of the *Zouaves*, would capture and hold the German first and second lines for 48 hours. During that time, the captured German positions would be wired with explosives, and then the French would withdraw. Ideally, the trenches would be blown again as the Germans re-occupied them. This was attrition warfare at its nastiest, well almost; the *45e Division* would also be on the scene when poison gas added another level of horror on 22 April 1915.

The fighting surrounding the mine detonations of 17 February 1915, at Roclincourt, illustrates two important points. First, it was taken for granted by the French that the Germans would be forced to counter-attack, causing punishing losses to them. The Germans did, in fact, oblige. The fighting advantage clearly went to the defender when attacks were launched over open ground in daylight, yet no-one seemed to question the assumption that lost ground should be retaken at all cost. The result of the German chlorine attack on 22 April 1915 just two months later, created much the same situation. It seems astonishing that General Quiquandon could be lured into making the same mistake of launching ill-conceived counter-attacks in the wake of the chlorine attack (future volumes in this series will provide an opportunity to examine the costly counter-attacks launched by the *Zouaves* of the *45e Division*).

In light of the above, the counter-attacks of the *3e Bataillon de Marche* are an interesting case. In November 1914, the *3e Bataillon de Marche* would likely have fixed bayonets and charged heedless of the danger. Their actions following the gas attack reveal a much greater reluctance to take useless risks. The *3e Bataillon de Marche* was placed on alert shortly after the chlorine attack, but orders to counter-attack did not arrive until 2:40 am, by which time the Germans had already dug in. After making contact with the Germans between Boesinghe and Lizerne, they made good use of the ground available, sent combat patrols into the dark to probe the enemy lines, and the intense firefights of the next few days were costly enough, but there were no attempts by the *3e Bataillon de Marche* to assault the new German line.[79] Many officers of the *3e Bataillon de Marche* would have remembered Lizerne, which was where they had first entered the battlefield the previous November, and was only a few kilometres distant from the *Maison du Passeur* which they had captured in December 1914. It is very possible that they also remembered the preparation necessary to succeed. A counter-attack on 9 May 1915 at different segment of the line was cancelled after artillery failed to prepare the attack properly. Repeated and costly counter-attacks were made by other battalions of the *45e Division* and the dogged, methodical fighting of the *3e Bataillon de Marche* makes for something of a contrast.

Second, the *45e Division* spent its formative months in a particularly violent sector, where some hard lessons about trench fighting were being learned. The trench systems in front of Arras were sophisticated, involving multiple lines of defense, strong points, communication trenches, dugouts and barbed wire. Combat took place underground as well as above, and petards (makeshift bombs produced by the unit itself) and grenades (bombs of industrial manufacture) were the weapons of choice in the close-quarters fighting. Raiding and quick attacks with limited objectives were the norm. The trench system in front of Ypres had none of this sophistication, where the defenses consisted of thin sandbag walls erected above ground. In many places, bodies had been used to reinforce the bulwark. Those sandbag positions were not interconnected and were not even bullet proof. It has often been maintained that the poor defensive systems reflected an emphasis on offensive rather than defensive war. Colonel Nicholson's account of the Canadian occupation of French trenches at Ypres, found in *The Canadian Expeditionary Force 1914 – 1919*, provides a good example:

> ...French and British methods of conducting a war differed considerably. This was most noticeable with respect to the forward defenses, where British policy...was "to hold the line at all costs." The French, however, believed in manning the front line only lightly; if attacked the infantry would retire, allowing the artillery's effective 75-millimetre field guns to...stop the enemy...In view of these different standards, it is hardly surprising that the state of the French front line came as a great shock...[80]

Nicholson's assertion may have some validity with respect to the French divisions that held the Ypres salient prior to the arrival of the *45e Division*. Yet, it becomes evident from the JMOs translated in this volume that the trenches in front of Ypres were as much of a shock to General Quiquandon as they had been to the Canadian and British divisions that took over parts of the salient from the French. Within days of arrival on the Ypres salient, Quiquandon embarked on an intensive program of improving the front line defenses. While the diaries of the *1er* and *3e Bataillons de Marche* record Quiquandon's orders of 19 April 1915, there was no time to implement them. The chlorine attack came only three days later. Strong points and a second trench line 50 metres further back would likely have been of little value under the circumstances, but the scheme of raiding and use of petards might have caused havoc against German positions stuffed with chlorine cylinders. Even a brief inspection of captured German trenches might have revealed the chlorine cylinders, giving credence to warnings that had been delivered by German deserters. The "what if" scenarios arising from the possibility of trench raids are as intriguing as they are moot.

The wartime service of the *Joyeux* prior to the Second Battle of Ypres was not without problems. Readers will note from the war diaries that there were several instances of desertion and absence without leave (AWOL) on the way to the front in October and November 1914. Such men were returned to Africa with little fuss. In one case on 12 November, a *Joyeux* remained at Perrache "watching the departure of the train" as the rest of the battalion continued toward the front. Apparently, no attempt was made to force him on board; he was a problem for the *gendarmes* at that point. There seems to have been little interest in having anyone in the battalion who didn't want to be there. A far more serious situation occurred on 17 March 1915, with a mutiny that is only mentioned tangentially in an entry for 11 May 1915. After the severe casualties at Roclincourt, reinforcements incorporated into the battalions included reservists from the *Groupes Spéciaux*, *Disciplinaires*, and most surprisingly, men from *Sections d'Exclus*. The *Disciplinaires* and *Exclus* were not supposed to be sent to fighting units; their training prior to the war would have been minimal for the *Disciplinaires* and non-existent in the case of the *Exclus*. Some of the reinforcements mutinied and, consequently, most of the reinforcement group, totalling 250 men in the *1er* and *3e Bataillons de Marche*, were returned to Africa.[81] While the integrity of the battalions was preserved, they would remain understrength, though not critically.

So it was that the *1er Bataillon de Marche d'Infanterie Légère d'Afrique* occupied a section of the trenches in front of Langemarck on 21 April 1915. As we have seen, the *1e Bataillon de Marche* was a fighting unit second to none. The *1er Bataillon de Marche* diary offers some hints that the *Joyeux* tried to resist in many cases, but retreating was the most sensible option and, given the devastating losses, some *Joyeux* evidently held on longer than they should have. In the aftermath of the gas attack, the diarist of the battalion could only guess at the number of casualties; indeed, it was the first time that casualties could not be listed by name.

♦ ♦ ♦

Convicted felons, an impoverished upbringing; the *Joyeux* were easy to underestimate. Mac Orlan was wounded in 1916, and he related a story of how he met a *Joyeux*, nicknamed Toto, as he hobbled along a road to reach his regimental aid post:

> On the Cléry road, lit by the solemn autumn sun, between the veils of a protective fog, marching slowly, legs apart, an old soldier of the colonial infantry held his entrails in his bare hands to keep them from falling through the gape of an unimaginable wound... I made a very great effort to pass the colonial, whose black beard appeared intricately detailed on a waxen face. He marched along the road slowly and silently. I could soon no longer see him, yet the

> relief from it proved ephemeral in duration. I leaned upright against an embankment and my face drained, bathed in sweat. I drank all the wine that remained in my two-litre canteen.
>
> Then someone beside me said from a cut in the embankment; "Hey! Buddy, you're letting yourself go?"
>
> The soldier offered me a canteen covered in khaki cloth and I drank everything in rectifying myself into a vertical position.
>
> - Don't stay there... I am wounded in the hand, but you can support yourself on my shoulder, we are going to try to make "fissa" (speed).
>
> We went along, coupled like that as if interpreting a classic vision on the evening of a battle, on the road from Cléry up to Feuillèvre where we found ourselves two places in an ambulance vehicle.
>
> The soldier who had parted with his canteen in a moment when the contents of a canteen were perhaps worth more than the skin of a man he didn't know, was called Toto. He was a 2nd class chasseur of the 3e Bataillon d'Afrique.[82]

The episode left a lasting impression on Mac Orlan; he had just passed by a hopelessly wounded fellow without offering any comfort, to be rescued from his own despair by someone who could have easily passed him by as well. Toto was an unlikely hero. From Mac Orlan's description of the time they spent in hospital, Toto was an effeminate young man, who spent his day preening himself in front of a mirror, and perfuming his blond hair. Stories of *Joyeux* going out of their way to help someone in need crop up in some unexpected places. Jude tells of *Joyeux* who donated all of their money to help some children who were orphaned when their parents died on a shipwreck.[83] The *Journaux* are replete with examples of *Joyeux* bringing back wounded soldiers under fire; like any good unit, they only reluctantly left a man behind. Readers should take note of an entry in the *1er Bataillon de Marche* diary for 9 January 1915, when *Joyeux* came to the aid of some soldiers who were dying of exposure, stuck in the freezing mud of a communication trench, completely exposed to fire in broad daylight; one of the *Joyeux* was wounded in the effort. On another occasion, an unspecified captain writes a report to his brigade commander that he saw badly wounded Algerian *Tirailleurs* still in the trenches and not evacuated after six days. To me, these examples of moral courage are even more compelling than the numerous examples of battlefield courage. Going out of the way to help a fellow soldier was certainly not unique to the *Joyeux*. We need to be wary of caricatures, and Toto's example alone is not enough to build the case for a reputation, but there is power in his story, because we don't always expect the lowest of the low to be so noble. That is the story of the *Joyeux*.

Notes:

1. Pierre Mac Orlan, *Le Bataillon de la Mauvaise Chance* (Paris: Les Éditions de France, 1933), 169.
2. Pierre Dufour, *Les Bat' d'Af'* (Paris: Pygmalion, 2004), 86. The Greek deities of the east and west wind, *Flore* and *Zéphyr,* were married according to mythology. The nicknames for the battalions are believed to have been derived from the popularity of a ballet by Charles Didelot (1767 – 1837) – *Flore et Zéphyr* – which featured dancers "flying" on wires. *Chardonnerets* translates as Goldfinches.
3. Paul F. Deschaume, *Un Ch'ti chez les Joyeux* (Versailles: TdB Éditions, 2008), 120.
4. Antoine Camus, *Les Bohêmes du Drapeau* (P. Brunet, Editeur – Librarie, 1863), 6.
5. Feriel Ben Mahmoud, *Bat' d'Af* (Éditions Mengès, 2006), 27. The words sung to the bugle call may be the earliest recorded reference to the *Joyeux*, but this may be a case of "which came first," as the nickname could easily have predated the song.
6. Mac Orlan, *Le Bataillon de la Mauvaise Chance*, 57.
7. Louis Garros, *Historama, hors série No 10 – Les Africains* (Paris: Editions Chaix-Defosses-Neogravure, 1970), 147.
8. Albert Londres, *Dante N'Avait Rien Vu, Biribi* (1924; Reprint, Paris: Arlea, 2010), 98.
9. Dr. Louis Combe, *Le Soldat d'Afrique – 1* (Paris: Henri Charles-Lavauzelle, 1912), 59.
10. Ibid., 58.
11. Joseph Dimier, *Un Régulier chez lez Joyeux* (Paris: Bernard Grasset, 1928), 85.
12. The *Armée d'Afrique* was not a formal military formation, but a term for the collection of units that made up the French North African garrison.
13. Anthony Clayton, *France, Soldiers and Africa* (London: Brassey's Defence Publishers, 1988), 50.
14. Ibid., 6.
15. Deputy Pierre Richard, quoted in Dufour, *Les Bat' d'Af'*, 38.
16. Ben Mahmoud, *Bat' d'Af,* 24.
17. Anthony Clayton provides a very good primer on European and African regiments of the *Armée d'Afrique* in *France Soldiers and Africa*, see chapters 8 & 9.
18. Clayton, *France Soldiers and Africa*, 89.
19. Lieutenant Colonel Mangin, *La Force Noire* (Paris, Librairie Hachette et Cie, 1911), 226-228.
20. See for example the report of the *1er Battalion Infanterie Légère d'Afrique* to *90e Brigade* Head-Quarters that badly wounded Tirailleurs had not been evacuated after six days. JMO *1er BMILA*, 30 November 1914.
21. Dufour, *Les Bat' d'Af'*, 243.
22. Ibid., 254.
23. Clayton, *France Soldiers and Africa*, 90.
24. Combe, *Le Soldat d'Afrique – 1*, 33.
25. General Staff, War Office, *Handbook of the French Army 1914* (Nashville: The Battery Press, 1995), 204.
26. 25,000 is the number reported for reservists of the *Infanterie Légère d'Afrique* in 1903, see Anonymous, "*Les Bataillons d'Afrique et leur Organisation Actuelle*" *Journal des Sciences Militaires*, Tome 18 (Paris: Imprimerie et Librairie Militaires, 1903), p 409.
27. War office, *Handbook of the French Army 1914*, 64.
28. Ibid., 66-69.
29. Combe, *Le Soldat d'Afrique – 1*, 23.
30. Ibid., 71.
31. Dufour, *Les Bat' d'Af'*, 50.
32. Ibid., 44.
33. Commandant Ordioni, *La Réorganisation des Bataillons d'Infanterie Légère d'Afrique* (Paris : Librairie Militaire R Chapelot et Cie, 1911), 26-27.
34. Albert Londres, *Dante N'Avait Rien Vu, Biribi*, 51-52.
35. Francis Doré, *Albert Londres N'A Rien Vu* (Paris : Eugène Figuière, 1930), 173.
36. Combe, *Le Soldat d'Afrique – 1*, 48.
37. Ordioni, *La Réorganisation des Bataillons d'Infanterie Légère d'Afrique*, 14.
38. Ibid., 13.
39. Dr. R Jude, *Les Dégénérés dans les Bataillons d'Afrique* (Vannes : B. Le Beau, 1907), 13.
40. Ibid., 8-9.

41. Ibid., 21.
42. Combe, *Le Soldat d'Afrique – 1*, 26.
43. Jude, *Les Dégénérés dans les Bataillons d'Afrique*, 28.
44. Doré, *Albert Londres N'A Rien Vu*, 69.
45. Ibid., 111-112.
46. Both Dufour and Ben Mahmoud assert that homosexuality was an established practice.
47. Bernard Naudin in *l'Assiette au Beurre, No 227 – Biribi* (Paris: E. Victor, 5 August 1905), 303.
48. Deschaume, *Un Ch'ti chez les Joyeux*, 119.
49. Jude, *Les Dégénérés dans les Bataillons d'Afrique*, 34.
50. Combe, *Le Soldat d'Afrique – 1*, 94.
51. Combe, *Le Soldat d'Afrique – 1*, 97-98.
52. Mac Orlan, *Le Bataillon de la Mauvaise Chance*, 127-128.
53. Ben Mahmoud, *Bat' d'Af*, 87.
54. Mac Orlan, *Le Bataillon de la Mauvaise Chance*, 94-95.
55. Combe, *Le Soldat d'Afrique – 1*, 2.
56. Mac Orlan, *Le Bataillon de la Mauvaise Chance*, 70.
57. Mac Orlan, *Le Bataillon de la Mauvaise Chance*, 77.
58. Combe, *Le Soldat d'Afrique – 1*, 21.
59. Mac Orlan, *Le Bataillon de la Mauvaise Chance*, 95.
60. Combe, *Le Soldat d'Afrique – 1*, 71.
61. Jude, *Les Dégénérés dans les Bataillons d'Afrique*, 44.
62. Joseph Dimier, *Un Régulier chez lez Joyeux*, 103-104.
63. Deschaume, *Un Ch'ti chez les Joyeux*, 113.
64. War Office, *Handbook of the French Army 1914*, 56.
65. See Appendix A.
66. War Office, *Handbook of the French Army 1914*, 74.
67. Jude, *Les Dégénérés dans les Bataillons d'Afrique*, 45.
68. Mac Orlan, *Le Bataillon de la Mauvaise Chance*, 142.
69. See for example, the cover of the *Historique du 1er Bataillon d'Infanterie Légère d'Afrique*. Anonymous, Berger-Levrault, undated, which depicts the Flag of Mazagran and counts the holes in each colour band.
70. Paul Guénin, transcribed in Pierre Dufour, *Les Bat' d'Af'*, 117.
71. Antoine Camus, *Bohêmes du Drapeau*, 7.
72. Combe, *Le Soldat d'Afrique – 1*, 18.
73. JMO *1er BMILA*, 31 October 1914.
74. JMO *1er BMILA*, 17 November 1914.
75. JMO *77e Division*, 1 February 1915.
76. Anonymous, *Historiques du 3e Bataillon de Marche et du 4e Bataillon* (Paris: Henri Charles-Lavauzelle, 1920), 6.
77. JMO *45e Division*, 10 January 1915.
78. JMO *90e Brigade*, 16 February 1915.
79. Anonymous, *Historiques du 3e Bataillon de Marche et du 4e Bataillon*, 16-22.
80. Colonel G. W. L. Nicholson, *The Canadian Expeditionary Force, 1914-1919* (Ottawa: Queen's Printer, 1964), 56.
81. Dominique Kalifa, Biribi (Paris: Editions Perrin, 2009), 161.
82. Mac Orlan, *Le Bataillon de la Mauvaise Chance*, 7-8.
83. Jude, *Les Dégénérés dans les Bataillons d'Afrique*, 89

A sergeant of the *4ᵉ Bataillon d'Infanterie Légère d'Afrique*, taken in 1893 at Gabès, Tunisia. The uniform of the *Joyeux*, with its conspicuous red trousers and dark blue coat was essentially identical to any other French infantryman. The first steps to provide a more suitable uniform were begun in November 1914. The *Joyeux* may have begun recieving the new khaki uniform in December of that year. (Photographer: unknown. Author's collection)

Coat button, *Infanterie Légère d'Afrique*, 1832-1844. (Photographer: Allan Lougheed)

Coat button, *Infanterie Légère d'Afrique*, circa 1914. (Photographer: Allan Lougheed)

Joyeux of the class of 1909 are escorted by *gendarmes* to be embarked for North Africa. (Photo Courtesy of the Bibliothèque nationale de France)

MÉNAGE
Monsieur et Madame... sans Bébé.

Supporters of the disciplinary corps used homosexuality to argue that there were "degenerate" men who needed to be kept out of the army. Critics pointed to homosexuality in an effort to demonstrate the inhumanity of the corps, as Bernard Naudin does in this case in a satyrical Illustration for *L'Assiette au Beurre*, 5 August 1905. In English the caption reads: Couple, Mister and Missus... without baby. (Artist: Bernard Naudin, copyright Estate of Bernard Naudin / SODRAC (2012))

A post card depicting the Flag of Mazagran. The white specks on the flag are bullet holes. (Photographer: Jean Geiser. Author's collection)

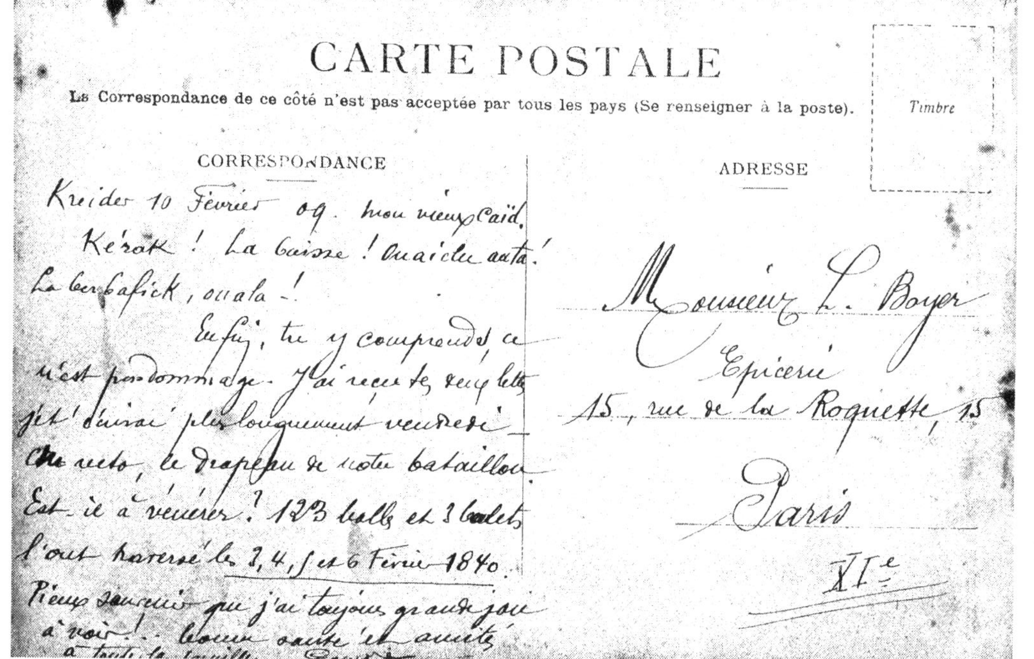

The post card was evidently sent home by a *Joyeux*, who writes “Kreider 10 February 09. My old caïd. […] finally, you understand it is not too bad there […] On the other side, the flag of our battalion. Is it to be revered? 123 balls and 3 bullets traversed it on 3, 4, 5 and 6 February 1840. Pious souvenir that I always have great joy to see…” (Author’s collection)

Looking north towards Lizerne, this road became the new fighting line of the 3e BMILA when they advanced after 2:40 am, 23 April 1915, and encountered Germans already dug in on the west bank of the Yser canal. The flat ground made any further advance impossible, but the road embankment offered enough protection to establish a new trench. The road runs parallel to the Yser canal, which is just beyond the tree line on the right-hand edge of the photo. (Photographer: Allan Lougheed)

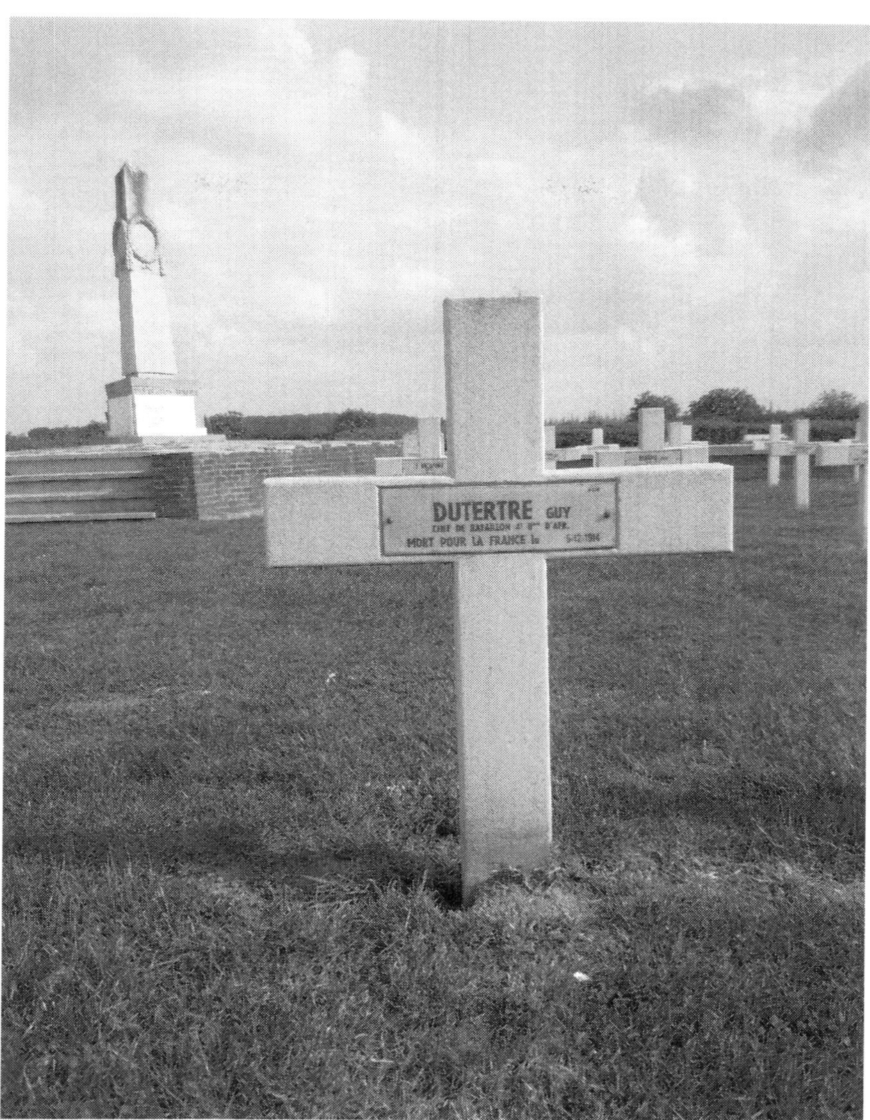

The final resting place of Major Dutertre, Commanding Officer of the *3ᵉ Bataillon de Marche d'Infanterie Légère d'Afrique*, killed 5 December 1914, during the attack on the *Maison du Passeur*, buried at St. Charles de Potyze Cemetery, Belgium. (Photographer: Allan Lougheed)

Part One

War Diary

of the 1er Bataillon de Marche d'Infanterie Légère d'Afrique

During the Campaign against Germany

From 14 October 1914 to 6 October 1917

---

14 October 1914

3 Cies de marche of the 2e Bataillon d'Afrique, constituted at Aït-Lias, left that post for Meknés, where they will be brought in three stages. They bear the numbers 1, 2, and 3.
1ere Cie de marche formed from elements of the 1e and 2e active companies
2e Cie de marche formed from elements of the 3e and 4e active companies
3e Cie de marche formed from elements of the 5e and 6e active companies

Officer Cadre

1ere Compagnie:	Lieutenant	**Sauvage**
	Reserve Lieutenant	**Villain**
2e Compagnie	Captain	**Wéber** OC the detachment until Meknés
	Lieutenant	**Izaac**
	Reserve s/Lieutenant	**Porte**
3e Compagnie	Captain	**Lormier**
	Lieutenant	**Blondé**

Strength at the departure from Lias

	NCO's	Corporals	Chasseurs	Horses
1e Compagnie	9	13	172	
2e Compagnie	10	16	169	
3e Compagnie	10	14	133	

	First stage to Ito ....38 kilometres	
15 October 1914	Stage Ito to El Hadjeb.................24 "	
16 October 1914	Stage El Hadjeb to Meknés.........32 "	

The detachment arrived at Meknés where it was received by Captain **Noël**, battalion adjutant of the 2e Bataillon d'Afrique, designated to take command of the Bataillon de marche.

The Battalion will stay formed in 3 companies until its arrival in France where it will be completed with four companies, by a Comp[ie] de marche of the 1er Bataillon and by reinforcements from the same battalion which will be distributed in the three companies.

The Battalion is thus Constituted at Meknés

—

Captain Commanding	Captain	**Noël**
Deputy Officer	Lieutenant	**Sauvage**
Supply Officer	Lieutenant	**Blondé**
1ere Compagnie	Captain	**Bidot**
	Lieutenant	**Leclerc**
	Lieutenant	**Villain**
2e Compagnie	Captain	**Wéber**
	Lieutenant	**Izaac**
	s/Lieutenant	**Porte**
3e Compagnie	Captain	**Lormier**
	Lieutenant	**Delbreil**

_____ Strength _____

550 NCO's, Corporals, and chasseurs
Sojourn at Meknés from 16 to 19 and 20

19 and 20 October

Embarkation at Meknés by railway of two echelons of equal force for Méhédya

The voyage was completed in two days by Dar-bel-Hamri and Kenidra

22, 23, 24, 25 October

Sojourn at Méhédya

26 October

Embarkation of the Battalion by the packet boat "Tomé" destined for Marseille.

30 October

Disembarkation at Marseille.

The Battalion is directed towards the "Parc de l'Exposition" where it encamped.

Table indicating the numeric state of the Officers, rank and file, and horses disembarked on the 30th.

Officers..........12
Effectives..........542
Horses..........7

31 October

The detachment formed by the 1er Bataillon d'Afrique entered into the composition of the Bataillon de marche as reinforcements of the first three Companies and, in addition, formed the 4e Compagnie.

	Captain	**Renaud**
	Lieutenant	**Lefévre**
1	Chief Warrant Officer	
1	Warrant Officer	
1	Sergeant-Major	
13	Sergeants	
12	Corporals	
3	Buglers	
163	Chasseurs	
194		

__ Battalion Order __

Battalion Order № 1
Organization of the
1er Bon de Marche
d' I.L.A.

On the date of 31 October 1914, The Bataillon de Marche is at last constituted by the [addition] of the 1er Cie of the 1er Bataillon d'Afrique which joined itself with the 3 Cies formed by the 2e Bataillon d'Afrique.

The Battalion is the 1er de Marche

By reading the histories of the Battalions that contributed to its formation, in commemoration of the **Moroccan** campaign, from which the new elements were directly provided, it is permissible to say that the 1er Bataillon "takes after it" and to hope that glorious new pages will be inscribed in the annals of the Bataillons d'Afrique.

Under the aegis of the Flag of **Mazagran**, the Captain Commanding, took in all confidence the Command of the 1er Bataillon de Marche d'Infanterie Légère d'Afrique.

From 1 to 10 November 1914.

Preparation and organization of material, combat train, regimental train, food, ammunition, etc... by the date of 9 November.

__ Battalion Order __

No 2
Promotions and Transfers
By virtue of the power which is conferred to him, and by decree on the application of the Interior Service, art. 23, The Captain Commanding the 1er Bataillon de Marche d'Infanterie Légère d'Afrique, promotes:

1° Sergeant –major of the 1er Cie, **Berthomet** No: Mle: 4054, Quarter-Master Sergeant of the same company.
2° Sergeants:

Of the 1ere Compagnie,	**Perret**, No Mle 3412, corporal of the same Coy
Of the 2e Compagnie,	**Péguy**, No Mle 3921, corporal of the same Coy
	Blondeau, No Mle 3087, corporal of the same Coy
Of the 3e compagnie,	**Renaudier**, No Mle 3742, corporal-medic of the S.H.R.

3° Corporals:

Of the 1er Compagnie;	**Tellier**, No Mle 2808 } chasseurs of the same Coy
	Meunier, No Mle 2911
Of the 3e Compagnie;	**Cornuaux**, No Mle 019642 } chasseurs of the same Coy
	Conzaux, No Mle 01794
Of the 4e Compagnie;	**Olzy**, No Mle 3233 } chasseurs of the same Coy
	Ethingre, No Mle 2376
	Marie, No Mle 2700
	Reverdy, No Mle 3225

By application of the decree on the Interior Service, art. 24, and the decision organizing the Bataillon d'Afrique de Marche, the following transfers are pronounced in the interest of the service:
The Sergeants, **Lovisi**, N^{o} M^{le} 3077 and **Guinot**, N^{o} M^{le} 3313 of the 4e Compagnie pass to the 1er Compagnie.
The Sergeant, **Fonquerni**, N^{o} M^{le} 3102, of the 4e Compagnie, passes to the 2e Compagnie.
The Sergeant, **Biaggi**, N^{o} M^{le} 2025, of the 4e Compagnie passes to the 3e Compagnie.
The Corporal, **Barriée**, N^{o} M^{le} 3647, of the 4e Compagnie passes to the S.H.R., as corporal-medic replacing corporal **Renaudier** promoted to Sergeant.
These promotions and transfers will date from 10 November.

N° 3
Promotion
By Presidential decree of 3 November 1914, inserted in the "Official Journal" on 6 November, Captain **Noël**, of the 2e Bataillon d'Infanterie Légère d'Afrique, is promoted Battalion Chief.

10 November

The Battalion received the order to depart for the front. It must embark at 22^{H}45 by railway destined for Bourget regulating station.

Four hours before the departure, Captain **Bidot**, commanding the 1er Compagnie, broke his right wrist by falling. He was admitted to hospital. At that time, many chasseurs in illegal absence were declared deserters. Others illegally absent and returned at the moment of departure were left at the depot of the Bataillons d'Afrique.

Nominal roll of the Officers on the day of departure

Head-Quarters	Commander	**Noël**
Deputy Officer Lieut		**Sauvage**
Supply Officer Lieut		**Blondé**
Medical Officer 2nd class		**Aubert**
1er Compagnie	Lieutenant	**Leclercq**
	dº	**Villain**
2e Compagnie	Captain	**Wéber**
	Lieutenan	**Isaac**
	s/Lieutenant	**Porte**
3e Compagnie	Captain	**Lormier**
	Lieutenant	**Delbreil**
4e Compagnie	Captain	**Renaut**
	Lieutenant	**Lefèvre**

Situation of numeric strength

Chief Warrant Officers...
Warrant Officers..
Sergeants Major..
Orderly Sergeants...
Sergeants..
Corporals...
Chasseurs..

	Totals
Horses	49

Embarkation on the 10th at Areng station at Marseilles at 22H45

12 November

Arrival at Bourget at 11H30.
One chasseur stayed at Perrache watching the departure of the train.
The Battalion was directed at 12H15 towards Aubigny at 10km west of Arras, to enter into the composition of the 10e Armée.
Sergeant Major **Terrasson** of the 2e Compagnie had to be left at the Creil ambulance.

13 November

Arrived at Aubigny at 7 hours in the morning. The Battalion is designated to form part of the Army reserve, received the order to encamp at the village of Agnières 1 km east of Aubigny.
The enemy is fortified in many trench lines 10 km to the N and N.E. of Agnières. To the West, at the village of Aubigny is found the HQ of the 33e Corps. To the East, at the village of Capelle Fermont, 1 km from Agnières, an artillery group is encamped.
10e Armée: General de **Maudhuy**
33e Corps: General **Pétain**

14 and 15 November

Rest at Agnières

16 November

The Battalion Chief received the order to constitute a machine gun section. The material and animals for two sections were conferred to the Battalion (section from the Corps and section of the 2e Bataillon de Marche which will arrive later).
At 15 hours, the Battalion received the order to go to encamp at Maroeuil, village situated a 7 km E. S.E of Agnières.
Departed Agnières at 16H30
Point of assembly; Laly Farm to the south of the village, at the junction of the road coming from Agnières to the National highway from Montreuil to Mézières.
Itinerary: Agnières road to National highway, National highway until the Maroeuil road junction.
Arrived at Maroeuil at 18H30.
The entire Battalion is encamped in a sugar refinery.
Our advanced lines, formed of several lines of trenches, cover the front of the Brigade sector, between Maison blanche hill 90, National highway from Bethune to Chateau Thierry and the crossroads situated to the N.N.W. of hill 109 (at the base from the S of Mont St. Eloi, map of 80000. Arras SE.)
The village of Maroeuil is occupied to the N.E. by the 1er Bataillon de marche, to the E by a battalion of Tirailleurs, to the S by a battalion of the 27e Territorial, to the W. by a battalion of the 2e Zouaves. (Divisional reserve, destined to constitute the relief troops on the sector front.)
At 20h30, the vicinity of the sugar refinery was shelled by German heavy artillery.
The instruction is to evacuate provisionally, the Battalion went to form itself 500m further S at the entrance to Etrun, then the bombardment having ceased, the encampment was reinstated at 22hrs. The rest of the night without incident.
From the 16th the Battalion formed part of the **45e Division**, General **Drude**, and the **90e Brigade**, General **Quiquandon**.
The General Staff of the Brigade can be found at Mareouil also.

17 November

At 13 hours, the Battalion was inspected by General **Quiquandon**.
At 14 hours the Battalion left the sugar refinery to encamp in the N.E part of the village.
The enemy is established at Neuville-Saint-Vaast and at la Targette.
Resupply orders for the 17th.
Resupply of the T.R. by Section 2 of the C.V.A.D. – 45e Division at Hermaville (W. exit eleven hours resupply in meat.
45e Division – Crossroads 1500m W. of Etrun at 14h30.
Evacuations – to the resupply station (cripples only.)
Labourers – The 1er and 4e compagnies furnished at 18 hours, each 100 labourers who were put at the disposal of the engineers for work in the trenches.
That detachment was surprised at the end of the work, towards 22h.30, by a searchlight. It suffered machine gun fire for some moments. The men dove for cover instantly, suffering no losses and returned without incident.
Groupe Franc – Some volunteers were asked for in the Companies to constitute a corps franc for a Forlorn Hope which will be employed in a coup de main. Effectives: 73 men, 17 corporals, 22 NCO's, Lieutenant **Izaac** (total of the volunteers of the Bon)

18 November

Resupply of the T.R. at Hermaville, same point of last night's meat resupply: crossroads 1500m W. of Etrun.
Evacuations: to the resupply station.

__ General Order № 121 __

I. General situation without notable change in the North, where the struggle diminished in intensity, without change on the front of the Division, were it not for a little more activity of the enemy infantry and artillery.
II....................
III...................
Rest for the Battalion.

19 November

90e Brigade General Staff brought to Etrun.
91er Brigade General Staff to Anzin St. Aubins
The Battalion is encamped today at Maroeuil

The 2ᵉ Cⁱᵉ today formed a posse of police at Mairie and eight posses were sent.
The 3ᵉ and 4ᵉ Cⁱᵉˢ each furnished 100 labourers for the engineers.
Departure of the detachment towards the work to be executed in the trenches of the front at 18 hours.
Returned at 5 hours on 20 November. Same resupply orders as last evening [for] 20 November.

20 November

Same situation as last evening.
The 2ᵉ Compagnie furnished 100 labourers with Lieutenant **Izaac** for the trenches.
Departure at 18 hours

Return at 3 hours on the 21st without incident
The Battalion received:
1° The order to furnish 3 companies to occupy the trenches of the 1st line, with a battalion of Zouaves.
Departure on the 21st at 3 hours.
2° The order to furnish 80 volunteers of the Corps franc at the disposal of Captain **Ayme** of the 2ᵉ Zouaves, to effect a coup de main on an enemy trench situated close to Maison Blanche.
Reconnaissance of the sectors in the afternoon by the officers of the Battalion.
Companies assigned for the occupation of the sectors:
1ᵉʳ, 3ᵉ, and 4ᵉ, Cⁱᵉˢ.
Because of that service the Corps franc could only furnish 5 Sergeants and 65 men and corporals.

21 November

Mission given to Groupe franc.
-" Instruction for the execution of a coup de main on Maison blanche." –

1 – **Goal of the operation**. – Clear the German trenches of their defenders to the east and close to Maison blanche, capture a machine gun supposed to be in the trenches, destroy the said trenches with charges and withdraw rapidly.
II – **effectives engaged**. – A groupe franc of 200 volunteers chosen in the 4 corps of the Brigade under the orders of Lieutenant **Ayme** of the 2ᵉ Zouaves. A small detachment of sappers is attached.
III – **Supporting troops**. – The Companies occupying the trenches neighbouring Maison blanche and said farm.
IV – **Execution** – A searchlight will illuminate:
21 November from 18h.50 to 19 hours, the zone from Aux-Rietz – La Targette
From 19 hours to 19ʰ3' the ground shelled by group **Lenoble**,
From 19 hʳˢ3 to 19h.25 again the zone Aux-Rietz – La Targette

Finally at close to $19^{h}25$, the zone Maison-blanche – La Targette together
At 19 hours group **Lenoble** will execute fire by salvoes on the trenches to clear them.
Duration of fire 4 Minutes.-
From the end of the fire, the Groupe franc will throw themselves on the German trenches.
Probable duration of the operation, from 15 to 20 minutes.
At close to $19^{h}15$, group **Fraichet** will execute fire by salvoes on the borders south of Aux-Rietz, La Targette, and Neuville St. Vaast.
All details of the execution were made by verbal instructions to interested parties.
V – **Contacts**. – As well as the detailed orders given, telephone contact was established between the post of Lieutenant **Ayme** at Maison blanche and the Artillery.
An artillery observation officer is attached to Lieutenant **Ayme**
VI – **Time** – A runner of each element of execution will come to obtain brigade time at 14 hours.
Assembly point–
The men of the Groupe franc of the Battalion received the order to have themselves at 3 hours in the morning at the junction of the Thérouanne causeway with the Maroeuil La Targette highway.
Following a delay in departure, only the men of the 2e, 3e, and 4e,Compagnies, in total 47 men and 4 Sergeants, found themselves at the place indicated and were taken by Lieutenant **Ayme**.
The 19 men of the 1er Cie and 1 Sergeant left with their Company and waited at the command post of the Sector until 5 hours. At that moment Lieutenant **Sauvage** arrived at that post, gathered the men of the 1ere and conducted them by the communication trench up to Maison blanche which was reached at 6 hours.
Strength of the Groupe franc of the Battalion at that time. –
66 chasseurs, 5 Sergeants.
Later, in the day towards 14 hours, Lieutenant **Izaac**, on the orders of the Battalion Chief, went to reinforce the group with 10 men.
Total effectives: 76 chasseurs, 5 Sergeants, 1 Lieutenant.

___ Report of Lieutenant Izaac ___

On 21 November, the General commanding the 90^{e} Brigade, ordered a coup de main on “Maison Blanche.” The goal of the operation was to clear the German trenches of their defenders to the east and close to “Maison Blanche,” capture a machine gun supposed to be in the

trenches, destroy said trenches with charges and withdraw rapidly. Lieutenant **Ayme** of the 2e Zouaves commanded 200 volunteers of the 90e Brigade and a small detachment of engineers. According to his orders, the groupe franc of the 1er Bataillon de Marche d'Afrique was divided into two groups for the assault.
1st group: Sergeant **Lamy** and 70 chasseurs or NCOs.
2nd group: Sergeant **Blondeau** and 10 chasseurs.
The 1st group must clear the ground of the German straight trenches and traverse those trenches to the right and left.
Lieutenant **Ayme** must go with them.
The 2nd group must stop the runaways from the left trenches and look to seize the supposed machine gun.
Lieutenant **Izaac** and 10 Zouaves must act with that group.
At 19 hours precisely, a searchlight illuminated the remote German lines, illuminating along the zone of the assault.
At the same instant, the 75s of group **Lenoble** executed a formidable fire by salvoes on the trenches to be cleared.The French infantrymen, crouched in our lines, bayonets fixed, heard a frightful uproar; earth sometimes flew among them, coming from shells striking 15 metres in front of our trenches.At 19 hours 4 minutes, the fire ceased abruptly, the searchlight extinguished itself; the whole line had already left for the assault in great silence.

1st Group Lamy. –
In one bound, they entered in the German trenches which were at 15 metres from the French trenches. The unwounded enemies were surprised, crouched down; the most brave tried to defend themselves with bayonet or with knife, two or three officers or NCO's with revolver.
The greater part fled or sought to flee in disorder.
The "Joyeux killing forty Germans with side arm, the signal to retreat was given; they quickly collected some helmets, rifles, bags, etc... and retired to the French trenches.

2nd Group Blondeau. –
He left behind Lieutenant **Izaac** followed by 10 Zouaves.
He ran at all speed towards the supposed place of the machine gun he had 100 metres to go.
Despite the icy ground and some barbed wire occasioning disagreeable falls, that group arrived at the left of the German trenches.
There too, there were runaways and enemies on the ground, killed or wounded by 75s. The signal to retreat stopped the élan of the group. They ran, skirting the German trenches to disengage the fire of a section of Zouaves that remained behind.
One heard again the cries of terror and pain of the Germans while the 2nd line enemy began to fire furiously. The group stopped in our lines without losses, after staying four minutes in open ground.
The intensity of the German fire increased.
The groupe franc of the "Joyeux" remained together nearby the

ordinary troops of the trenches in case of counter-attack.
The Germans only dared to carry that out by fire.
The bullets rattled, and large calibre shells fell all around "Maison blanche."
The "Joyeux" therefore stayed the whole night.
Among them could be found men passing a third sleepless night and circumstances having forced them to take no food since the 21st in the morning. The night was icy, one chasseur had his feet frozen.
Our losses are, with the Groupe Franc, for the 21st and the 22nd.

Rossé	Killed at the French trench		
Secondi	Mortally wounded	dº	
Culpin	wounded	dº	
Druon	wounded	dº	
Floire	wounded at the French trench		
Mauconduit	wound with side arm at the assault		} all these
Bazet	dº		} wounds
Savary	dº		} are light
Métail	dº		}

21,22 and 23 November

Duty in the trenches, Brigade Order received on the 20th.
For a relief of 21 November, 3 Companies of the 1er Bataillon d'Afrique will go to the trenches where they will relieve:
1°, 1 Company of Zouaves of the 1st line
2°, 1 Company of Zouaves of the 2nd line
3°, 1 Company of Tirailleurs of the 3rd line
Roster: 1er, 3e and 4e Compagnies.
Effectives engaged: 162 rank and file
2 Officers

Events as follows.

The 1er Compagnie had furnished the following detachments:
A. 1 platoon at Maison blanche until the 23rd at 4H45
B. 1 Section to the west of the Arras to Bethune highway flanking Company **Lormier**; placed on the 22nd November at 10H30, it was relieved on the 23rd at 4 hours.
C. 1 Section in reserve in the trenches of the 2nd line.
On the 22nd towards 20 hours, a lively enough fusillade appearing to come from the Territorial platoon reinforcing Company **Lormier** was heard. The Company did not have to intervene in it.
The platoon at Maison blanche alone fired some salvos on isolated Germans (8 to 10 cartridges per man).

Losses:
Killed – nil
Wounded – **Harpinaud** Chasseur 2nd cl. lightly wounded in the left thigh on the 22nd at 11 hours by a projectile.
Munitions:
The spent cartridges have been replaced by cartridges abandoned in

the trenches.
The provisioning remains complete.
Food:
As usual. The company vehicle provided food until kitchens were installed on the sunken road at 500 metres to the west of the trenches. (road says "the electric poles").

Report of the 3e Compagnie
Effectives engaged: 107 men
2 Officers

Events occurred.
The company had been reinforced during the night of the 21st to 22nd by a platoon of the 27e Territorial.
Munitions
The only fire carried out was one cartridge by a section
Provisioning of munitions complete.
Losses: nil

Report of the 4e Compagnie

One section in the 1st line	} first and second lines
One half section supporting the artillery	} situated to the West and
The rest in 2nd line	} on the border of Ecurie

Transfers:
Lieutenant **André** of the 2e Bataillon d'Afrique, adjutant of Lieutenant-Colonel **Pouget**, coming from occidental Morocco and disembarked at Bordeaux, arrived at Maroeuil on the 21st with his batman and a horse. Posted to the Battalion on the date of the 21st, Major **Noël** conferred the command of the machine gun section to him.

23 November.

The 1er Compagnie furnished a detachment of 100 labourers with their cadres to be put at the disposal of the engineers. Departure at 6 hours, return on the 24th at 4 hours 30. On the outward journey, the group had a chasseur grievously wounded in the head by a ball. Chasseur 1st class **Lefaon** was directed immediately to the aid post at Thérouanne.
Resupply of the T.R. by the section II of the CVAD Hermaville, West exit at eleven hours.
Resupply of meat; effected at the same point and at the same time as the 22nd.

Congratulations;
The Battalion Chief received yesterday from the General of the Division. In the course of a meeting, the General of the Brigade had highly marked his satisfaction with the bearing of the volunteers of the Battalion, in the course of the operation that was effected in the evening of the 21st to the 22nd November (assault on the German

trenches).
The volunteers of the Battalion had been clearly remarked upon for their spirit, by the chiefs and comrades of the other Corps; they are now acknowledged to "have guts," that they carry on. They as well as the Battalion have the right to be proud of being thus honoured.
The Commander praised them for their tour wholeheartedly.

__ Battalion Order Nº 5 __

Promotions
Following the operation of capturing the German trenches by the group of volunteers of the Battalion, in the night of the 21st to the 22nd November 1914 and by the application of art. 23 of the regulations of the "Interior Service," The Chief of the Battalion made the following promotions:
1st to the rank of Corporal Bugler:
Of the S.H.R. Nº Mle 1641 **Tindy**, Bugler of the 2e Compagnie.
2nd To 1st Class of the 1er Compagnie:

	Nº Mle	3307	**Culpin**	2nd Class of the same Compagnie
	"	4189	**Mauconduit**	dº
	"	3569	**Harpinaud**	dº
2e Cie:	Nº Mle	3346	**Floire**	dº
4e Cie:	Nº Mle	2787	**Métail**	dº
	"	2748	**Bazet**	dº
	"	2798	**Savary**	dº
	"	3198	**Druon**	dº

The promotions will date from 24 November 1914.

24 November

Rest in the encampment at Maroeuil.

25 November

The 2e 3e and 4e Compagnies did duty in the trenches at 3 hours in the morning in the sector of the centre (Bethune-Chateau Thierry highway, Arras to Neuville St. Vaast road, to the south of Maison blanche).

26 November

Operations of the Groupe franc under the command of Lieutenant **Izaac** in the night of 25 to 26 November 1914.

On 25 November 1914, the groupe franc (2 officers 80 rank and file) received the following order from the General commanding the 90^{e} Brigade

"clear of their occupants and destroy with charges a sap head and its communication trench undertaken by the Germans to the North of Ecurie, to the west and near the Ecurie road to Neuville St. Vaast."

A detachment of engineers is attached to Lieutenant **Izaac** who must execute the order. Company **Millet** of the 2^{e} Tirailleurs is in support.

26 November at 5 hours, the 75s of the Artillery (group **Lenoble**) fired 10 canon shots on the designated communication trench. The 10th shot was the signal to launch the assault.

Lieutenant **Leclercq**, Sergeant **Moureaux** and ten brave chasseurs jumped into the head of the Sap, running along the communication trench with bayonet, chasing in front of them those Germans thrown into a panic and succeeding in killing four. Two groups of twenty chasseurs supported in the open ground to the right and left of the communication trench; the engineers commenced to prepare their mines in the head of the sap. The rest of the detachment was ready to act with bayonet. At $5^{H}10$, 7 German mines exploded producing disorder in us, understandably enough.

Sergeant **Moureaux** and chasseur **Demortier**, caught between the German trenches and the mine, ran at that trench, **Moureaux** was wounded in his hand at point blank range in taking the rifle of a German. At 5 hours 15, the signal to retreat was given, the groupe franc returned to our lines. **Moureaux** and **Demortier** came back bringing two wounded.

The head of the Sap is still unscathed, the cords having been cut by us, at the moment of the disorder produced by the explosion of the German mines. But the Communication trench was largely destroyed by the German mines themselves.

The enemy, protected by shields, would rebuild the communication trench, while a violent counter-attack by fire was produced at that point and around it.

Lieutenant **Millet** commanding the Support Company was killed.

At $16^{h}45$, four cases of melinite prepared ahead were thrown into the head of the Sap which was destroyed as well as a part of the communication trench rebuilt by the enemy. A new counter attack by fire, very violent, obliged the groupe franc to stay the night. They only returned to the camp on the 27th at 6 hours.

Disappeared: **Créon** of the 1er Cie at the moment of the explosion of the German mines.

Wounded:	**Allain**, of the 2e Cie	d°
reservist	**Gauthier**, of the 2e Cie	d°
	Houley	d°
	Massiera	d°
Sergeant	**Moureaux**, of the 2e Cie (infantry ball point blank)	

Fort of the 4e Cie (struck by a shell returning to camp)

Lieutenant **Izaac** reports:

Citation of the
Army
Accorded
Lieutenant **Leclercq**, “Very beautiful conduct during an assault, keeping a cool head, despite the explosion of German mines, returned to our lines in good order, killing an enemy with his own hand.” –
Sergeant **Moureaux**,” Caught between an enemy barricade and a mine in a communication trench, ran at the barricade, instantly making an end of the enemy. Wounded himself, brought back two wounded of his group to our lines, with marvellous sang-froid.” -
Demortier, “Caught between an enemy barricade and a German mine followed his chief to the barricade instantly finishing off the enemy. Carried a gravely wounded man to our lines over a run of a hundred metres under very violent enemy fire.” -
Allain
“Jumped bravely into a communication trench occupied by the enemy, pursuing them with bayonet until the moment of the explosion of a German mine, there grievously wounded and burnt. Gave proof of the energy, while wounded, to forget to feel sorry for himself to keep up the morale of his comrades.” –
Corporal **Tindy**,
“ Jumped first with bayonet into a communication trench occupied by the enemy and did excellent work there. Not for the first time.” –

In that operation, Lieutenant **Leclercq** with 10 men received the following order “On 10 shell strikes, your group will sortie from the French trenches, will jump into the German sap, will drive out the occupants and will secure their return at all costs by the communication trench in fifteen minutes. Signal to retreat; sudden siren blasts. You will be supported on the right and left. –
At the signal, and following the instructions received, Lieutenant **Leclercq**, Corporal **Tindy**, the chasseurs **Goy** and **Legrand**, jumped into the head of the sap, as well as Sergeant **Moureaux** with six chasseurs gaining around forty feet and jumping into the communication trench to cut off the retreat of the occupants. Those fled at the arrival of the first four assailants. It had been impossible to engage them, one of the two, who was hidden in an armoured sentry box situated around 45 metres from the head of the Sap, was killed by a knife thrust after his rifle was grabbed.
Fearing to be assailed by Germans who had hastily constructed a barricade around one hundred and fifty metres from the head of the sap, Sergeant **Moureaux** and four chasseurs charged up to that place.
Some minutes passed when 7 mines situated in the communication trench at 20 metre intervals from one another exploded causing the chasseurs of the groupe franc to tumble over each other.
Fifteen minutes after its entrance into the communication trench, the

groupe franc beat a retreat, though not having heard the signal to retreat, without leaving any of them in the enemy lines.
4e Compagnie: 2185 **Carré** Etienne, chasseur 1st class killed in the trench
2772 **Seube**, wounded during his service on sentry
2286 **Branche**, wounded during the return of the Company to the encampment

27 November

Machine gunners:

1503 **Billon**	2nd class	} wounded at their post in the trenches
3337 **Massierat**	dº	}
4327 **Marochin**	dº	}Killed at their posts
2767 **Descollaz**	dº	}

28 November

Rest in camp

29 November

Five Sections and the machine gun section do duty in the trenches of the Sector
The groupe franc participated in a counter-attack to retake a trench of the sector and to disengage trench 4, strongly menaced by the enemy (Bavarian).

Report of Lieutenant Izaac

On the affair of 29 November.
On 29 November 1914, at 13 hours 3, the groupe franc of the 1er Bataillon d'Afrique, received the order to assault the German trenches, to the left of a line composed of the Zouaves and chasseurs à pied.
The distance to be covered was about 80 metres.
After the preparation by the group of 75s of **Lenoble's** Artillery, the line of attack left for the assault at the precise hour.
In a magnificent élan, the greater part of the "Joyeux" arrived at the trench; very few killed or wounded by the enemy fell or stopped.
A hand to hand struggle ensued. The Germans, caught in their trenches, too crowded, defended themselves badly and made our men kill fifty with bayonet or shot point blank. A large enemy reinforcement coming from the rear and our left, some mines, some grenades shot from neighbouring communication trenches, made some chasseurs hesitate then return.
Their chief who had been lightly wounded and bruised by a shell, fell, some chasseurs put themselves around him, while rumour spread

that the Lieutenant was dead. The false rumour brought back many "Joyeux" to the friendly barricade, where furthermore, too many Zouaves crowded.

Sergeant **Salviny**, corporal **Tindy**, and some braves stayed in the German trench firing point blank without pity at all enemies except for a prisoner taken by Sergeant **Salviny**; that small group maintained itself for about 3 hours at the German trench, then perceiving the French retreat of the left wing, returned in good order by a communication trench to our lines.

Our losses were:

9 killed, 8 missing, 14 wounded (including 4 very lightly).

Killed

1er Cie **Sicre** corporal
2e Cie **Legrand** 2nd class
" **Lacour** "
3e Cie **Gradeler** Sergeant
" **Bourdat** Corporal
4e Cie **Montaz** Jean 2nd class
2268 **Pouilly** Joseph "
" **Lecotten** Laurent "
2294 **Lagache** Charles "

Missing

2e Cie **Bournez**
" **Guillomont**
3e Cie **Chauveau**
" **Lang**
" **Audubert**
" **Gilet**
" **Pelet**
4e Cie **Lorang** x

Wounded

1er Cie **Coquant** Sergeant
" **Coutant** 2nd class
" **Gardé** "
2e Cie **Izaac** Lieutenant
" **Gantereau** 2nd cl
" **Gaillie** "
3e Cie **Conraud** Corporal
" **Demortier** 1st cl
" **Buguet** 2nd
" **Ribery** "
4e Cie **Petit** Corporal
" **Métail** 2nd cl
" **Savary** "
" **Clément** "

All the chasseurs having taken part in the assault are to be congratulated.

All the braves who stayed with Sergeant **Salviny** and Corporal **Tindy** Are to be Reported for their truly magnificent conduct.

Salviny Sergeant:

'Entered the assault in a German trench, maintained himself there for three hours with a handful of men, inflicting serious losses on the enemy. Returned in good order bringing back French wounded that were on his way and took a prisoner. Returned last.

Tindy Corporal:

"Entered into a German trench, maintained himself there with some men in that trench. Took command of thirty chasseurs à pied, Zouaves, and chasseurs légère with authority, succeeding with his energy to bring them back to face the enemy."

Coquant Sergeant:

"Although lightly wounded in a French trench, left for the assault. Killed numerous Germans with his own hands until the moment when he was wounded for the 4th time."

Lerche 2nd class:

"Already prisoner of the Germans, and freed by two Zouaves, returned to the hand-to-hand combat with spirit and success."

Hérouin 2nd class:

"Spirit and sang-froid in hand-to-hand combat, during which time he

inflicted serious losses on the enemy."
Bazet 2nd class:
"Very beautiful conduct under fire, witnessed by Lieutenant **Léoni** of the 2nd Zouaves."

Eneman, Sauzet, Rousseau, Lorang, Savay, Detrez, Lecotten, Clément, Roussin, Métail, Oswald, Moutay, Pouilly, Lagache, Petit corporal.

"Maintained themselves for three hours with their Sergeant in an enemy trench, returned in order bringing back French wounded."

Report of Captain Wéber

On the affair of 29 November:
On 29 November 1914, at 4 hours, three sections of the 2e Cie (Captain **Wéber** and reserve s/Lieutenant **Porte**) went to occupy the trench of the 1st line isolated who found themselves forward of the village of Ecurie.
That trench also had to be occupied by 3 Sections of the regiment de marche of the Tirailleurs, but following an error, they did not arrive.
The occupied trench was separated from a neighbouring trench by an open space of around 80 metres, battered by the fire of two German machine guns and which could only be crossed at night.
In crossing the open passage, chasseur **Basserie** was lightly wounded in the lower leg, that did not stop him from fighting the whole day.
Scarcely installed, the company recoiled from gunshots and bombs from three different sides. To the front, on the right, and to the rear, they found German trenches.
At 8 hours, 1 corporal and 3 chasseurs were already killed and four chasseurs wounded.
The occupied trench was continued by a German trench which was only separated by a barricade of sand bags that had been destroyed many times in the day and rebuilt.
Other barriers were also established to the rear. On several occasions the Germans tried to penetrate into the trench but were immediately repulsed by the 4e Section commanded by s/Lieutenant **Porte** who occupied the extremity of the trench.
Although the situation was very difficult and though the length of the trench to be guarded was excessive for so few men, everyone, NCO's and chasseurs, competed in zeal and spirit to conserve the trench.
All those who were in the trench merited to be cited, because they had no less defiance and after having dressed the wounded or placed the dead in the shelter in the trench, each went back to his

spot to fight.
In 24 hours, those three sections lost 1/6th of their strength, that is to say:

Dead		Wounded	
Laffont	Corporal	**Vacher**	2nd Class
Bertheaux	2nd class	**Thirion**	"
Lanchez	"	**Basserie**	"
Pujat	"	**Lecompte**	"
		Puillotin	"
		Renard	"
		Sulot	"
		Challard	"

———

___ Report of Lieutenant Léoni of the 2e Zouaves ___

———

On the subject of the beautiful conduct of Sergeant **Salvini** during the attack on the German trench of 29 November.
"Sergeant **Salvini** of the 1er Bataillon d'Afrique was beside me in the German trench, and demonstrated great courage and great energy during the whole time that we stayed in the enemy trench.
He was the last to leave and always remained in contact with the enemy who were massed in their trench shelter.
That NCO merits to be reported to Command with a view to obtaining a well merited recompense."

30 November

Duty in the trenches:
3 Sections of the 3e Compagnie
2 Sections of the 4e Compagnie, Capt. **Lormier** and Lt **Lefévre**

Killed	Wounded	Missing
Vincelot Sergeant		**Nouyon**
2781 Clément Alphonse 4e Cie		
2082 **Camps** Marnis 2nd class		
Pointel d°		

Cartridges spent 15,000

Incidents:
Two bayonet attacks were made by the Germans, the 1st on the 30th towards 18 hours without importance. The 2nd towards midnight had been more serious.
Each attack was preceded by thrown bombs and grenades. The two attacks were repulsed vigorously by the 1er Section under the orders

of Chief Warrant Officer **Lahargouette**, supported by the fire of the other sections. All the chasseurs were very well composed, showing calm and sang-froid.

The Captain reported the following points on which it is necessary to attract the attention of the superior authorities:

1. The bad influence on the morale of the men who occupy that trench, who find themselves lost on the field of battle for the whole day in consequence of communications with the W trench.
2. Difficulties and dangers of going over there on clear nights.
3. Gravely wounded (Tirailleurs) were in the trenches for 6 days.
4. Number of dead lying in the trenches without having been able to be buried for want of tools.
It would be necessary for all detachments to bring general tools for doing urgent work.
The trenches will very likely be captured if care is not taken. (grenades provisioned)

From 1st December
To 2nd December

Duty in the trenches:
Company **Leclercq** 4 Sections 1 section of the 3e Compie

Killed	Wounded
Passereau of the 1er Cie	**Giovanai**
	Pascaud
	Canelli

From the 2nd
To the 3rd
December

Duty in the trenches Ecurie Sector
2e Compagnie 4 sections Captain **Wéber**
4e Compagnie 1 Section

Killed	Wounded
Petitjean 4e Compagnie	**Marri** of the 4e Compy
Aubert Corporal of the 2e Cie	**Leroy**
	Hecaën
	Gainche
	Monnereau
	L’hôte
	Barreau
	Dumont
	Charpentier
	Baumer
	Brillant
	Léost

Borelli

Machine gun Section:
Voiton and **Grosjean**

Report of Captain Wéber

From 2 to 3 December, the company occupied isolated trench No 4. The situation was still more difficult than the preceding days the Germans having progressed and continued to throw bombs.
The barrier separating trench No 4 from the German trench was destroyed each time by bombs and fire of the infantry.
Towards eleven hours they attempted a serious attack against the trench preceded by the throwing of numerous bombs.
That attack was repulsed but with serious losses. One corporal killed and 8 chasseurs wounded.
Finally towards 15 hours a serious barrier was able to be established. Two other barriers simply permitting passage were established to the rear.
The barriers were no longer demolished and we were permitted to hold the Germans at a distance where their throwing of bombs would not seem to produce much effect.
Some petards were also thrown during the night by some soldiers of the engineers and produced greater effect.
Twenty rifles were shattered by bullets.

From the 3rd to 4th December

Duty in the trenches:
3e Cie 3 Sections}
4e Cie 3 Sections} Captain **Renaut**

Killed			Wounded	
Lindsal	Corporal	3e Cie	**Meyer** of the 3e Cie	
Hérambourg	2nd cl	d°	**Dantal**	d°
Roux	d°	d°	**Blanc**	d°
Gorenflot	d°	d°	**Giaccardi**	d°
			Genay of the 4e Cie	

From the 4th to the 5th December

Duty in the trenches
3e Cie 2 Sections}
1er Cie 3 Sections} Lieutenant **Leclercq**

Wounded

Armengaud of the 3e Cie
Crapez 2nd cl
Raveleau bugler
Taisne of the 2e Cie died
of his wounds at Ecurie

From the 5th to 6th December

Duty in the trenches:
1er Cie 1 Section }
2e Cie 4 Sections} Captain **Wéber**
Machine gun Section.

From the 7th to the 8th December

The entire Battalion did duty in the night of the 6th to the 7th until 8 in the morning, service was done from this date for a period of 48 hours alternating with the 4e Battalion of the 2e Zouaves.
Different elements of the Battalion intervened in counter-attacks against the Germans who seized a barricade established on the Lille highway and a neighbouring trench (trench No 7).
Killed:
Girard of the 1er Cie
Marchal of the 1er Cie
Diamiano dº
Wounded:
Machine gun Section
Cavallera 2nd class
Boudehem dº
Vatrin dº
Darson Sergeant
Mourot Sergeant of the 2e Cie
Enemann 2nd class dº
Carour dº
Cuvelard dº
Montagne dº
Clépier 2nd Class of the 3e Cie
Césari dº
Ney dº
Darrot dº
Ripouill Corporal
Balocq dº
Armando dº

From the 9th to 10th December

Rest in camp at Etrun, the Battalion having received the order to occupy the camp of the 2e Zouaves.

From the 7th to the 8th **Report of the Machine gun section**
On the 7th at 6h15, the chasseur on sentry at the guns reported to Sergeant **Darson** that trench No 8 situated to the west of the Lille highway seemed to be occupied by the Germans.
Having verified the fact, Sergeant **Darson** traversed the gun onto that trench where the Germans installed metal plates.
Cold and insufficient grease impaired the normal functioning of the guns.
The Sergeant ordered the infantry to fire to hinder the work of the Germans, having been unable to put the guns back in a working state.
The Germans responded with musketry fire
Towards 8 hours, Sergeant **Darson** was lightly wounded in the head
He bandaged himself in the trench and kept command of the section.
At noon Sergeant **Darson** transported his guns to Ecurie to repair them and get them back on point.
At 14 hours he put his guns back in battery against trench No 7. A German machine gun was established in that trench and directed its fire on our sandbag loopholes which were more or less put out of action. Two chasseurs were wounded, **Boudehen** in the hand, **Vatrin** in the foot.
The Germans attempted to sortie from the trench, the fire of the machine guns stopped them in their movement.
Towards 18 hours, the fusillade resumed. The Germans tried again to sortie from their trench, and directed the fire of their guns on our machine guns. However, a stoppage occurred in one of our guns, and under and intense fire, corporal **Dauzat** put it back in order, during his work he was hit in the hands and face, from splinters of rock or earth produced by the bullets on the loopholes.
The piece functioned anew and the fusillade ceased at that point.
Distinguished in the course of that attack and to be recommended are:
1° for the Military Medal
Darson Sergeant.
"Commanding a section of machine guns, gave fire with purpose and energy at a German threat resulting in the capture of one of our trenches; lightly wounded in the head, kept command of the section and only left the trench once relieved by another unit twenty hours after having been wounded.
2° for a citation
Dauzat corporal
"Number 1 of a Section of machine guns, under violent fire of musketry, and of machine guns, which had destroyed the loopholes of our machine guns, had put back in order a piece which a stoppage rendered unserviceable. Was lightly injured by projectiles of earth or stone."

According to general order no 144, the situation is unchanged on

the front of the Division, the enemy showed some activity around the Lille highway and in front of trench 8 in the subsector of the 1er Zouaves and pushed out Saps to the north of Roclincourt and on the trenches of the 3e Zouaves to the east of the old cemetery.
Same mission of the Division.
On the 9th in the evening, a reinforcement of 140 men arrived at Etrun coming from the depot of the camp of Garrigues.

10 and 11 December

The entire Battalion did duty in the trenches in its usual subsector in the night of the 9th to 10th December, on the 10th in the morning towards 8 hours, the reinforcement detachment was taken to Ecurie, distributed to the companies. It therefore participated in trench duty immediately.
Relief of the Battalion in the evening of the 11th.
Losses during the days of the 10th to the 11th.

1er Compagnie: 4207 **Chenat**, chasseur wounded
3262 **Lesage** dº
3018 **Nedelec** dº
2e Compagnie: 2238 **Rémy**, Jules chasseur wounded
3370 **Levollre**, August dº
Rte **Lespinasse** dº
1641 **Tindy** Maxime, Sergeant wounded
Rte **Rideau** Maurice chasseur wounded
3e Compagnie 3278 **Magne** chasseur wounded
Rte **Castagnet** dº
4e Compagnie 2700 **Marie** corporal wounded
3474 **Eucat** chasseur wounded
2788 **Vieroch** dº
Dubois Henri (of the reinforcement group) wounded.

11 and 12 December

General Order Nº 145

1° General situation without notable change.
On the front of the Division the enemy seems to show less activity and to want, after the coups de main that we have attempted, to adopt a defensive attitude.
2° The offensive actions of the Division will be pursued energetically

12 and 13 December

Rest in camp at Etrun.

___ General Order № 146 ___

1° Nothing new in the general situation on the front of the Division, heavy enough fusillade to the North of Roclincourt, the German activity seems concentrated on trench 8 near the Lille highway.
2° Same mission of the Division.

___ General Order № 147 ___

1° Nothing new on the front of the Division, resumption of activity on the part of the enemy heavy Artillery and bombardment of trench 8 by "minenwerfers."
2° Same mission of the Division.
The Battalion must do duty in the trenches
On the 13th in the evening received the order to delay its departure (16H15) until the arrival of a written order.
At 17H45 it was alerted by the following order:
"Take arms and proceed by Auzin St. Aubin – St. Catherine, to the farm of the Ganvrian windmill to 1000m to the north of the Junction of St. Catherine" –
The Battalion will fall in to the east of the Bethune Highway –

___ General Order № 33 ___

The General commanding the 33e A.C. cited to the order of the Army Corps;
Izaac Lieutenant of the 1er Bataillon de marche d'Afrique.
"gave proof of sang-froid, of courage, and initiative, in the course of a night attack that was crowned with success.
Led the group that he commanded to the assault with bayonet and caused considerable losses to the enemy."
Lamy Sergeant
"During the assault and in the trenches, during a violent return fire, showed excellent qualities of spirit and coolness."
Tindy chasseur 1st class
"entered first in an enemy trench and was remarkable for his energy and his good humour."
Mauconduit chasseur
"Wounded in the arm during a night assault, stayed in the trench and assured his service there for 10 hours repeatedly bandaging himself."
Floire chasseur
"Placed as a sentry in a dangerous post, refused to allow himself to be relieved. He was wounded at that post."

13 and 14
December

Duty in the trenches.

1er Compagnie:	4087,	**Constant**	chasseur wounded
	3372,	**Bézine**	dº
	4114,	**Troispoux**	dº
	Rte,	**Magand**	dº
	4220,	**Dozière**	dº
2e Compagnie:	3348,	**Raymond**	dº
	3992,	**Flocard**	dº
	3985,	**Lebonniee**	dº
	4269,	**Mercier**	dº
	Rte,	**Martin**	dº
3e Compagnie		**Lormier**	Captain wounded
	3754,	**Lang**	chasseur wounded
	Rte,	**Saunal**	dº
	2482,	**Bauduin**	dº
	Rte,	**Croustillières**	Sergeant wounded
4e Cie	2119	Lepoutre Jean	bugler killed

15 to 16
December

Duty in the trenches:

1er Compagnie:	**Pezaire**	Sergeant wounded
	5547, **Prévost**	2nd class wounded
2e Compagnie:	**Lerche**	Corporal wounded
	Pégny	Sergeant wounded
3e Compagnie:	**Lévy**	2nd class wounded
S.H.R.:	**Hanchard**	2nd class wounded

17 to 18
December

Duty in the trenches:

1er Compagnie:	**Desmaroux**	2nd class wounded
	Truiquet	dº
2e Compagnie:	**Chaffard**	dº
3e dº	**Faubel**	dº
4e dº	**Ambs**	dº
	Baud	dº
	Oswald	dº
	Robert	dº
	Bouche	dº
	Lequin	dº
	Noury	1st class killed

19 to 20
December

Duty in the trenches

1er Compagnie:	**Bagault**	chasseur 2nd class wounded
	3126 **Lapeyre**	dº
2e Compagnie:	3282 **Raas**	dº
	Boterel	dº
	Marty	dº
	Mérin	dº
3e Compagnie:	**Delportrie**	dº
	Badin	dº
	Rémy	dº
4e Compagnie:	**Nagard**	dº
	Crespel	dº
	Morini	dº
	Rte **Marioujol**	dº
	Gendron	dº
	Hazebrouck	dº

G.Q.G. 7 December 1914

10º Armée
33º Corps d'Armée
General Staff
1er Bureau
No 3720 /1

Order Nº 35

Copy

The General Commanding the 33e Corps d'Armée cited to the order of the Army Corps:
Chasseur 2nd class **Legrand** of the 1er Bon M.I.L.A.:
"Despite the explosion of seven mines, stayed in the German lines for twenty minutes"
Chasseur 2nd class **Goy** of the 1er Bon M.I.L.A.:
"Despite the explosion of seven mines, stayed in the German lines for twenty minutes"
Chasseur 2nd class **Bazet**, corporal **Petit**, chasseurs 2nd class +**Eneman**, **Sauzet**, **Rousseau**, **Lorang**, **Savary**, **Détrez**, **Boursin**, **Oswald**, **Clement** (wounded), **Métail** (wounded), **LeCotin** (killed) **Moutay** (killed), **Poilly** (killed) **Lagache** (killed) of the 1er Bon M.I.L.A.:
x "Very beautiful conduct under fire, kept themselves three hours with their Sergeant in the enemy trenches and retired in good order bringing back French wounded."
Chasseur 2nd class **Thély** medic of the 1er Bon M.I.L.A.:
"Assured by himself, at a dangerous point, with the greatest calm and the greatest devotion, the care of numerous wounded."
Chasseur 1st class, **Demortier** of the 1er Bon M.I.L.A.:
"Valiantly fought in the affair of the night of the 25th to 26th November

1914, was not left affected by the explosion of the mines, brought back under intense fire one of his wounded comrades."

Signed: Petain

Certified True Copy
Chief of General Staff
Signed: illegible

---

21 to 22 December

Duty in the trenches:

2^{e} Compagnie:	2832,	**Moreau**	Chasseur 2nd class wounded
	Rte,	**Nicol**	d^{o}
	4263,	**Forest**	d^{o}
	4301,	**Buisson**	d^{o}
3^{e} Compagnie:	2923	**Corsand**	d^{o}
	3825	**Rigaud**	d^{o}
	"	**Adam**	d^{o}
	1984	**Desnoylle**	d^{o}
4e Compagnie:	5623	**Rondin**	d^{o}
	Rte,	**Bichambis**	d^{o}

Medical Officer's aide **Greffier** coming from the auxiliary Doctors of the 97e Infantry Regiment passed to the 1er B^{on} de marche of the Infantrie Légère d'Afrique
Mr. **Porte** S/Lieutenant of the 2e Compagnie evacuated for illness.

22 to 23 December

Rest in camp

23 to 24 December

Captain **Renaud** of the 4e Cie, returned from Haute-Avesnis.

	Grivey Sergeant		"	"
	Fontant	d^{o}	d^{o}	d^{o}
	Scheyder 1st class		d^{o}	d^{o}
	Clement	d^{o}	d^{o}	d^{o}
x	**Graziani** Sergeant of the 1er Cie			d^{o}
	Devilliers	d^{o}	d^{o}	d^{o}
	Scavino corporal		d^{o}	d^{o}
	Richard	d^{o}	of the 2^{e} Cie	d^{o}
	Carrot	d^{o}	d^{o}	d^{o}

Duty in the trenches.

1er Compagnie:	**Pradeille** wounded and evacuated		
2^{e} Compagnie:	**Forest** chasseur 2nd class wounded		
	Mouton	d^{o}	killed
3^{e} Compagnie:	**Poignant**	d^{o}	wounded

	Briaggi Sergeant	wounded
4e Compagnie:	**Valani** chasseur 2nd class	wounded
	Chariot dº	
	Loriot dº	
	Pianet dº	

24 to 25 December

Change of camp
The Battalion goes to camp at Anzin-St. Aubin

25 to 26 December

Duty in the trenches:

1er Compagnie:	**Santenac** chasseur 2nd class wounded	
2250	**Bricent**	dº
	Combarel	dº
	Lagache	dº
	Gilhodes	dº
	Marlézy	dº
	Granger	dº
	Rivoton	dº
2e Compagnie:	**Olivier** corporal wounded	
	Sulot chasseur 2nd class wounded	
	Seignard	dº
	Vignal	dº
	Montagne	dº
Rte	**Assier**	dº
3380	**Junca**	dº
	Furno	dº
3e Compagnie:	2643 Ajoux Louis	dº
4e Compagnie:	**Orchampt** Sergeant-Major killed	
	David chasseur 2nd class wounded	

26 to 27 Decber

Rest in Camp

27 to 28 Decber

Duty in the trenches

28 to 29 Decber

Rest in Camp

29 to 30 Decber

Duty in the trenches

1er Compagnie: **Clinchard** chasseur 2nd class wounded
Fanget dº
Ronstant dº
2e Compagnie: 4115 **Cherrier** dº
3582 **Martines** dº
Rte **François** dº
3e Compagnie: **Schmulz** dº
Rutillet dº
4e Compagnie: **Roussel** chasseur 2nd class wounded
Sherbier dº
Justice dº

30 to 31 December

Rest in camp

From 31 December 1914
To 1 January 1915

Duty in the trenches
1er Compagnie: 3861, **Duhéme** chasseur 2nd class wounded
2e Compagnie: 3857, **Hécaen** dº
Richard dº
4e Compagnie: 6251 **Hoquette** dº
3489 **André** dº
2785 **Fromentin** dº
During the night from 31 December to 1 January, the Battalion was alerted following the threat of an attack; the Coys proceeded to their emplacements in reserve in the 2nd line until 7 hours in the morning, at 7 hours returned to camp.

1st to 2 January

Rest in camp

2 to 3 January

Duty in the trenches:
2e Compagnie: Rte **Abriol** chasseur 2nd class wounded
Rte **Bouisset** dº
Rte **Grime** dº
4257 **Lecompte** corporal wounded
Fargnes chasseur 2nd class wounded

3 to 4 January

Rest in camp

4 to 5 January

Duty in the trenches:
The 1[er] C[ie] in reserve at the model farm (Lille highway) furnishing a platoon to participate in the retaking of craters created by the explosion of the charges of German mines.
The cooks of the four companies setup at that farm, left their stoves to participate in the assault.
Missing: **Viriou** and **Robert**

3[e] Compagnie:	3321	**Pautrier** chasseur 2nd class wounded	
	3929	**Bordeneuve**	d°
	2888	**Baril**	d°
		Françon	d°
1er Compagnie:		**Bidot** captain wounded	
	716	**Hillarion** 2nd class wounded	
	705	**Pit**	d°
	4090	**St Just**	d°
	3883	**Vroland**	d°
	3687	**Scavino** corporal wounded	

During that counter-attack, the men of the Battalion having participated there were remarked upon by the other corps for their bravery and their spirit.

5 to 6 January

Rest in Camp

6 to 7 January

Duty in the trenches

7 to 8 January

Rest in camp

8 to 9 January

Duty in the trenches
Following bad weather, the trenches and communication trenches were in a frightful state.
The men bogged down in the sticky muck and ran a real danger (notably the Zouaves who go out for relief)
Several men of the Battalion, with makeshift tools, did not hesitate to put themselves nearly uncovered and exposed in an open field some hundreds of metres from the German trenches to rescue men stuck in a communication trench all night and threatened with death from exposure or suffocation.
Those distinguished:
2533 **Perrin** Sergeant
3286 **Grivey** d°

Rte **Martin** 2nd class

1er Compagnie: 3347 **Legrand** chasseur 2nd cl wounded
3137 **Leturcq**
2969 **Foucher**
2e Compagnie: Rte **Rigaud** dº
" **Martin** dº
534 **Deconihout** Sergeant killed
3e Compagnie: 2725 **Roubé** chasseur 2nd class wounded
2138 **Verpoest** dº
3911 **Guillemain** dº
4e Compagnie: 3130 **Ezzaoui** dº
2787 **Métail** dº
3286 **Grivey** Sergeant wounded

9 to 10 January

Rest in camp

10 to 11 January

Duty in the trenches

11 to 12 January

Rest in camp

12 to 13 January

Duty in the trenches
1er Compagnie: 2107 **Colier** chasseur 2nd cl wounded
3141 **Carré** dº
4131 **Jonés** dº
2859 **Montziol** dº
" **Seccia** dº

13 to 14 January

Rest in camp

14 to 15 January

Duty in the trenches
15 January the Battalion was alerted and proceeded at 11^{h}30 to Anzin St. Aubin
At 18^{h}30, the 4e Compagnie received the order to proceed to the factory at Roclincourt.
15 January at 4h20, the commander of the Coy, called to proceed to the Command Post of the carrier pigeon loft, received the following order from the Commander of the Segment. "Attack and occupy

former trench no 7."
The company brought itself immediately to the place of attack, French trench to the west of the Lille highway.
The following dispositions were taken;
1st line of attack, Lieutenant **Lefèvre** with 60 men bayonets fixed tasked with falling on the enemy trench
2nd line, Chief Warrant Officer **Berthet** with 25 men bringing petards.
3rd line, Warrant Officer **Cazanova** with 15 men bringing tools and sandbags
The start off took place at 7 hours after the explosion of a mine Trench 7 was occupied the 1st line who in their dash suffered particularly from the fire of machine guns installed along the embankment of the Lille highway.
The Germans evacuated the trench precipitously leaving some cadavers, the communication trench extending that work to the other German trenches was rapidly obstructed by dead enemies.
At the moment where the three lines could reunite, a very heavy bombardment of the occupied trench commenced on the part of the Germans. Bombs grenades and petards raged.
The Commander of the Company reported rapidly that the situation was untenable and after some minutes of occupation he ordered a withdrawal.

On returning to the French trench, from a strength of 100 men he counted:
One officer wounded, Mr **Lefèvre**
One Chief Warrant Officer missing, **Berthet**
Killed:
2414 **Provost** Celestin, bugler of the 4e Cie
5304 **Pinault** George, 2nd class dº
Wounded:
956 **Humblot** August, Sergeant of the 4e Cie
1486 **Guillotel** Eugène, dº
2655 **Machecourt** René corporal of the 4e Cie
3833 **Olry** Gaul dº
2111 **Bury** Alfred chasseur 2nd class of the 4e Cie
2791 **Renard** Joseph dº
3495 **Surot** Fernand Victor dº
043 **Lèglise** Elei dº
2758 **Pastor** Antoine dº
" **Gousset** Alexandre dº
3230 **Mathieu** Charles dº
2755 **Chardonnet** Louis dº
" **Brülé** Theophile dº
3387 **Bénard** Léon dº
2256 **Theirry** Anet dº
2798 **Savary** Emile, chasseur 2nd class of the 4e Compagnie
Missing:
1396 **Michot** Jean, Sergeant of the 4e Compagnie
3604 **Potel** Jean, dº

3087 **Toutain** Alphonse, d°
3225 **Reverdy** Marius, corporal of the 4e Compagnie
Montel Francis d°
671 **Ménissier** Alfred bugler of the 4e Compagnie
3987 **Piglione** Jean, Chass 2nd cl of the 4e Compagnie
2207 **Quéval** Maurice d°
2799 **Yen** Victor d°
2780 **Gaudin** Desiré d°
" **Blasco** Manuel d°
3216 **Baulois** Maxime d°
3609 **Ducasse** Felix d°
2616 **Pélerin** Alexandre d°
2105 **Boesten** Ernest d°
" **Lemailre** Alfred d°
" **Thomas** Antoine d°
2750 **Couzin** Jean d°

1er Compagnie:
Killed:
2856 **Charpentier** Julien chasseur 2nd class
3876 **Goy** Henri d°
Wounded:
3016 **Ramel** Alphonse chasseur 2nd class
2100 **Petit** Henry d°
" **Louis** Edouard d°
" **Dorizon** Henri d°
" **Delacourt** d°
4005 **Laphaine** George d°
3274 **Arrillon** Marcel d°

2e Compagnie
Killed:
Rouxel Ernest chasseur 2nd class
Wounded:
4002 **Voissard** Jean chasseur 2nd class
3087 **Blondeau** Jules Sergeant

3e Compagnie:
Killed:
4055 **Beretti** Antoine Sergeant
Wounded
2931 **Malvergne** Jean chasseurs 2nd class
" **Charrier** Abel d°
" **Faivre** Alexis d°
1958 **Escappé** Alfred d°
2912 **Puo** Louis d°
3994 **Tissier** François d°
3785 **Ruello** Lucien d°
2104 **Gras** Jules d°
4286 **Bétrancourt** Louis d°
3957 **Histe** Léon d°
0769 **Domon** Louis d°

___ Order of the Division № 65 ___

In the course of the combats of the 14 to 15 January, The troops who struggled in the sector of the Lille highway have made proof of the most beautiful qualities of spirit and bravery. The General commanding the 45e Division congratulated them.
He cited to the Order of the Division,
"The Company of the Bataillon d'Afrique commanded by Captain **Renaud** and the **group of volunteer scouts** of the same Battalion who were particularly distinguished during those two days have greatly contributed to the success of our operations."

___ Order of the Division № 68 ___

The General commanding the 45e Division cited to the Order of the Division:
Stretcher-Bearer Team of the 1er Bataillon de Marche d'Afrique
"Since the Battalion has been on the front, particularly during the affairs of 15 to 20 January, assured with the greatest Courage and the greatest self-sacrifice, the transport of the wounded to the aid post, despite difficult terrain and often battered by fire.'
Salanne Warrant Officer:
"Detached with his Section in immediate contact with the enemy, had assured the execution of the different orders given with sang-froid and intelligence during the whole day, those that had the effect of keeping the positions conquered in the morning."
Berthomet Sergeant Major
"Same motif."
Richard Sergeant
"Threw himself into a Sap which came to be abandoned by the Germans and gave a beautiful example of courage and sang-froid to the chasseurs placed under his orders in throwing petards despite enemy fire."
Lejafé Sergeant
"By his sang-froid maintained the good order of his Section when a German bomb killed one man and wounded three."
Arson chasseur 2nd class
"Gave proof of courage in maintaining himself despite enemy bombs in a trench occupied in part by the adversary."
Petit chasseur 2nd class
"Same motif."
Perrin Sergeant;
"Gave proof of much sang-froid, energy and a spirit of devotion in directing, in broad daylight uncovered at about 400 metres from the enemy, a team of rescuers bringing aid to soldiers deeply mired."

Monthessuit Bugler
"Made part of a group of volunteer scouts, was remarkable for his spirit. Assured guard of 5 German prisoners of whom three were killed during the journey from the small German post to the French lines."
Garvignon corporal of the group of volunteer scouts
"In jumping into a German trench, cut the cords armed to fire a mine that also prevented the Germans from blowing it up."
Pastor chasseur 2nd class
"Brought himself to the German trench with remarkable spirit, and killed several enemies. When grievously wounded, accompanied his chief of the group until the end of the operation."
Chesnay chasseur 2nd class
"Brought himself forward with perfect spirit, showed great sang-froid during the occupation and returned in the lines after having assured the return of two wounded."
Deschamps chasseur 2nd class
"Very beautiful attitude during an attack on a trench and his occupation despite adverse fire."
Mallre chasseur reservist
"Under fire, came to the aid of his wounded Lieutenant and brought back a grievously wounded comrade."
Clément chasseur 1st Class
"Followed his company commander and made every effort for his protection and returned to the line with the last wounded."
Dubrulle chasseur 2nd class
"Wounded in the face by the blast of a petard, stayed on the front until the last moment."
Martin chasseur 2nd class
"Wounded providing aid, in broad daylight and in the open, to soldiers mired in a communication trench about 400 metres from the enemy."

15 and 16 January

Rest in camp

16 and 17 January

Duty in the trenches

17 and 18 January

Rest in the camp

18 and 19 January

Duty in the trenches

19 and 20 January

Rest in camp

20 and 21 January

Duty in the trenches

20 January, the groupe franc of the Battalion, under the command of Lieutenant **Lahargouette**, the 2e Compagnie under the command of Captain **Wéber** and a platoon of the 3e Compagnie with Warrant Officer **Mertrand**, in concert with the Zouaves, had to attack trench 7. The signal of which was given by the explosion of a mine near the Lille Highway after which the enemy trench will have been bombarded by the Artillery.

At the given signal, everyone went over the top, but the platoon on the left of the 2^{e} Cie and the platoon of the 3^{e} Cie were immediately stopped by the shells of 75s that had not yet lengthened their fire. Nevertheless the groupe franc and the 1er Peloton of the 2^{e} Cie penetrated the German trench and were able to bring back 6 prisoners.

The operation having not succeeded, a new attack was ordered undertaken by the other platoon of the 3^{e} Cie but the Germans having received reinforcements, they did not succeed any more than the first, few men reached the German trench, the others were stopped by infantry fire, machine guns, and bombs.

The third attack took place at 10 hours, the 1er Cie was able to reinforce the Battalion and 4e Cie stayed in reserve in the trenches. The third attack was also stopped by violent fire and everywhere by enemy machine guns.

In that day, the Battalion experienced the following losses:

1er Compagnie:

Killed:

4053 **Berthomet**, Sergeant Major
4194 **Gasté**, Théophile, corporal
4001 **Patry**, Ernest chass 2nd cl
2696 **Herbet**, Gabriel -d^{o}-

Wounded:

3674 **Lecca**, Toupaint, chass 2nd cl
3559 **Lorret** François, -d^{o}-
3003 **Rouys** Robert, -d^{o}-
4189 **Mauconduit**, Georges -d^{o}-
0601 **Miguel** Marius -d^{o}-
3307 **Culpis** Albert -d^{o}-
2744 **Jérès** Victor -d^{o}-
04014 **Olive** Eugène -d^{o}-
2763 **Roy** Emile, -d^{o}-
4082 **Heintz** Emile -d^{o}-
3861 **Guignier** Georges -d^{o}-
3950 **Ledouce** Albin -d^{o}-

Missing
Girard Maurice -d°-
2131 **Loridans** Ernest -d°-

2e Compagnie:
Killed:
3909 **Drouard** Troyrer, Sergeant
03523 **Leloup** Arthur chass 2nd class
Wounded
2795 **Furois**, Gaston Chass 2nd class
2081 **Orosco**, Mathias -d°-
3e Compagnie:
Killed:
3632 **Jeannot**, Armand, corporal
3061 **Nicolini**, Alfred, chass 2nd class
Mr. Potot, Henry, Captain,
Wounded:
3918 **Griffon** Gustave, Sergeant
1864 **Jaurey** Jean, ~~chasseur 2nd class~~ Sergeant
3416 **Coquelin** Joseph, Sergeant
3112 **Lamy** Armand, Sergeant
Le Ray François corporal {charged a machine gun and killed the machine gunner [...]
Sougné Alphonse chass 2nd class
2922 **Sténégri** Joseph -d°-
Jumeau Gaston -d°-
2272 **Gardot** André -d°-
0758 **Boilot** Charles -d°-
2932 **Barreau** Pierre corporal
2141 **Cervaix** Eugène, chass 2nd class
2797 **Perrenet** Léon -d°-
3139 **Moillet** Victor -d°-
3856 **Avenel** Faldonie -d°-
2867 **Le Bars** Eugène -d°-
Missing:
01019 **Boulay**, Ernest, chass 2nd class
Bruchon Alphonse -d°-
4e Compagnie
Wounded
Rte **Evanno**, Joseph chasseur 2nd class
" **Maffre** Germain, -d°-
2350 **Mor** Lucien, -d°-
3121 **Ben Taïel** Amed -d°-
Rte **Virlouvet** René -d°-
" **Quié** Jules -d°-
2789 **Duval** Pierre -d°-
2115 **Perrotey** Charles -d°-
" **Leclercq** Léon -d°-
2200 **Lucignanni** Albert -d°-
Rte **Canot**, Alexandre -d°-

" **Pillet**, Julien -d°-

Missing

Colombel, chasseur 2nd class

2348 **Dubrulle** Ernest -d°-

Bousiver -d°-

Dubois -d°-

Durand, Frédéric -d°-

Israël chasseur 2nd class

Marmin -d°-

Couzinet -d°-

Following the days of the 15 to 20 January, the General Commanding the 10e Armée presented the following order:

___ Order of the Army № 45 ___

The General commanding the 10e Armée cited to the order of the Army:

The 45e Division d'Infanterie

"Placed for three months in a particularly difficult sector, exposed to incessant attacks from an aggressive and enterprising enemy, which was cited as a model of the 6th German Army by its Chief the Prince of Bavaria, the 45e Division held its positions.
It turned each attack of the adversary with remarkable energy.
Under the impulsion of its Chief, General **Quiquandon**, it clearly retook the moral ascendancy over the enemy at last by attacking in a war of saps and mines without respite."

____ Order of the Division № 70 ____

The General commanding the 45e Division cited to the order of the Division:

Fontant; Sergeant: "Brought himself forward brilliantly at the head of the platoon he commanded."
Tournu: Sergeant-Major, "Brilliantly conducted his group in the combat of 20 January."
Michée, Sergeant: "made proof of ardour, spirit, and sang-froid – in the combat of 20 January."
Lejalet, Sergeant: "After the death of his Section Chief, took command of his unit and brilliantly led the attack."
Rivière: Sergeant, "Showed much spirit and heartiness in the course of 3 successive attacks."
Le Ray, corporal "same motif"
Lecacheur, corporal "Brilliant conduct in the attack of German trenches. Took six prisoners."
Menu, Chasseur, "same motif"
Pierrons -d°- "same motif"

Molier -d°- "same motif"
Boudon -d°- "same motif"
Marty -d°- "same motif"
Billiat -d°- "Brought himself with bravado up to a German trench."
Virlouvet, chasseur " Very brave in the attack – was wounded"
Bentayeb, chasseur "same motif"
Beiziers, chasseur "Showed much spirit and heartiness in the course of 3 successive attacks."
Leroy, chasseur, "same motif"
Caumont -d°- -d°-
Piles -d°- -d°-
Lebars -d°- -d°-
Aubrefald -d°- -d°-
Lestrap -d°- -d°-
Jumeau -d°- -d°-
Guilot -d°- -d°-
Saulnier -d°- -d°-
André -d°- -d°-
Blénot -d°- -d°-
Cleis -d°- -d°-
Hilaire -d°- -d°-
Lahargouette, 2nd Lieutenant "when lightly wounded, gave the finest example of energy and courage and spirit as his group of scouts assaulted a German trench three times."
Berthomet, Sergeant Major. "Brilliantly conducted his group in the combat of 20 January and was killed shot in the head."
Drouard, Sergeant "Very beautiful conduct in the course of three attacks executed on 20 January. Was killed."

21 and 22 January

Rest in camp

22 and 23 January

Duty in the trenches
1er Compagnie
Wounded
3352 **Salençon**, chasseur 1st class
3901 **Debord**, chasseur 2nd class
2415 **Trapp**, -d°-
2347 **Dimnet** -d°-
Missing
4178 **Coutant**, chasseur 2nd class
3237 **Garaet** -d°-
3354 **Créon** -d°-
2e Compagnie
Missing
2332 **Lefévre**, chasseur 2nd class

3e Compagnie
Killed
3742 **Renaudier**, August, Sergeant
019695 **Oguer**, Félix, chasseur 2nd class
3284 **Flambeax** Louis -do-
Constant Maurice -do-
4007 **Vinet** François -do-
Rte **Papaïx** Fernand corporal
Chardonnet Louis -do-
Wounded
2083 **Miranda**, chasseur 2nd class
3599 **Legendre** -do-
2299 **Renaudin** -do-
Missing
" **Garreché**, Marcellin, chasseur 2nd class
3129 **Bitton** makloud -do-
3235 **Le Gall** Mathurin -do-
3923 **Le Geylon** François, -do-
4e Compagnie
Wounded
2718 **Henry**, Lucien, chasseur 2nd class
" **Druet** Eugène -do-
2306 **Dossinet** Alphonse -do-
3969 **Mouret** Jules -do-
3276 **Lavoute** Roger -do-
3428 **Créach** Paul -do-
Missing
(3225 **Reverdy**, Marius, corporal) counted twice
" **Arnaud** Barthelemy -do-
Rte **Lescure** Joseph chasseur 2nd class

23 January the Battalion received the order to go to camp at Anzin-St.Aubin.
In the night of the 23rd, the horse, Jaick, escaped from its stable.

24 January

At 14 hours the Battalion arrived at Hermaville for rest

25 to 28 January

Sojourn at Hermaville.
On 27 January, the Battalion Chief awarded on parade the Knight's Cross of the Legion of Honour to Captain **Renaud**
On 28 January the Battalion proceeded to Anzin, in the course of the stages Colonel Codet Commanding the 90e Bde awarded to the Battalion Chief the Officer's Cross of the Legion of Honour which was conferred to him with the following words:
"was singled out in the defense of his sector and the furious counter-attacks that were made against the Germans who attempted to seize

our trenches.
Showed great energy and beautiful bravery leading his Battalion under fire with the greatest energy."

From 28 January
To 13 February

The Battalion did duty in the trenches in the evening under the following conditions;
3 Companies at Roclincourt or in the first line trenches.
1er Compagnie – available – at rest at Anzin-St.Aubin
Every three days that compagnie relieved one of the Companies of the first line.
1er Compagnie.
Wounded
2347 **Dimnet**, Albert, chasseur 2nd class
Missing
(Rte **Lescure**, Joseph, chasseur 2nd class) double employment
3e Compagnie
Wounded
2299 **Renaudin**, Louis, chasseur 2nd class
2681 **Sombre**, Alexandre

31 January

1er Compagnie
Wounded
Dizmel, chasseur 2nd class
Delastre -d°-
Leclercq Lieutenant
Huquet chasseur 2nd class

1 February

1er Compagnie
Wounded
2863 **Delastre**, Paul, chasseur 2nd class
4e Compagnie
2261 **Grusenmayer**, Paul, chasseur 2nd class
2668 **Marris** Desire Georges -d°-

2 February

4e Compagnie
Wounded
4038 **Sirot**, Gaston, chasseur 2nd class
2676 **Hermann**, Gaston, -d°-

3 February

2e Compagnie
Wounded
Rte **Thébaud**, Louis chasseur 2nd class
3983 **Dupuis**, Hector, -d°-

4 February

The group of volunteer scouts under the command of Warrant Officer Darson and comprised of Sergeants Michlée and Gondonnière, 3 corporals and 42 chasseurs, received the order to cooperate with a company of Zouaves to attack trench 7, the appropriate signal having to be given by the explosion of two mines. At the signal to attack, at 3 hours, the group exited the trenches and fell upon the German trench. That last, full of mud, did not permit the chasseurs to advance rapidly and the Germans had the time to retire with two machine guns, however a barrier was immediately established to assure the conservation of the trench.
To the side, the Zouaves, like those of the volunteers of the Battalion the operation succeeded, the Zouaves occupied the trench and consolidated and the scout group received the order to regain the French trenches.
1er Compagnie.
Wounded
4020 **Sages**, André chasseur 2nd class
2e Compagnie
Killed
4250 **Faget** Louis, chas 2nd class
Missing
2310 **Bonnefaut** Lucien, Antoine chasseur 2nd class
Rte **Vigouroux** Alfred, -d°-
" **Léost**, Gabriel -d°-
S.M. **Valentin** -d°-
3e Compagnie
Wounded
3285 **Bunel** Gaston Henri, chasseur 2nd class
3278 **Magné** Auguste -d°-
4e Compagnie
Wounded
2200 **Lucignani** Albert, chasseur 2nd Class
Killed
" **Servoise** Emile Desiré chasseur 2nd class

5 February

3e Compagnie
Wounded
2738 **Jourdain** Robert, corporal
Rte **Le Strat** Louis, bugler

d° **Perronet** Emile, Ch 2nd class
4e Compagnie
Wounded
3558 **Boursin** Francis corporal
8389 **Beuriot** Victour, Chasseur 2nd class
438 **Albouy** Lucien Henri -d°-
2202 **Marmin** Victor Louis -d°-
2169 **Dumont** Marius -d°-

6 February

1er Compagnie
Wounded
2476 **Richard**, Victor, chasseur 2nd class
4139 **Lamadon** Claude, -d°-
15530 **Le Poder** Louis, -d°-
3e Compagnie
Rte **Sonilhac** Victor, Louis chasseur 2nd class

7 February

2e Compagnie
Wounded
8433 **Paget** Emile chasseur 2nd class
04528 **Garcin** Elie, -d°-

8 February
9 February

1er Compagnie
Wounded
4063 **Decaeus** Gaston, chasseur 2nd class
4e Compagnie
4878 **Degat**, Antonin, chasseur 2nd class
7842 **Lamblain** Louis -d°-

10 February

3e Compagnie
Wounded
Rte **Allanet**, Emile, chasseur 2nd class

11 February

1er Compagnie
Wounded
3719 **Dupré** Paul, Sergeant
7345 **Raissaut** Robert, chasseur 2nd class
3e Compagnie
3784 **Rousselle**, René chasseur 2nd class

0600 **Fernandez** François, -d°-
7703 **Proux** Marcel, -d°-
5804 **Nicolic** Charles -d°-

12 February

1er Compagnie
Wounded
7576 **Bachelier** René, chasseur 2nd class
Rte **Favre** François -d°-
2e Compagnie
Wounded
Rte **Bonsignour** chasseur 2nd class
3356 **Taxdo** -d°-
Rte **Legouin** Victor -d°-
Rte **Ballier** Charles -d°-
3516 **Colombo** Louis -d°-
2271 **Devilliers** Eugène -d°-

13 February

3e Compagnie
Forêt, Paul, chasseur 2nd class wounded
2e Compagnie
Wounded
Rte **Quartz**, Vincent chasseur 2nd class On the evening of the 13th the Battalion went to camp at Hermaville
Chasseur Dubois of the 1er Compagnie fell in the course of the march on the pavement and died of a fractured skull.

14 February

Rest - at Hermaville
Arrived – reinforcement – of 250 men under the command of Captain Bidot.

15 and 16 February

Rest – at Hermaville
Captain Bidot was attached to the 3e bis R**é**giment de Zouaves by a decision of the General OC the 45e D^{on}.
Lieutenant Tremsal joined the Bat^{on} coming from the 80e R**é**gmt d'Infanterie, he is attached to the 4e Compagnie.
On the 16th at 6^{H}30' the groupe franc with an effective strength of 4 Sergeants, 5 corporals, chasseurs under the command of Lieutenant **Sauvage** were sent to the mill at Roclincourt to cooperate with an attack on the 17th directed against the German lines.

17 February

On the 17th at 14 hours the Battalion left Hermaville to go to Anzin, it was attached to Sector B. Two companies must occupy the first line trenches, the others will rest at Anzin. The relief will take place in two days.

____ Attack of the 17th ___

Order of the attack:
An attack will be made on the German trenches situated to the west of the Lille highway and extending
- From that highway to the sunken road (about 500m E
- of the Lille highway)

Troops of the attack
3 Companies and 4 groups of scouts including that of the Battalion.
The signal of the attack will be given by the explosion of a mine at 5 hours 45
Protection of the attacks:
The companies and the machine gun sections that occupy the trenches, to the right and left of the zone of attack will protect the assaulting troops with their fire - against the flank attacks, directing their fire on the trenches facing their front.
Artillery:
The groups Arnaud and Lenoble will protect the columns by forming a barrage to the E, in front, and to the W.
Scaling ladders have been distributed at a rate of twenty per company or scout group
A section of labourers taken into each reserve company will be, if necessary, attached to the sappers of the engineers who, following the attacking troops, will have to rapidly face the German trenches to the north and create the necessary barriers, they will also establish connecting communication trenches with our trenches.
Execution:
The explosion was produced at 6H30, immediately the scouts of the Battalion, whose objective is a little to the east of the Lille highway, bounded onto the German trench, where a certain number of dead and wounded were lying hit by the explosion of the mine. Some Germans exited their rest dugouts, some sought to defend themselves and were killed, the others surrendered. A German lifted a white object and advanced toward the group of chasseurs; at some steps from them he raised his rifle and fired on the chasseurs. Those who perceived it immediately thrust with bayonet, as well as four Germans who were found behind him. Meanwhile, Lieutenant Sauvage, an Warrant Officer of the Zouaves and some chasseurs stormed the door of a rest dugout that held a Lieutenant and four Germans who were made prisoners.
Lieutenant Sauvage with some men launched themselves into the

communication trench leading to the second line which they reached at the same time as a group of scouts from the Zouaves. The Germans ran away down the communication trench to the third line or towards the right part of the trench.
Estimating that the number of men available to him did not permit him to pursue, Lieutenant Sauvage established a barrier towards the right and consolidated the 2nd line trench facing north. Little by little the Germans from the right part of the conquered trench advanced with petards to the established barrier.
The scout group pursued the consolidation of the trench, while some responded to the attack – by throwing some petards from their side.
Towards noon a German company, 2 officers and 5 NCOs at the head, sortied from the trenches and of the third line while skirmishers advanced toward the trench that we occupied. The rapid fire opened immediately made fifty Germans fall including the ranks at the head; one of the officers fell wounded and died in our trench. Lieutenant Sauvage mounted the men on the parapet to wait for the attack, he received, at that moment a ball in the right arm.
The Germans turned about and quickly regained their shelter, having left about 80 dead on the ground.
The fusillade resumed from one part and another as well as the launching of bombs and petards. The artillery also directed its fire on our trenches. The scout group was hard hit by the bombardment, the thrown petards and bombs.
At 17 hours Lieutenant Sauvage who stayed in the trenches with the survivors received the order to return his group to Roclincourt, a unit coming to occupy the conquered trenches.
The machine gun section, which to the left of the Lille highway, had to flank the attack, took part, replacing one of its jammed machine guns with a German machine gun, Sergeant Dauzat received a ball to the right hand. In the morning the action of the pieces was jammed at different times by the explosion of bombs or petards. One of them buried one of the pieces in the ground and rendered it momentarily unusable.
At 18 hours, the 3e and 4e Cies were taken in service in the trenches and the 2 others were installed at Anzin in camp on alert.
During that day the soldiers, - whose names follow – were cited to the order of the Division.

___ Order of the Division № 87 ___

General Quiquandon, Commanding the 45e Division cited the order of the Division:
Hérie, chasseur 2nd class
'calm bravery in keeping his particularly dangerous post under threat from petards and bombs, launching petards at one time himself at the assailants"
Mamessier, Sergeant
"Very great bravery, and spirit attacking a German trench. Tenacity

keeping conquered ground, despite bombs and petards."

Gauthier	corporal	Same citation
Pierron	-d°-	-d°-
Drogrez	-d°-	-d°-
Piles	chasseur 2nd class	-d°-
Charrier	-d°-	-d°-
Cheneval	-d°-	-d°-
Bichard	-d°-	-d°-
Piedbois	-d°-	-d°-
Renaud	-d°-	-d°-
Lemaire	-d°-	-d°-
Cauvin	-d°-	-d°-

___ General Order ___

The General Commanding the 33e Corps d'Armée cited to the Order of the Army Corps:
Floire, chasseur
"Very great bravery and spirit attacking a German trench, tenacity keeping the conquered ground despite bombs and petards. Already cited and wounded."

Deviller, Sergeant.
"Very great bravery and spirit attacking a German trench, tenacity keeping the conquered ground despite bombs and petards. Was wounded."

___ Extract of Order No 655 D. ___

Mr. Sauvage, Alfred, Lieutenant of the 1er Bataillon de Marche d'Infanetrie Légère d'Afrique.
Has been promoted - in the Order of the Legion of Honour with a rank of Knight.
"In the course of an attack on 17 February against the German trenches, remarkably conducted the group of volunteer scouts which he commanded. Wounded in the arm, was not bandaged for three hours after, and kept his command until the evening."

Signed: Joffre

___ Extract of General Order No 649 D ___

The Military Medal is conferred to the veteran whose name follows:
Tindy, M.H.J. Sergeant of the 1er Bataillon de marche if the Infanterie Légère d'Afrique'
"Non-commissioned Officer of remarkable courage and spirit. Again came to be remarked upon and was wounded. He made proof of his remarkable courage and spirit in the course of the day of 17 February."

Signed: Joffre

Wounded in the course of that attack

1er Compagnie
6881 **Petit** Pierre, chasseur 2nd class
3e Compagnie
2912 **Joguin** Rouxell, chasseur 2nd class
4e Compagnie
7850 **Verrier** claude, chasseur 2nd class
5404 **Gay** Marcel, -do-
7756 **Roud** Emile -do-
Killed
1er Compagnie
8322 **Cauvin**, Alfred, chasseur 2nd
2e Compagnie
5267 **Bursin** Eugène. Chasseur 2nd class
3e Compagnie
1833 **Michlée** Benjamin, Sergeant
" **Abeillon**, Auguste Chasseur 2nd class
3271 **Finet**, Camille, -do-
Missing
1er Compagnie
7670 **Gilbin**, Edmond, Chasseur 2nd class
8311 **Boismartel** Gustave -do-
6882 **Didier** Alide -do-
8568 **Depagne** Eugène -do-
7662 **Stampff** Charles -do-
4e Compagnie
2099 **Rouquet**, Léon, chasseur 2nd class
1828 **Lemaïtre**, Alfred -do-

18 February

The 1er and 2e compagnies received the order at 14 hours to bring themselves in reserve to the factory at Roclincourt
The machine gun section abandoned the craters where they were in position to go to establish themselves at the sunken road, to parry a possible counter attack. In the course of the day the Germans vigorously bombarded our trenches and overwhelmed them – with bombs and petards. In the course of the bombardment, the Battalion endured the following losses.
Wounded
3346 **Floire**, Edmond chasseur 2nd class
1641 **Tindy**, Maxime, Sergeant
4004 **Piles** Pierre chasseur 2nd class
4115 **Charrier** Jean -do-
7746 **Melay** Claude, corporal
3e Compagnie
2574 **Rose**, Joseph, chasseur 2nd class
2953 **Combes**, Louis -do-
4e Compagnie
2690 **Sauvan** Charles chasseur 2nd class
2414 **Testa** Louis corporal

2188 **Alette** Fernand chasseur 2nd class
2321 **Lebrun** Henri -d°-
3450 **Kergosien** Pierre Marie -d°-
3745 **Meschino** Henri chasseur 2nd class
8502 **Lequeval** Michel -d°-
3052 **Tomaso**
4269 **Mercier** Adrien -d°-
s.m. **Brouse** -d°-
s.m. **Ducard** -d°-

Killed

4e Compagnie

7774 **Montreynaud** Joseph chasseur 2nd class
7450 **Jacques** Clement -d°-
3429 **Druant** Grullmann -d°-

Missing

4e Compagnie

8215 **Gourdy** Pierre, chasseur 2nd class
2149 **Marquez** Louis -d°-
s.m. **Roure** Louis-Joseph -d°-
2099 **Rouquet** Léon -d°-
1828 **Lemaitre** Alfred -d°-

19 February

The Germans continue their attacks by launching petards and bombs.
In the course of the day the Battalion endured the following losses:
Wounded

1ere Compagnie

3327 **Victor** Louis, chasseur 2nd class
7575 **Talavera** André -d°-
7332 **Calvet** Jules -d°-
2275 **Arson** Gustave -d°-
5306 **Mollette** Colette -d°-
3342 **Combarel** -d°-
2215 **Castel** Eugène -d°-
5543 **Barbarin** Georges -d°-
5239 **Perrin** Gaston -d°-
5327 **Brun** Joinisse -d°-
5352 **Guston** Alfred -d°-
5893 **Chomel** Marius -d°-
6848 **Dupuis** Joseph -d°-

2e Compagnie

s.m. **Lollier** Léon chasseur 2nd class
4097 **Moreau** André -d°-
7490 **Dutto** Dominique -d°-
7206 **Gradelet** Albert -d°-
3135 **Jacomino** Louis -d°-
4316 **Hémon** Louis Joseph -d°-
Rte **Duchet** -d°-

3387 **Laplaud** Léonard -d°-
6140 **Dubois** Robert -d°-
7018 **Decroix** Maurice -d°-
3e Compagnie
8013 **Lenorey** Joseph chasseur 2nd class
7507 **Dijoud** Emile -d°-
7381 **Thépault** Yves corporal
Goudard chasseur 2nd class
7095 **Robinet** -d°-
3826 **Thiely** -d°-
3363 **Hanez** -d°-
5681 **Beauce** Marc -d°-
5861 **Laureau** Eugène -d°-
3818 **Nouhet** Clovis -d°-
7747 **Vallier** Joseph -d°-
3542 **Canu** Louis -d°-
3594 **Rousson** Paul -d°-
2691 **Evain** Joseph -d°-
4e Compagnie
s.m. **Danès** Emile, chasseur 2nd class
s.m. **Perrez** Mouchy -d°-
7979 **Perrot** Henri -d°-
s.m. **Colas** Auguste -d°-
7640 **Phylippe** François -d°-
s.m. **Giry** Moise -d°-
2968 **Mars** Achille -d°-
6859 **Chapentier** Alphonse -d°-
2790 **Hazebrouck** Louis chasseur 2nd class
8424 **Landrin** René -d°-
3095 **Ducou** Georges -d°-
s.m. **Lingelser** Alfred -d°-
s.m. **Mamessier** Gussaye Sergeant
8419 **Dubois** Pierre chasseur 2nd class
Ducat Aimé -d°-
1001 **Darmon** Moïse -d°-

20 February

The 3e and 4e Compagnies return from the trenches
Wounded
1er Compagnie
5239 **Perrin** Gaston chasseur 2nd class
6327 **Brun** Joinisse -d°-
5352 **Guston** Alfred -d°-
5893 **Chomel** Marius -d°-
5398 **Garatini** François -d°-
7826 **Vincent** Emile -d°-
6737 **Colombe** Charles -d°-
2001 **Dahan** Maurice -d°-
2953 **Buchimiller** Henri -d°-

s.m. **Moll** Jean -d°-
6922 **Guerardi** René -d°-
7612 **Picard** Auguste -d°-
0864 **Massot** Eugène -d°-
8274 **Mallard** Raymond -d°-
7869 **Bourdet** Eugène -d°-
s.m. **Dervaux** Louis -d°-
s.m. **Lesouple** Emile -d°-
2e Compagnie
2112 **Chavalle** Prudent -d°-
7459 **Céria** Lucien -d°-
3683 **Nielle** Henri -d°-
Courrier Remy Corporal
7389 **Abgrall** Charles chasseur 2nd class
2370 **Delattre** François -d°-
2970 **Pelletier** Jean chasseur 2nd class
2972 **Maréchal** Henri -d°-
3e Compagnie
s.m. **Denigot** Henri, chasseur 2nd class
s.m. **Gaffet** Gabriel -d°-
3982 **Guigot** Georges -d°-
3999 **Lemarié** Louis -d°-
4e Compagnie
s.m. **Aerif** Isaac -d°-
" **Catgrotia** -d°-
2779 **Mizzi** Fernand -d°-
" **Lesqumaud** -d°-
2924 **Vaudenay** Pierre -d°-
7821 **Jarcelat** Léon -d°-
8401 **Desomme** Jean Baptist -d°-
Killed
1er Compagnie
3490 **Dubois** Marcel bugler
8323 **Bouffay** Marcel chasseur 2nd class
Missing
1er Compagnie
" **Girard** Maurice chasseur 2nd class
2131 **Loridans** Ernest -d°-

21 February

The 3e and 4e Cies left Anzin-St. Aubin and went to camp at Pont-de-Gy.
Wounded
2e Compagnie
2469 **Cuvelard** Jules chasseur 2nd class
3423 **Mérour** Joseph corporal
2956 **Dumont** Louis chasseur 2nd class
2199 **Lecomte** Jules -d°-
3590 **Marzin** François -d°-

4e Compagnie
3391 **Charrat** Pierre chasseur 2nd class
5969 **Faure** Claude -d°-
2278 **Demester** Louis chasseur 2nd class
6417 **Lacroix** George -d°-
1452 **Jacotin** René -d°-
Machine gun section
8376 **Kuestel** Henri chasseur 2nd class

22 February

On 22 February the 3e and 4e Cies received the order to leave Pont-de-Gy to bring themselves to Bavincourt where they arrived in 18 hours.
Wounded
H.R. Section
6004 **Favergon** Francois chasseur 2nd class
1er Compagnie
1828 **Devillier** Joseph chasseur 2nd class
6477 **Giraud** Eugène chasseur 2nd class
4230 **Guiraud** Jules -d°-
3132 **Soria** Sauveur -d°-
2e Compagnie
7770 **Vernay** Louis -d°-
7018 **Decroix** Maurice -d°-
7948 **Semeriva** Charles -d°-
Rte **Prévot** Paul -d°-
1er Compagnie
3439 **Mallet** Henri -d°-
50312 **Toron** Jean Antoine -d°-
2979 **Klein** Henri -d°-
5864 **Casale** Jacques -d°-
0563 **Brunon** Claude -d°-

23 February

The 1er and 2e Compagnies received the order to leave the trenches and went to camp at Etrun.
Missing
1er Compagnie
6391 **Favier** Jacques chasseur 2nd class

24 February

The 1er and 2e Compagnies received the order to leave Etrun and bring themselves to Bavincourt where they arrived at 17 hours
That movement of the Battalion to Bavincourt was the execution of General Order N° 209 by which the 45e Division was relieved from the front and placed in Army reserve.

25 February

In execution of special order n° 241 prescribing to the 45e Division to put five Coys and 6 machine gun sections at the disposal of 10e Corps to relieve a Division of Cavalry, the four coys of the Battalion and its Machine gun section were brought into Rivière at 20 hours.

The 3e and 4e Compagnies and the MG Sect went to occupy the trenches while the 1ere and 2e stayed in reserve at Rivière

26 February

The losses were the following:
Wounded
3e Compagnie
3316 **Chaulet** Armand chasseur 2nd class
7495 **Payot** Léon d^{o}
4e Compagnie
2827 **Boismin** Jules d^{o}

27 February

The 1ere and 2e Compagnies go to relieve the 3e and 4e Cies in trenches who return to camp at Rivière
Wounded
1ere Compagnie
6058 **Verdier** Raymond, chasseur 2nd class
2e Compagnie
s.m. **Saunal** François chasseur 2nd class
Killed
1er Compagnie
3477 **Herce**, chasseur 2nd class

28 February

Sojourn at Rivière

1st March

The Corps received a section of machine guns on carriers and constituted a Machine gun Platoon administered separately – of which Lieutenant André took command
The 3e and 4e Compagnies relieved the 1er and 2e Compagnies at 22 hours.
Wounded
1er Compagnie
8431 **Desrousseau** Albert chasseur 2nd class
7420 **Mélier** Louis d^{o}
Killed
4161 **Hudenou** Ernest d^{o}

2 March

In execution of special order N° 9 prescribing the relief of all the units of the 91er Brigade including the machine gun section on the whole front of the 10e C.A. the Battalion rejoined Bavincourt where it took camp
Wounded
3e Compagnie
2653 **Lafosse** Albert chasseur 2nd class
1er Compagnie
7745 **Legigan** Marcel-d°-

3 March

Rest

4 March

As of the 4th the instruction and training of the troops resumed daily.
In the morning it executed an inspection.
The evening was consecrated with an exercise in field service

From 5 to 19 March

Sojourn in Bavincourt
On 9 March the Battalion was provisionally attached to the 10e Corps d'Armée from the point of view of command, administration and discipline.
On the date of the 20th by decision of the General Commander in Chief the Commander **Trousson** took command of the 1er Bataillon de marche of the Infanterie Légère d'Afrique.

20 March

By note of service of the Commander of the 10e C.A. the Battalion was put at the disposal of the 19e Division
In execution of that order the Battalion left Bavincourt on the 20th, to go to camp at Duisans and left the camp on the 21st to bring itself to Roclincourt. The general services in billets at Anzin
Two and a half coys (the 3e and 4e Compagnies) did duty in the trenches, the rest of the Battalion, 1 and ½ coys remained available at Roclincourt

21 March

Duty in the trenches
The service was organized as follows:
One Company ½ in the first line
One Company in the 2nd line

One Company ½ rest at Roclincourt
Each day the units alternate between themselves

22 March

A section of machine guns was put in battery (1st line)
The 2nd section remained available in Roclincourt
During the day the Baton endured the following losses

Wounded
Machine gun platoon
Richard chasseur 2nd class

23 March

Wounded
1er Compagnie
4214 **Pasteau**, Gustave, chasseur 2nd class
3174 **Montmayrand** Louis -d°-
3e Compagnie
3776 **Laurens**, Pierre -d°-
3931 **Desqueyroux** Jules -d°-
4e Compagnie
2801 **Sieg** Fréderic -d°-

24 March

Killed
1er Compagnie
Mr. Toulza Albert, Lieutenant.
Wounded
1er Compagnie
Mouton, Alfred, Chasseur 2nd class

25 March

Wounded
1er Compagnie
3999 **Roger**, Pierre Chasseur 2nd Class

26 March

The Battalion was on alert all night, some airplanes having reported the assembly of Germans which seemed to presage an attack on Arras.

27 March
Wounded
2e Compagnie
Rte **Pinagot** Auguste, chasseur 2nd class

3668 **Labussière** Paul, -d°-
3647 **Bienvenu** Albert -d°-

28 March

In the night of 28 to 29 March, the Battalion was relieved by the 3e Bataillon de March d'Infanterie Légère d'Afrique and went to camp at Wanquetin, where it arrived at 6 hours in the morning.

29 March

Rest

30 March

From 30 March, the instruction and training of the troops was resumed daily
In the mornings it executed inspection parades, the evening was consecrated with an exercise in field service.

1, 2 and 3 April

Sojourn at Wanquetin
By decree of 22 March, the Lieutenants Tremsal and Blondé are promoted to Captain

4 April

Captain Faulin joined the ambulance
The Battalion received a reinforcement of 150 chasseurs coming from the Depot of Aix. At 14 hours it left Wanquetin to relieve the 3e Bataillon d'Infanterie Légère d'Afrique in the trenches of Roclincourt.
The service was assured in the same conditions as the previous sojourn, that is to say a Compagny and a half in the 1st line, a Company in the 2nd line, a Company and a half in reserve at Roclincourt.
One of the machine gun sections was in the 1st line, and the 2nd section was in reserve at Roclincourt.

5 April
1915

In the night of the 4th to the 5th some patrols were launched in front of the trenches seeking, by making prisoners, to identify the German troops newly arrived and holding the trenches in facing us.
In the course of one of the patrols chasseurs Picard and Bouveau of the 1er Compagnie lost their direction, believing to be returning to our lines, came up against the German barbed wire entanglements. Taking fire, they turned around to reach our trenches.

Bouveau was wounded in the shoulder, the two chasseurs continued to progress towards our lines by crawling.
Picard, in his turn was wounded and alone succeeded in reaching our lines.
However, Bouveau left for dead on the ground, returned to the trenches on the 12th of April after having stayed for 7 days between the two lines.
Picard was cited to the order of the Army Corps for the following motif:
"Taking part in a patrol for which he was present voluntarily, was wounded seeking to bring back one of his wounded comrades to our lines."
In the course of that day the Baton endured the following losses:

	Wounded
	1er Compagnie
2940	**Bouveau** Louis chasseur 2nd class
7612	**Picart** Auguste -do-
02	**Valéro** Mariaus -do-
5015	**Lefoye**r Louis -do-
	3e Compagnie
5198	**Ledez** Pierre Corporal

Killed
1er Compagnie
2936 **Paulain** chasseur 2nd class

6 April and
7 April

Wounded
1er Compagnie
2759 **Marbézy** Léopold chasseur 2nd class

8 April

Execution of note No 2380 of the 10e Corps d'Armée dated 7 April:
The 1er Bataillon de Marche d'Infie Légère d'Afrique will be relieved that night by a Baton of the 19e Divon d'Infie.
It will bring itself immediately after to Wanquetin, where it will be taken the next day towards 13 hours by automobile to the destination of Frévent to embark itself by rail at 18 hours. The teams will return from Wanquetin to Frévent by road; they will have to arrive there before 17 hours.
The Battalion to find at the Frévent station 1 day rations for the rail way and 2 days of disembarkation.
The Battalion left Roclincourt in the night of the 7th to the 8th and went to camp at Wanquetin.
At 14 hours it was taken by automobile to the destination of Frévent,

where it arrived at $16^{H}30$ and where it departed by rail towards 21 hours.

9 April

Disembarkation at Esquelbecq where the Battalion received the following order: N° 313 of the D.A.B.
The two Bataillons d'Afrique of the 45e Division will make movements in the following conditions to the area south-west of Woesten, where they will be at the orders of the General commanding the 20e C.A..
The Battalion disembarked on 8 April will be brought on the 10th to Proven and on the 11th to Woesten
The Battalion disembarked on 9 April will be brought on the 11th to Proven and on the 12th to Woesten.
Encampment in the region of Esquelbecq

10 April

Sojourn at the camp of last evening

11 April

The Battalion went to camp in the region of Proven

12 April

The Battalion went to camp in the region of Woesten

13 April

Lieutenant Harion of the 4e Compagnie was evacuated.
Captain Wéber took over the function of Captain Adj Major
Captain Tremsal took command of the 2e Compagnie
The Battalion did duty in the trenches of Langemarck
3 Cies and a Machine gun section in the 1st line
A Cie and a machine gun section remain available at Langemarck.

14 April

In the course of the day the Battalion endured the following losses
Wounded
1er Compagnie
3128 **Limousin** Pierre 2nd class
6118 **Fromont** Emile chasseur 2nd class
3497 **Cholet** François do
7099 **Boutbien** Albert do
4020 **Sages** André do
3188 **Braun** Emile do
2e Compagnie
2312 **Pierron** Paul chasseur 2nd class
3577 **Béthencourt** Vincent do

3e Compagnie
" Théaudière Jean chasseur 2nd class
Killed
2e Compagnie
3274 **Carrot** Petrus Corporal
3e Compagnie
3136 **Ivorra** Mariano, chasseur 2nd class

15 April

Losses
Wounded
1er Compagnie
4242 **Mérin** Paul chasseur 2nd class
3786 **Fournier** Louis Emile do
3752 **Bestin** Jules Marie do
Killed
2e Compagnie
2829 **Kerrirzin** Stanislas, chasseur 2nd class
The Battalion entered the composition of the 45e Division which took place on the 15th April in the Detachment de l'Armée de Belgique
Copy of the special order of 14 April 1915 of the General OC the D.A.B. (N° 727)

I. Mr General Quiquandon, OC the 45e Don. will take on 16 April at noon the command of the Groupement d'Elverdinghe
II. He will dispose of :
1◦ the units of his division, except for the units enumerated in paragraph III below
2◦ of the 87e D.T.
3◦ of engineer companies 4/2 7 and 4/3 7
4◦ the two batteries of 120H (of the 1er Regt of foot artillery provided from the Belgian Zone)
Of two batteries of 95 (33e and 34e batteries of the 5e regiment of heavy artillery)
Of a battery of 75 (52e Battery of the 15e Regiment)
5th provisionally of squadron M.F.35
6th Companies of Belgian labourers N° 38, 39, 41, 42, and 43.
III. A brigade of Infantry, general staff and of the 45e A.D. and two batteries of that group will have to be encamped in Army reserve in the area of Crombeke, Vestvleteren, Eykhoeck.
The Algerian Auxiliary Saphis will form two squadrons on the front as the divisional squadrons of the 45e Don.
The other squadrons will be maintained provisionally in the zone of their actual encampment.
The general commanding the Groupement d'Elverdinge will address to the General OC the D.A.B. the proposal on the subject of the periodic relief of units.

IV. In the Groupement d'Elverdinge, the command of the artillery will be exercised provisionally by Mr. Lieutenant Colonel Pruche, OC the 27e A.D.
Command of the engineers will be exercised provisionally by Mr. Commander Savournin, chief of staff of the Engineers of the D.A.B.
Mr. the Military S/Intendant 2nd Class Bel of the 87e D.T. will assure the direction of the Intendance Service of his Division.
Mr. the Head Doctor Collinet of the 45e Division will assure the direction of the health service, while conserving the direction of the health service of his Division.

Signed: Putz

In consequence of the above order

I. The H.Q. of the 45e Div will operate as of 16 April at noon at the Chateau d'Elverdinghe

II. The reserve groupement (1 Infie Brigade, 1 H.Q. of the group of two Batteries of the 45e A.D.) will be placed under the orders of Colonel Mordacq.

III. Two squadrons of Auxiliary Saphis under the orders of a Squadron Chief will bring themselves to Kruystraete (E of Bambecque) tomorrow by Wormhoudt and Herzeele – Passage leading to the West entrance of Wormhoudt at 9 hours.

IV. The H.Q. (1st and 2nd echelons and telegraphists left at Esquelbecq and the ambulance 4/45, forming a single column under the orders of Captain Madrange will bring themselves to Elverdinghe tomorrow by Wormhoudt, Watou Bridge, Poperinghe.

Departed Esquelbecq at 6H30

16 April

Losses
Wounded
3e Compagnie

2397	**Chassain** Maurice, chasseur 2nd class	
05011	**Lebouc** Lucien	do
8098	**Rilhac** Jean	do
3129	**Lacroix** Alphonse	do

Killed

3651	**Delporte** Léon, Corporal

General Order No 1 dated 16 April – thusly defines the service of the Groupement d'Elverdinghe.
I. The service of the Groupement d'Elverdinghe will be assured – in the conditions fixed in the adjoining table.
III. Occupation of the sector.

a) 87e D.T. without modification
b) 45e Division (less the elements in Army Reserve) 1st line, support, and reserves of sector to the E of the Yser Canal, 1 Bataillon d'Afrique, 1 Infantry Regiment, 1 battalion of the 2nd Regt of the Brigade.

Groupement Reserve {1 Battalion of Inf to the S of highway
---------------------------- {1 Battalion at Elverdinghe
(3 Battalions) {1 Bataillon d'Afrique between
{Elverdinghe and Woesten

IV. Employment of Artillery
The Artillery of the front will be put under the orders of the Lieutenant-Colonel Commanding the 45 A.D. who will be billeted at Boesinghe
It will be divided in 3 groupements
a) Groupement to the South of Zuydschoote (1 group of 75 Maj Perrin)
b) Groupement to the East of Boesinghe (2 Bies 90, 2 Bies 75, 1 Bty 95)
c) Groupement to the East of Pilkem, Ypres (4 Bies 90, 2 Bies 75 Maj Lenoble)

The two Batteries of 120 H, the Battery of 95 and the Battery of 75 anti-aircraft, will stay at the disposal of the Colonel OC the Arty of the Groupement.

V. Employment of Engineers –
No modification is brought to the actual service of the engineers; The divisional coys remain at the disposal of the General of the Division.
VI. Reliefs
The 90^{e} and 91er Brigades will alternate for the relief in the sector of Langemarck by periods of eight days.
The relief of the 91er Brigade by the 90^{e} Brigade will commence in the night of 21 to 22, the relief of the 90^{e} by the 91er Brigade will commence in the night of 29 to 30 April and so on.
The Bataillons D'Afrique will alternate for the relief of their sector by periods of 4 days.
The Bies of Arty in reserve will alternate for the relief with the Bies on the front, following the orders given by the Colonel OC the Arty
----

17 April

Losses
Wounded
4^{e} Compagnie
2258 **Berthon** Henri Corporal
7356 **Toiron** Albert Chasseur 2nd Class

3377 **David** Louis do
Killed

4e Compagnie

201- **Terrier** Gaston Chief Warrant Officer

In the night of 17 to 18 April the Battalion was relieved by the 3e Bataillon d'Afrique and went to camp around Woesten

18, 19, 20 April

Sojourn in camp

21 April

The Battalion left the camp at 17 hours to relieve the 3e Baton d'Afrique.
Lieutenant Bourion sick stayed in camp.
By note dated 19 April, the organization of the sector of Elverdinghe was thus defined:
"Mission"
The mission of the Groupement d'Elverdinghe is to hold the ground between the Belgians on the left and the English on the right on the front actually occupied and to intervene, should the need arise, by counter-attacks on the flank against all German offensives. That mission is essentially defensive.
The goal is not therefore to advance forward of a determined line. Nevertheless, the intention of the General is not to stay completely inactive, but on the contrary, to conserve the moral ascendancy over the enemy by raids rapidly executed on the points particularly susceptible.
1 – Infantry and Engineers:
Repartition of the Sector and mission in each Sector.
The zone of the Groupement d'Elverdinghe is divided into two Sectors of which the boundaries have been fixed (Sketch attached to General Order N° 1 of 16 April).
A – Sector of Boesinghe, under the orders of a Brigade Commander (87e D.T.) camped at Boesinghe and having under his orders;
5 Battalions in the 1st line (1st line and supports)
1 Battalion in the 2nd line (permanent occupation of the bridgehead of Boesinghe).
3 Battalions in reserve.

The Commander of the Sector must:
a) hold the 1st line trenches of the sector
b) hold the Bridgehead of Boesinghe (West part).
c) Be ready to counter-attack, either in his sector, or the flank towards the North, on one or the other side of the Yser Canal.

B. Sector of Langemarck, under the orders of a Brigade Commander (45e Division) camped at Elverdinghe and having under his orders:
3 and a half Battalions in the 1st line (1st line and supports)

½ Battalion on the 2nd line (permanent occupation of the bridgehead at Boesinghe)
1 Battalion in reserve
The Commander of the Sector must:
a) – Hold the trenches of the 1st line of the sector.
b) – Hold the bridgehead of Boesinghe (east part)
c) – Be ready to counter attack, either on his sector, or on the East side of the Canal in the Direction of Steenstraat, or in the direction of St. Julien Kerselaere.
Reserves:
One reserve of the groupement at the disposal of the General Commanding the groupement is placed under the orders of the General Commanding the 87e D.T. (camped at Woesten) comprised of:
3 Battalions of the 87e D.T. under the orders of a Regiment Commander (87e D.T.)
2 or 3 Battalions of the 45e D.I. under the orders of a Regiment Commander (45e D.I.) camped at Elverdinghe.
The reserve must be in a state to intervene either in the sector of the Groupement or on the two sides of the Yser, to the North of the line of Bixschoote Zuydeshoote or in the general direction of Elverdinghe – Paschendaele.
Occupation of the trenches and work in the sectors.
The trenches must be strongly organized to be in continuous function by the minimum strength.
(a). They must be continuous, that is to say that all the elements have to be connected between them with walls of sand bags, communication trenches, etc... organized for firing
(b). They have to be doubled in behind by a line connected by communication trenches (average distance between those two lines about 50 metres)
(c) They must have obstacles in front, with widely spaced secondaries
In each sector, behind the 1st line, several strong points will be created which will be connected to the trenches by communication trenches.
Finally, communication trenches need to be established between the 1st line trenches and the bridge head at Boesinghe.
These works must be undertaken immediately in the order of urgency below:

1 { a – work of the first line trenches
{ b – Strong points and communication trenches between the strong points and the first line trench.

2 { c – Doubling the trenches of the first line
{ d – communication trenches from the Bridgehead at Boesinghe to the trenches

The work of the 1st line trenches (1st and doubles) will be effected by

the troops occupying the sector.
The strong points and communication trenches will be made by the engineer Coys of the Division to which will be attached pioneers of the inf[ie].
Mr. Commander of the engineers of the groupement will come to an agreement with the Commander of the sector for fixing the emplacements of the strong points, the sighting of the communication trenches and to give all the necessary execution orders. (the propositions made by the Captain OC company 17/m were approved) A general plan of the work will be given according to the agreement above to the General OC the groupement who will definitively determine the bases.
The works in the sectors will be undertaken immediately. They will be pushed with the greatest activity.

Works to be effected by units other than those in the 1st line.

_A_ Engineer Coys 4/2 7, 4/3 7 – The Companies will be utilized according to the orders given by the Commander of the engineers of the groupement. A portion of those units will be obligatorily charged with the operation and the eventual destruction of the bridges and foot bridges over the Yser.
B – A line of defense will be organized on the west side of the Yser Canal, following the general line of Pypegale, Lizerne, Boesinghe, Toordhof farm. Mr. Commander of the Sector and the Commander of the engineers will agree between themselves for the sighting of the line and the liaison between the two sectors by Boesinghe.
The works will be effected by the 3 Battalions in reserve of the sector (87e D.T. and a reserve of the Groupement (45e D.I.)
C. Gabions, fascines, etc...
The battalions in reserve of the Groupement (87e D.T.), the Brigade in reserve of the Army, the Territorial Brigade resting in camp will construct the gabions, fascines, etc... following the instructions which they will be given by the commander of the engineers of the groupement. Some propositions will be addressed by the Commander of the engineers of the groupement concerning the transportation of the materials of the fabrication workshop to the engineer park.
Engineers –
The engineer park will construct and will keep in permanent supply 30000 petards and 20000 hand grenades, illumination fuses and other trench devices for feeding the parks of the Divisions. It will constitute at Boesinghe, the park of the 45e Division.
Pioneers.
There will be attached to each company of engineers a team of pioneers of 100 men, furnished by the Infantry regiments of the 45e Division. 35 men by each regiment of Zouaves furnished to the 17/M Cie.

	{ 100 men furnished by a brigade to the 10/3 Cie
87th D.T.	{100 -- 4/2 7

{100 --- 4/3 7

The platoons of pioneers will be constituted immediately and for 25 April at the latest (except for those of the 4/2 7 Cie which will be constituted care of the General of the 87^e D.T. after the arrival of the BrigadeTerritoriale N° 186).

Reliefs in the Sectors

87^e D.T. The relief in the Sector of Boesinghe will be governed by the General OC the 87^e D.T. according to current behaviour,186^e brigade must also participate in service after its arrival. Some requests for automobiles will be addressed in good time for transport on the front of the brigade for rest and replacement in the rest area by the brigade relieved from the front.

45^e D.I. _a_ the two Bataillons d'Afrique will alternate between themselves for periods of 4 days.

(b) the 90^e and 91er brigades will alternate between themselves for periods of 8 days.

The relief will be by halves (1st night of the 21 to 22 regiments in the first line, following night, regiments in 2nd line) The frontline commanders of the 45^e D.I. will govern the relief of the units in the interior of the sector.

Guard of the Bridges.

In each sector, a special unit will be charged with guarding the bridges and foot bridges. That unit will be near to the reserve of the sector (87^e D.T.) and in reserve of the groupement (45^e D.I.) An instruction will be remitted by the commander of the sector to the Commander of that unit which will assure the execution under the responsibility of the Commander of the Sector.

Notebook of the sector

Each commander of a sector and s/sector will establish a notebook which will be transferred in case of relief, and in which will be indicated all information on the enemy. (It is prohibited to provide any indication there on the French works.)

The notebooks of the sector Commanders will be addressed to the General OC the groupement on the 1st, 10th and 20th of each month.

II Artillery The field artillery (7 batteries of 75, 6 batteries of 90) plus a battery of 95 will be divided in three groupements under the orders of the Lt. Col. OC the 45^e A.D. OC the Artillery of the front.

1^e Groupement Lenoble	{ 2 Bies of 75 }	Mission: batter the front of the 45^e D.I.
or Arnaud	{3 Bies of 90 }	
2nd Groupement	{2 Bies of 75 }	Mission: batter the front
De Tristan	{2 Bies of 90 }	of the 87^e D.T. between the E boundary and the Tilleul farm
3rd Groupement Perrin	{3 Bies of 75 }	Mission: batter the front
	{1 Bty of 90 }	of the 87^e D.T. to
	{ 1 Bty of 95 }	the W of Tilleul farm and flank the Yser Canal towards the north.

Heavy Artillery, (2 bies 120h and 1 Bty 95) and the anti-aircraft battery, retain their special mission and are under the direct orders of the Lieut. Col. OC the Arty of the groupement.
III. Aviation The Squadron M.F. 35 must be in position to respond to the needs below;
a. Adjust the fire of the Artillery on direct request made by the Lieut. Col. OC the Arty of the Groupement.
b. Reconnaissance and photography of the enemy lines. A daily reconnaissance will be effected and reports will be made each evening.
c. Long range reconnaissance, the reconnaissance will be ordered by the Gen OC the groupement, some propositions will be made whenever it is useful by the Captain commanding the squadron.

22 April

The service of the Battalion in the trenches is assured in the following fashion:
Three Companies: (2, 3, and 4) and a machine gun section are in the first line: the 1er Cie and 2nd machine gun section in reserve at the village of Langemarck: the whole under the command of Captain Battalion adjutant major **Wéber**
Maj Trousson {The Battalion Chief commanding the sub-sector Y had his command post behind Pilkem at the Auberge de Lièvre

22 April

At ten hours, s/Lieut Ernst of the 3e Cie was struck by the same bullet in the arm and the side.
Towards 17 hours, a thick cloud, about 3 metres high was carried between the German and French trenches. The north wind that blew that cloud towards our lines and brought

[A hand-written report is inserted here. The diary entry continues afterwards.]

Moroccan Division
1er Bataillon de Marche
d'Infanterie Légère d'Afrique

Copy

Report of Captain **Tremsal** of the 1er Baton
De marche d'Infanterie Légère d'Afrique on the subject of the affair of 22 April 1915.

22 April 1915 towards 16 h30, I left my observation post in a house in the ruins of the village of Langhemarck (Belgium), where I had adjusted the fire in the afternoon of our Artillery, to take some rest before the work of the night.

At the moment when I left the loft where I was observing the fire, I saw a Drachen[*] rise behind the German lines. I ordered the Sergeant who accompanied me to return to his shelter as a precaution to avoid revealing the location of the command post and I regained my post.

I had scarcely stretched out to take a little rest, when I heard a lively enough fusillade erupt. I thought at first of a skirmish, the very clear and very sunny weather, the solidity of the trenches, the confidence that I had in my men left me very reassured in the eventuality of an attack. I had, however, only just risen when the fusillade redoubled in intensity, the machine guns rattled and after several minutes the cannon sounded. Convinced therefore of a serious attack, I dove out of the cellar to see what was happening when the climax of the escalation came.

I encountered a man of my company coming in all haste from the neighbouring trenches about 200 metres from the command post which was not connected to those by any communication trench. That man shouted to me: “My Captain there is no more way to hold there, they have struck us with poisons.” I left on the road, the village was flattened by projectiles and I perceived an enormous cloud several metres high, yellow in the centre and green on the edge, masking and discolouring the landscape. The cloud concealed our trenches which the occupants were obliged to evacuate in all haste. I made at once to leave my reserve section commanded by Lieutenant Chevalier and installed it at the edge of the village behind the ruins of the houses then regrouped the men who fell back from the trenches around me, shouting to them: “The Joyeux have never lost a trench, rally to me!” All the men who heard me quickly joined themselves to the reserve section, but after some minutes, the asphyxiating cloud came upon us. A horrible sensation of burning took hold of us in the throat, our lungs refused to receive that poisoned air. A blood tinged dribble came from the nose and mouth in quantity so abundant that the whole breast of my great-coat was covered. The suffocation by asphyxia began to make itself felt.

To stay there was impossible, I shouted the order to retreat, which was effected by crossing the park of the Chateau de Langhemarck under a hail of shells and bullets. Anyone who fell short of breath, unable to get back up immediately, died there. Finally, after superhuman efforts, gasping and suffocating, we arrived, [...], at the exit of the park where we threw ourselves down at the foot of the parapet wall.

The gas, very likely stopped by the parapet wall of the park and dissolved by a pond found in the park, no longer rendered the air unbreathable, a strong odour of chlorine alone substituted. Rallying my men with Lieutenant Chevalier, about thirty in total, I installed them in the trenches constructed exactly at the level crossing of the Langhemarck station at less than five hundred metres from our evacuated trenches. I did not find the reserve Coy of the Bat[on] (Lieut.

[* A type of German observation balloon]

Vincent) in those trenches, which I had hoped to meet there.

Considering [illegible] to have to be the easiest to hold, since the effects of the gas were no longer mortal, hoping always that the fire of the French reserves of Pilkem were going to work and judging the maintenance of the support point at Langhemarck to have great importance for us, I resolved to resist on that point. Not long after settling in, I saw Captain Lormier of the Battalion coming with a group of men. I told him briefly of my intention and put myself at his orders. He responded to me: "I am going to go to take orders from Wéber." The Captain commanded the Bat^{on} and he went away with his staff in the direction of the west (of Pilkem).

The command post could be found at the N exit of the village of Langhemarck. I had in vain attempted a relief by telephone at the start of the attack. Everyone was talking on the different lines so that it had been impossible. Surprised by the direction taken by Captain Lormier, I resolved to go myself to the command post, at some hundred metres on my left. I ran there alone, but I did not find anyone there. I returned to my men, who calm and resolute, awaited the enemy in the trenches. It was about 17^{H}15 or 17^{h}30. Nothing presented itself in front of us to the right and the left, some isolated shell bursts. At several different times, I changed positions to see if anything was coming from the direction of Pilkem. The French Artillery was killed, I finally remarked to Lieut. Chevalier on the seriousness: "but N. de D. [**] where the f... is our Artillery." I knew at that moment it had fallen into German hands.

I had covered my men by two patrols, one to the right and S to a church, the other to the left at the N exit of the village. Moving to see what they were doing, I perceived by the gap in the road on my left and behind me, a long line of German skirmishers who encircled the village by enveloping it. I wanted immediately to face to that attack and could no longer dream of holding the corner of the village where I was installed, so drew nearer to the line of retreat of Pilkem. I was ignorant therefore that that village had fallen to the power of the Germans and that I was completely surrounded. I gave the order to leave the trench in column behind me to gain the line of the W to E railway from Pilkem to Langhemarck. The movement was executed as if on parade, it was effected at the start without encounter, thanks to the defile of abandoned railway coaches in the station. It was at that moment past 18 hours. On coming to the end of some coaches, I found Captain Renaud of my Bat^{on}, who had wanted, him too, to hold until the end, and came alone or with one man, I cannot be precise. He had been wounded in the head because he wore a dressing. I agreed with him saying: "The wretches, this is their "war." I didn't finish, because an explosion very close by threw me on the railway as well as 5 or 6 men who were closest to me. I fell face down against the ground helped immediately by my orderly,

[* N. de D. = Nom de Dieu, meaning "in the name of God"]

private Colin, reservist of the 349e Régiment d'Infanterie, on strength with the 1er Bon de Marche. d'Inf^{ie} Lég^{re} d'Afrique, who despite my orders to try to save his own life, refused to leave me and whose courageous attitude astonished me, bayoneted and crossed with two German soldiers there who wanted to finish me. It was at that moment 18h.15 or 18h30.

I greatly regret not being able for the moment to request for the men of the 1er Sec of the 2e Cie of the 1er B^{on} de M d'Inf^{ie} Lég^{re} d'Afrique, for Lieut. Chevalier and for private Colin, the recompense that those braves have merited in the atrocious circumstances of the battle of the 22 April 1915,

I hope to be able to do it on my return from captivity.

Signed: Tremsal

Certified True Copy
P.C. 2 February 1917
[stamped] Battalion chief du Guiny
OC1^{er} Bataillon de Marche
Infanterie Légère d'Afrique

[The war diary continues:]

on our Companies asphyxiating vapours of chlorine and nitrous products.
Behind the cloud, Germans in close lines approached our trenches, of which the defenders, [illegible] asphyxiated were obliged to retire to avoid the non-breathable atmosphere that gripped them.
The Germans advanced straight on the men who fell back suffocated walking with pain.
However the 1er Cie, which at the sound of the fusillade had brought themselves towards the railway, garrisoning the hedges that faced the trenches, were struck in their turn by the asphyxiating vapour. They commenced their retreat by following the railway which they soon abandoned under fire of artillery and musketry of the Germans. Many men of the 1er Cie or the Coys in the trenches fell near the station. Whereas the ones withdrawing towards the S.E. thus escaped the movement of the Germans, which became more evident by the railway and to the west.
The Chief of the Battalion, whose attention had been aroused by the fusillade asked for communication with Langemarck the trenches. The telephone lines did not function. Only the Artillery asked for orders and the Commander, who only knew of the attack from the noise of the fusillade, which grew in intensity, ordered the artillery to fire vigorously.
The Cannonade and the fusillade soon became so violent that it was impossible to obtain the least communication. At that moment a certain number of men arrived at the ridge of the Command post and said that the Germans, after having asphyxiated the units in the

trenches, pursued them in the direction of the railway. The German shells soon covered the ridge of the Auberge de Lièvre, the whole plain with Marmites [*] and 77 shells.

Meanwhile, the asphyxiating vapours arrived at the command post and the shell bursts of the railway therefore indicated the increasing approach of the Germans.

Gathering sixty men who descended from the trenches, the Chief of the Battalion ordered the abandoning of the Command post and to retreat in the direction of Ypres; The route to Boesinghe was in effect sprayed with shells, and a little to the west of the railway the Germans came firing.

The chief of the Battalion with deputy Lieut. André and the 60 men who gathered there directed themselves towards the farm where the T.C. of the Battalion was halted.

The road was not practicable, the vehicles were abandoned and the horses were led across country.

Pursued by Artillery and infantry fire the small group retired in the direction of Ypres in the impossibility of facing the enemy, only 4 or 5 men still having their rifles.

The Yser canal was reached towards 19h30 and the men retreated by the footbridges which presented themselves while the chief of the Battalion consolidated on the North side of the canal with 40 men (sappers) and a section of Zouaves from a neighbouring unit to prohibit the passage of the bridge on barges.

That done, towards 22h30 the Chief of the Battalion sought to recuperate, with some men who accompanied it by other elements of the Battalion, without being able to reunite a single detachment.

The next day, some men who had retired on Ypres rejoined at Woesten.

Following that affair, the Battalion was reduced to the following strength:

1. Officers

M.M. Trousson		Chief of the Battalion Commanding
Aubert		Medical Officer
Blondé	Captain	supply officer
André	Lieutenant	deputy officer
Bourion	d°	4e Compagnie

2. NCO's 29
3. Corporals and Chasseurs 263

In the course of the day of the 22nd, the Battalion had lost:

Killed or missing;

Officers	9
NCO's	40
Corporals and chasseurs	368

Evacuated;

Officers	1
NCO's	3
Corporals and Chasseurs	160

1 Machine gun Section (complete)

1 machine gun (The 2nd having been brought back by Crs **Puel** and

Pechin complete, the mounting and the support of that 2nd piece)
The telephone equipment
4 baggage vehicles
1 tools vehicle with its set
and all of the billeting party, armament and equipment.

23 April

Fifty men who retreated to Ypres rejoined the Battalion, which to reform it, were left at camp in the area of Woesten.
A certain number of men still persist in having traces of intoxication, some cases of bronchitis, pulmonary congestion from the absorption of gas is manifest.

24. 25. 26. 27 April

Sojourn in camp

28 April

In view of an attack to definitively chase the enemy from the west side of the canal (General Order of Operations N° 5), a company was formed with elements which remain of the Battalion that will reinforce the 3e Bataillon de marche d'Afrique (General order № 7)
The state of fatigue of the 3e Bataillon de marche d'Afrique that was engaged from the 23 to 27 makes it leave to rest in camp.

29 April

The attack of last evening must be continued (orders № 6 and № 9) the formed Company makes ready to intervene.
In the course of a bombardment effected by the Germans of the zone of the encampment, of the reserve units, the Battalion suffered the following losses:
Wounded:

26/4	1er Cie
	7689 **Marçay** Armand chasseur 2nd class
	7535 **Ferry** Del d°
27/4	4823 **Gaudrea** Sergeant of the 2e Cie
	7638 **May** chasseur 2nd class of the 3e Cie

30 April

Sojourn in Camp
By note № 98 PC/S of 30 April 1915, Mr. The General OC the D.A.B. made known that the "Groupement d'Elverdinge" is disbanded.

1st May

A company de marche is formed, with elements available to the

Battalion, under the orders of Lieutenant **Lefèvre**, returned 27 April from the Depot, it reinforces the 3e Bataillon d'Afrique. Alert at $0^{\underline{H}}30$ in execution of General order N° 13.

___ General Order Nº 13 ___

For the operations of 1st May 1915.
The intention of the General OC the 45e Division is to attack with the maximum forces available, in the direction: Zwaanhoff Farm, Boesinghe railway crossing, Langhemarck and the Ypres-Steenstratt road, then ultimately on plateau 20, 21 (NW of Pilkem) with the support of elements placed on the west bank of the Canal.
The right of the attack will be supported on the Ypres – Steenstraatt road.
In consequence:
I. – a) The 3e bis Zouaves and the 3e Bataillon d'Infanterie Légère (reinforced with elements of the 1er B^{on} d'Afrique and Cie 17/1M Engineers, placed under the orders of Colonel Mordacq, will be charged with the principle attack. Those elements will be reunited today 1st May at four hours at the S of Zwaanhoff farm where Mr. Colonel **Mordacq** will send them the orders necessary to place them as close in proximity as possible to their line of attack.
The attacking troops will be provided with petards, grenades and sand bags care of the engineer park, then will transport those devices for three hours to the level crossing of the railroad (500 metres W of the command post of Colonel **Mordacq**) at the disposal of Colonel **Mordacq**.
b) The 87e D.T. reinforced with the régiment mixte and the Group of the 58e (**Perrin**) will be charged with covering the left of the attack by holding in an inviolable fashion, the west bank of the Canal on the front it occupies.
It will assure in addition, guard of the lines behind the front.
If the attack reaches farm 14, the crossing of the Canal will be affected in conformation to orders given by Mr. the General **Couillard**.
The elements that will have to cross the Canal, will attack on plateau 20, 21 (NW of **Pilkem**) in the direction of Bixshoote aligning on the right with the troops of the principle attack.
c) The elements actually under the orders of Colonel **Mordacq** and not referred to in the above Art. under the orders of Colonel **Etienne**, will be tasked with consolidating the position occupied and assuring the inviolability of the front to the E of the régiment mixte.
Major **Trousson** will be adjutant to Colonel **Mordacq**
II. The 1er Régiment de marche de Tirailleurs will continue its mission of supporting the Artillery.
Their chief will cooperate to that effect with Mr. Colonel **Fracque** of the 45e AD.
III. Artillery

The Artillery (less the group of the 58e) will prepare and support the attack of the Infantry.
The field artillery following the particular indications that they have been given.
The heavy artillery, destroying the strong points between the railway bridge and Pilkem and to the South.
The adjustment of fire will commence during the day.
IV. Cavalry. –
The two squadrons of Auxiliary Spahis, will extend themselves to the west of Elverdinghe at the disposal of the General OC the 45e D.I.

Company **Lefèvre** arrived at 4h.30 at the emplacement indicated. Towards 12^{h}30 the German heavy artillery violently bombarded our trenches that bordered the east bank of the Canal. Company **Lefèvre** was obliged to displace to the S.
In the course of the bombardment, the company suffered about thirty losses. It gained the point which it had to bring itself to attack in small groups.
Our artillery executed fire for effect from 15^{H} to 15^{H}10, but at the moment of the last minutes of fire the artillery lengthened its fire, the Germans with their large artillery fired a barrage in front of our trenches which obstructed the attack we were to produce.
The attack had to be attempted anew at 16^{H}40. After ten minutes of artillery fire, the infantry launched themselves, but had to return to their lines under violent musketry fire.
At 19h^{rs}, a last attack was attempted in the night, insufficiently prepared by the artillery which had several pieces neutralized by the bombardment, the men who went forward following Lieut. **Bourion** were obliged to stop after having run about a hundred metres.
They dug a trench immediately to which the first line troops aligned themselves during the night.
In the course of the day, the German artillery violently bombarded the trenches and the ground up to the battery emplacements. Notably, they sent a 1/2 dozen "380" shells.
In the course of the day, the Battalion suffered the following losses:
Wounded 1st

4e Cie: **Lefèvre**,	Lieutenant
2026, **Marini**, Titus	Sergeant
2925, **Gautheron** Paul	Corporal
2213, **Lecaille** Louis	2nd cl
3186, **Couzinet** René	"
Rte, **Briant** Eugène	"
1077, **Legland** Basile,	2nd cl
2405 **Vervisch** Evariste,	"
Machine gun Platoon:	
2883 **Péchin**	Corporal
2871 **Marie**	2nd cl

The night of 1st to 2 May was occupied with consolidating the conquered ground.

2 May

A special order of Colonel **Mordacq** prescribed that the offensive will not be pursued on 2 May on the E bank of the Canal and to organise ourselves in a manner to assure the possession of the conquered ground.
Coy **Lefèvre** dedicated the day to organizing the conquered trench.
Around 10 hours, the German artillery violently bombarded the trenches.
Arrival of Lieut. **Sauvage** and s/Lieut. **Lahargouette**.
Lieut. **Lefèvre** wounded, is replaced in command by Lieut. **Bourion**.
Following the attack of 1st May, the following recompense was accorded to the Battalion.

____ Order of the Brigade Nº 40 ____

Colonel Mordacq Commanding the 90e Brigade cited to the order of the Brigade:
Baudon Corporal of the 1er Bon de M. d'Infie. Légère d'Afrique.
"Made proof of the greatest bravery in the course of the attacks of 1st May 1915."

Druet	Chasseur	"Same citation"
Guichard	dº	dº
Juillet	dº	dº
Baugeard	dº	dº
Melet	dº	dº
Turquin	dº	dº
Blineau	dº	dº

P.C. 8 May 1915
Colonel Mordacq CO 90e Brigade
Signed: Mordacq

___ Order of the Division Nº 102 ____

General **Quiquandon** OC 45e Division cites to the order of the Division, the veterans whose names follow:
Ibran Quartermaster Sergeant of the 1er Bon de M. d'Inf. Légère d'Afrique

Laurain	dº	dº
Bazy	Sergeant	dº
Calousdian	dº	dº

"Have constantly exerted an example in the course of the attacks of 1st May and placed themselves at the head of the most brave."

At Q.G. 16 May 1915
Signed; Quiquandon

3 May

Change of encampment

4 May

Change of Encampment
The T.R. and the S.H.R. go to camp at Crombeke under the command of Lieutenant **Sauvage**.
The orderlies are encamped at Woesten under the orders of Captain **Blondé**
The Headquarters corps and Lieut. **André** proceeded to 90e Brigade.
The Bat^{on} Chief is put until new orders at the disposal of the Colonel OC the 90e Bde.
S/Lieut. **Lahargouette** rejoined Lieut. **Bourion**.
The Battalion, near the front at Boesinghe, is at the disposal of the General OC the 91er Brigade.

5 May

The Battalion returned to the sector to the E of the Boesinghe bridge at Zwaanhoff farm.

6 May

The Battalion is alerted at 22^{H}30
The Germans launched some asphyxiating shells. The Artillery fired a barrage to parry a German attack.
In a minute all returned to calm
The Battalion passes to the first line.
In the course of that day, the Battalion suffered the following losses:
Wounded:

1er Cie:	7699	**Combes** Gustave chasseur 2nd class	
3e Cie:	2774	**Chavarin** Louis d^{o}	
		Birkel Adolphe	chasseur 2nd class
Machine gun Platoon.			
	2862	**Blestel**	chasseur 2nd class
	0670	**Gachel**	d^{o}
	3161	**Vallée**	d^{o}
	4152	**Moreau**	d^{o}
Killed:			
4e Cie		**Duthe** Emile	chasseur 2nd class

7 May

Violent bombardment:
Losses: Wounded:

1er Cie:	2813	**Soison** Raymond	2nd class
2e Cie:	2602	**Pinto** Gérome	"

	2736	**Guillot** August	"
3e Cie:	3493	**Bondon** Jules	Corporal
	3548	**Lanchec** Jean	2nd class
	Killed:		
4e Cie:	Rte	**Calvat** Francis 2nd class	

8 May

The bombardment continues.
Losses:

1er Cie:	6797	**Gojon** Jules	2nd class
2e Cie:	3695	**Cousinon** Gustin	"
3e Cie:	2901	**Marty** Elie	Corporal
	2944	**Dupay** Alexandre	2nd class
4e Cie:	2712	**Angot** Léon	"

9 May

Preparation to attack by artillery at 14 hours.
The infantry could not attack following insufficient preparation by artillery.
At $17^{\underline{H}}20$, new preparation by artillery
Finally, no attack, the artillery having been unable to fire for effect.
Losses: Wounded:

1er Cie:	2886,	**Lecuticz** Zéphirin,	2nd class
2e Cie:	7392,	**Quéval** Edouard,	"
3e Cie:	3200,	**Nicolas** Joseph,	"
4e Cie:	3637,	**Desuroire** Charles,	"
Machine gun Platoon:			
	3515,	**Haraud**	2nd class

10 & 11 May

The Battalion is relieved at 4h in the morning and goes to camp at a farm NW of Elverdinghe.
Following the affairs of the 1st days of May, have been cited,
1° to the Order of the Brigade N° 40.
Corporal **Bondon** and chasseurs:
Druet, **Guichard**, **Juillet**, **Baugard**, **Melet**, **Turquin**, **Blinot**
With the following mention:
"Made proof of the greatest bravery in the course of the attacks of the 1st May."
2° to the order of the Groupement N° 2.
Bouron Lieutenant.
"At the head of his troops, launched himself heroically to the assault of the German trenches, which were at more than 300 metres. Taken immediately under fire from machine guns,nevertheless succeeded in advancing 60 metres, then conserved the conquered ground."
Lefèvre Lieutenant:
"Had remarkably organized the elements at the head of an assault

column, had been wounded reconnoitring the ground to be attacked."
Henry Camille Stretcher-bearer Corporal
"Had since the arrival of his battalion at the front given numerous proofs of his devotion and courage. At the time of the attack of 22 April had been able in the company of another Corporal to take the greatest efforts, bringing back to our lines a Captain and two asphyxiated [men] and assured their evacuation."
Veling, Felix, Raoul, Corporal.
At the time of the attack of 22 April, had been able in the company of another corporal to take the greatest efforts, bringing back to our lines a Captain and two asphyxiated [men] and assured their evacuation. Seriously hit himself, also had to be evacuated. "
Pechin René, Corporal
Puel Henri, Corporal
"In the attack of 22 April, had brought back a machine gun that a gunner could no longer transport. Gave in that circumstance a beautiful example of energy and overcoming the suffering that was produced by the absorption of asphyxiating vapour."
Béthencourt Victor, chasseur 2nd class
"Was wounded bringing aid to his mortally wounded Corporal."
Losses: Wounded:
3e Cie: 3200 **Nicolas** Joseph chasseur 2nd class
Up to 27 May: Some debris of the Battalion (90 men able to take arms and including the number falling little by little to 40) were placed at the disposal of the 3e Bataillon de Marche d'Afrique and constituted a group under the command of Lieutenant **Harion** assisted by s/Lieut **Lahargouette**; Lieutenant **Bourion** having been evacuated for illness on 8 May.
During that period, the S.H.R. and the T.C. were encamped at Crombeke with the T.R.

4 May, Major **Trousson** sent the following report to the 45e Division.
The present report is intended to make a redistribution of the personnel and material necessary for the reconstitution of the 1er Bataillon de Marche d'Infanterie Légère d'Afrique. Execution of the prescriptions of [illegible] of the General Order No [illegible] dated 3 May:
1° Actual situation of the Battalion from a "Personnel" point of view.
In the combat of 22 April, the Battalion lost:
10 Officers, 40 NCOs, 523 men.
Since that date and notably the attack of 1 May, it lost additionally:
1 Officer, 7 NCOs, 70 men
Being in total:
11 Officers, 47 NCOs, 593 men.
Including only:
2 officers, 11 NCOs, about 200 men evacuated, possibly able to return more or less, after a delay of 15 days to three months.
There remains in the Battalion:
The complete S.H.R.
All the animals and their drivers.

The 4 Sergeant-Majors of the companies and the Quartermaster of the Machine gun platoon.

Those aside, there only remains as combatants:

5 Officers (3 Lieutenants having returned before yesterday coming from the depot

5 NCOs

80 men (That last statistic is approximate, the men available having been put at the disposal of the 3e Bon d'Afrique since 1 May and the losses have not yet been totalled.)

The Battalion therefore no longer exists as a tactical unit.

2° Reconstitution of the personnel

To reconstitute the Battalion such as it was at its formation, it requires:

4 Captains.

12 Lieutenants (9 for Coys, 1 Machine-gunner, 1 Chief Adjutant of the corps, 1 Supply)

1 Medical Officer

2 Cavalry NCOs attached to the chief of the corps

2 Chief Warrant Officers

47 Sergeants including 4 machine-gunners for completion as a formation and 12 Sergeants per Coy and 2 per Section of Machine guns.

Around 800 men for the Coys including 16 buglers (with entrenching tools and camp kit)

Instructed personnel of 2 sections of machine guns without drivers

1 Chief Armourer

3° Reconstitution of material

It requires:

1 Battalion telephone equipment

1 light vehicle of tools with explosives and tools for them.

4 ammunition vehicles

1 4-wheel vehicle for transport of wounded

4 complete Machine guns with reload magazines and sacs

72 cases of machine gun cartridges

8 ordinary stretchers

1 rolling stretcher

4° Precautions to take for the reconstitution. –

It is also absolutely necessary that the cadres (officers and NCOs) provided entirely of the active army and chosen among the ranks having the proficiency of soldiers of the Battalion.

The last reinforcements sent were comprised for the most part of the worst in North Africa. Following an unimaginable aberration, they comprised exclus,[*] men from special groups, and disciplinary cases. About a third of those reinforcements deserted en route. The remainder brought indiscipline to the battalion (mutiny of 17 March at Bavincourt). It is important that the apparent behaviour is not renewed and that men sent comprise none of the chasseurs in the

[* Exclus = men from a Section d'Exclus were normally deemed unfit to bear arms due to a prison sentence longer than 2 years.]

categories above (exclus, special groups, disciplinary cases, or men condemned by a court marshal, to create indiscipline, desertion, refusal to obey, voices of defeatism or outrages against superiors). Finally, it will be necessary to proceed with the reconstitution behind the front, and to dispose of about fifteen days to amalgamate and put in hand all the necessary elements.
The Commander requested the dissolution of the Bat^on^. Awaiting an official decision.
On 10 May, Captain **André** received a tasking to constitute a Machine gun Coy that will be at the disposal of the 90e Brigade. The organization commenced at Crombeke. Detached provisionally from the Battalion, it was afterwards attached to the 1er Tirailleurs. Chief Medical Officer **Aubert**, is attached to the ambulance of the 153e Division.

12 May

Losses. Wounded:

Machine gun Platoon:	3026, **Duval**	Chasseur 2nd class
	2595, **Roche**	d°
	3712, **Brical** Frederic	d°

17 May

Killed:
Machine gun Platoon:

	2759.	**Rochée** Auguste	chasseur 2nd class
2e Cie,	7498.	**Guichard** Léon	d°
	Missing:		
2e Cie	7360	**Vilquez** Féliciez	chasseur 2nd class
	3699	**Dussaussois** Maurice	d°
4e Cie	109	**Davesnes** Maurice	Corporal
	2718	**Fleury** Victor	d°

18 May

Losses : Wounded

1er Cie	3745,	**Richard** Albert	Sergeant
2e Cie	3925,	**Ripouill** Théodore	Corporal
	Rte	**Rideau** Maurice	2nd class
	2962	**Willems** Ferdinand	"
	3643	**Loir** Georges	"
	3036	**Morelli** Jean	"
	3688	**Blanchet** Eugène	"
3e Cie	2974	**Deglos** Ferdinand	"
	5348	**Toutain** André	"
	3485	**Plot** Félix	"
	4125	**Sabourault** Ernest	"
	4292	**Mazurier** Jules	"
	3460	**Gonet** Jean	"

6123 **Thoumire** Léon "
2819 **Roullaud** Toussaint "
Rte **Mouton** Jean "
2800 **Moretti** Paul "
7916 **Riviere** Michel "
3139 **Pizanelli** Ferdinand "

Machine gun Platoon:
8242 **Tuillet** Marée chasseur 2nd class
4252 **Valentin** Eugène "
7938 **Noblet** Henri "

19 May

Losses: Wounded
1er Cie 3116 **Giaccardi** Antoine chasseur 2nd class
7339 **Janvier** Louis "

22 May

By decision of the Minister, the Battalion must be reformed and the Battalion Chief received the order to proceed with the reconstitution. A first reinforcement of 83 men come from Algeria and Tunisia arrived 22 May with s/Lieutenant **Robbe**

23 May

Captain **Bebas** of the 3e Battalion and Lieutenant **Boizeau** of the 2e Battalion arrived at Crombeke.

24 May

Losses. Wounded:
2e Cie 2088 **Allette** Fernand Chasseur 2nd class

25 May

Reserve Lieutenant **Azéma** left from the 2e Bat^{on} d'Afrique with a detachment of 100 men and 69 chasseurs, 3 Corporals, 2 Sergeants, 2 Sergeant-majors
Losses.
3e Cie 4002 **Jézéquel** Théodore chasseur 2nd class
6508 **Quérel** Raoul "
" **Joussaud** Jean "

26 May:

Losses:
2e Cie 3580 **Martinez** Henri chasseur 2nd class
3065 **Bézin** Abel "

27 May

The Battalion Chief received the order to camp his newly arrived reinforcement elements, machine gun platoon, group marching with the 3e Bataillon de marche, in the area of Eikkok were it will be able to prepare the reorganization of the Coys.

28 May

Repartition of the companies:

1er Compagnie:	s/Lieutenant **Lahargouette**
2e Compagnie:	Captain **André** and Lieutenant **Harion**
3e Compagnie:	Captain **Debas** and Lieutenant **Azéma**
4e Compagnie:	Lieutenant **Robbe**
Machine gun Section	Lieutenant **Boizeau**

29 May

Four s/Lieutenants come from the 1er Regiment of Zouaves and newly promoted are attached to the Battalion.

1er Compagnie	s/Lieutenant **Troncy**
2e Compagnie	s/Lieutenant **Fournier**
3e Compagnie	s/Lieutenant **Chauveau**
4^{e} Compagnie	s/Lieutenant **Lungaretti**

31 May

In the afternoon, a detachment of reinforcements from the 4^{e} and 5^{e} Battalions arrived at Eickhok
It comprised two officers.
Lieutenants **Salviani**, **Gayle** and 269 men and NCOs.
The effectives of the battalion are thus brought to about 620 men and to 16 officers.
Special order of 31 May, for the relief of the 91er Brigade, in the night of 1st and 2 June, brought that the battalion will be in reserve of the sector in the farms to the west of the railway (near the level crossing) Notre Dame chapel to Boesinghe road.

1st June

Departure of the Battalion at 13h30
The emplacements scouted out were occupied at 22 h^{rs} the chasseurs bivouacked or used shelters

2 June

In the night of the 2nd to the 3rd, the 1er Compagnie brought itself to the Yser Canal (west bank) to hold the Zwaanohf footbridges including those to the north up to the sector of the 153^{e} Division.
Duration of the mission. From 21 hours to 3 hours

The 3[e] and 4[e] compagnies improved or constructed shelters.

3 June

Night of 3 to 4.
Same mission except executed by the 2[e] Compagnie
Two chasseurs were wounded by stray bullets

1[er] C[ie]: **Leborgne**
Pavie

Medical Officer **Aubert** was reattached as Chief Medical Officer of the 1er B[on] de marche d'Afrique, 50 men of the 3e Compagnie were furnished to transport 58mm shells from the Brigade Command post to the 1st line without incident.

4 to 5 June

The 1er Cie furnished 100 labourers to effect work in the region of Mortèse farm to the right of the sector and on the east bank of the Yser Canal.
The 4e Cie also furnished 100 labourers for work to be executed in the left part of the sector to the north of Zwaanhoff farm.
The 3e Cie furnished 50 men for the transport of 58mm shells from the Brigade command post to the 1st line trenches
The chasseurs were remarked upon for the spirit of their work in a dangerous zone.

Wounded during the work, by bullets or by shells:

1er Cie	**Mazère** chasseur 2nd class	
3e Cie	**Stoëmans**	"
4e Cie	**Andréau**	Sergeant
	Jéromechasseur 2nd class	
	Héroné "	
	Colin	"

(To report, the good timing of the stretcher bearers, 2 wounded in relieving the wounded).

5 to 6 June

The 2e Cie furnished 100 labourers in the same conditions as the 1st evening, the 3e Cie, 100 workers to continue the work of the 4e Cie.
Execution of a communication trench towards Zwaanhoff farm.
1er Compagnie:
Ibram Louis Quartermaster Sergeant wounded by a bullet at the edge of the bivouac
Tarrot 2nd class killed by a bullet while ensuring his service of cooking in the kitchen area
3[e] Compagnie:
Stoëmans chasseur 2nd class lightly wounded by a shell burst

6 to 7 June

The Command Post of the Battalion, bordering camps of the 3e and 1er Cies was lightly bombarded.
The 4e Cie furnished 100 men to go to work in the sector of the Zwaanhoff farm.
Relief:
The 90e Brigade is relieved by British troops.
The 1er Bataillon de marche left its emplacements at 20 hours to go to billets at Eikhok.
Installed in billets at 24 hours without incident.

8 to 13 June

Rest and diverse work of organization and reconstitution in the camp
The Battalion received on the 8th a reinforcement of:
1 Lieutenant (Mr. **Santini**) 1 Sergeant-Major, 5 Sergeants, 8 Corporals, 196 men.
Lieutenant **Santini** is attached to the 4e Compagnie and the men and NCOs were repartitioned among the companies
On the 10th the Machine gun Platoon drew its equipment from the park at Rouggsbruge.
The reconstitution is expedited by Lieutenant **Boizeau**
On the 11th, Parade at 10 hours
The Colonel commanding the 90e Brigade awarded the "Croix de Guerre" to Captain **Wéber**, Lieutenant **Sauvage** and Sergeant-major **Salvini**.
On the 11th appeared an order to relieve the new sector occupied by the Division. Front Lizerne – Boesinghe.

___ Special Order N° 54 _ Relief ___

I. The 90e Brigade will relieve the 91er Brigade in the night of 12 to 13 June
II. North Subsector.
(a) Six Coys of the 1er Tirailleurs will deliver troops to the 1st line (7e Zouaves and 102e Territal).
(b) The 76e Territorial will relieve the units of the 2nd line (102e Territal).
(c) Two Coys 1er Tirailleurs and the 3e Bon d'Afrique (the 2 Coys of Tirailleurs to the North.) will relieve the troops in reserve at the disposal of the Colonel OC the forward zone (7e Zouaves)
Commandant of the Subsector: Lieutenant-Colonel **Bourgeois**
III. South Subsector.
(a) Six Coys of the 2e Zouaves will replace the units of the 1st line (3e Zouaves and territorials).
(b) The 80e Territorial will relieve the troops of the 2nd line (100e Territorial)

(c) Six Coys of the 2^{e} Zouaves will relieve the troops in reserve at the disposal of the Colonel Commanding the forward zone (3^{e} Zouaves).
Commandant of the South Subsector: Lieutenant-Colonel **Deschizelle**
IV. The 1er B^{on} d'Afrique will replace the 2 Battalions of the 186^{e} Brigade in the 3rd line. Two Coys to the North of Woesten, 2 Coys to the South (Woesten excluded).
V. The relief of the 3 lines and of the reserve will take place at 21 hrs 21 h$^{\underline{rs}}$, passage of the relief elements of the 1st line at 19h.45 at Woesten for the North Subsector and 20 hours at Elverdinghe for the South Subsector.
VI Machine guns. 5 Sections in the North Subsector (Machine guns 1er Tirailleurs) 76^{e} Territorial, 3^{e} B^{on} d'Afrique.)
6 Sections in the South Subsector (Machine guns 2^{e} bis Zouaves, 80^{e} Territorial) The eleven sections in the first line.
VII. Passage of the companies: usual disposition.
Nevertheless, the Corps Chiefs, Bon Chiefs and captains of units charged with the relief tomorrow will make reconnaissance of the new sector and will take instructions at the same time. A report will be addressed on that subject to the Colonel OC the 90e Brigade, 12 June, before 16 hours.
VIII C.P. Woesten.
The Battalion Chief and Coy Commanders, will go in the morning of the 12th, to reconnoitre the emplacements.
The relief was postponed to the night of 13 to 14 June.

13 to 14

Service to the Corps of
M^{in} A.M^{or} Rockéas
Repartition of the units:
4e Cie to the N of Woesten ensuring contact with the Belgians at the point situated at the crossing of the Landvoorbeck creek and the road Eikhok hill 9 Boochhock.
1 Section at the N corner of the woods situated to the E of Boochhock on surveillance.
3 section at the windmill of the In den Hockuit.
3^{e} Cie, to the E of Woesten.
1 Section at the windmill.
3 Sections billeted at 600m to the N.E. of the windmill.
2^{e} Cie, a half section to the E Elverdinghe road at 800 m S of Woesten.
A ½ section to the W of the same road.
3 Sections 800m S of Woesten and 400m to the W of the Elverdinghe road.
1er Cie, 1 Section astride the Elverdinghe - Boesinghe road at 300 metres to the E of Elverdinghe.
3 Sections at 800m to the N of Elverdinghe near the railway.
Machine gun Platoon. (in billets, not entered into the composition of the 3rd line forces as per instructions.).

At farm hill 19, near the road to the N leaving from the [illegible] Cabaret
Command Post: at Woesten near the Mayor's office.
Installation complete at 22 hours.

14 June

Occupation of the 3rd line execution of diverse work of repair and cleaning of the shelters and trenches.

19 to 20 June

Relieved at about 17 hours and return to billets at Eickhock

22 June

S/Lieutenant **Chauveau** was evacuated on an ambulance for sprain.

24 June

Arrival of a reinforcement from East Morocco from the 1er Baton d'Infie Légère d'Afrique that composed itself as follows:
1 Captain Mr. **Miseret** and 178 men of the troops.
Lieutenant **Lefèvre** of the 4e Cie returned from convalescence and attached to the 3e Bon de marche d'Infanterie Légère d'Afrique, was at his request, transferred to 1er Battalion. He is assigned to the 1er Cie.
S/Lieutenant **Lahargouette**, passed from the 1er Compagnie to the Machine gun Platoon.

26 June

____ Special Order № 59 _ Relief ____

I. The 90e Brigade will relieve the 91er Brigade in the night 27 to 28 June.
II. North s/sector – (a) two Coys of the 1er Tirailleurs and 2 Coys of the 1er Bon d'Afrique, will relieve the active troops of the 1st line (3e Mixte Zouaves et Tirailleurs)
(b) two Coys of the 1er Baton d'Afrique will relieve the 2 counter-attack Coys of the 3e Mixte Zouaves et Tirailleurs.
(c) The 79e Territorial will relieve with 2 Coys the units of the 1st line (73e Territorial.) and with one Battalion the Coys of the 2nd line (73e Territorial) reserve of the s/sector
(d) Two Coys of Tirailleurs and the 3e Bataillon d'Afrique will relieve the troops in reserve at the disposal of the Colonel OC the forwards zone (3e Mixte Zouaves et Tirailleurs).
Commandant of Subsector: Lieut-Colonel **Bourgeois**
III. South subsector

(a) 4 Coys of the 2e Zouaves will relieve the 4 Coys of the 3e bis Zouaves in 1st Line
2 Coys of the 80e Territorial will replace the 2 Coys of the 74e Territorial in 1st line.
(b) 2 Coys of the 2e bis Zouaves will relieve the 2 Coys of the 3e bis Zouaves (counter-attack Coys)
(c) The 80e Territorial will relieve with 1 battalion, the 2nd line battalion (74e Territorial) reserve of the subsector
(d) 6 Coys of the 2e bis Zouaves will relieve 6 Coys of the 3e bis Zouaves in reserve at the disposal of the Colonel OC the forward zone.
(e) The platoon of the 24e Dragoons, will replace the platoon of 7e Chasseurs.
Commandant of the s/sector: Lt-Colonel **Deschizelle**.
IV. - 3rd Line – A Battalion of the 1er Tirailleurs will relieve the Battalion of the 73e Territorial to the N of Woesten, two Coys 79e Territorial and 2 Coys of the 80e Territorial will replace to the S of Woesten the Battalion of the 80e Territorial
Commandant of the 3rd line: Lt-Colonel OC the 80e Territorial.
Major of the encampment of Woesten: Bon Chief of the 1er Tirailleurs.
V. The relief of the 1st and 2nd lines will take place at 22 hours
Passage of the relief elements of the 1st line { at Woesten at 20h45
{ at Elverdinghe at 21h
Relief of the 3rd line at 17 hours
VI. Machine guns – 1st line. North s/sector 6 sections, (3 of the 1er Tirailleurs. 2 of the 1er Bataillon d'Afrique, 1 of the 79e Territorial.
South s/sector. – 6 Sections (4 of the 2e bis Zouaves, 2 of the 79e Territorial.
North s/sector. – 1 Platoon of the 3e Bon d'Afrique. 1 Section of the 79e Territorial
South s/sector. – 1 Platoon of the Coy of the 90e Brigade.
The Coy of the 90e Brigade (available Platoon) will camp at Woesten, passage of instructions, usual dispositions.
VII. – The Battalion Chiefs, Company Commanders of the 79e Territorial, the Lieutenant of the Platoon of the 24e Dragoons, will make on 27 June before 9 hours, a reconnaissance of the emplacements of their units.
VIII. Command Post of the 90e Brigade. – Woesten.

___ Modification to Special Order Nº 59 _ Relief ___

The 3rd Regiment of the 174e Brigade being put at the disposal of the Colonel Commanding the 90e Brigade, Art. IV of special order No 59 is modified as follows:
One battalion of the 1er Tirailleurs, 2 Coys of the 79e Territorial and two Coys of the 80e Territorial will relieve the Battalion of the 73e

Territorial to the N of Woesten.
The 76^{e} Territorial will relieve the Battalion of the 74$^{\underline{e}}$ Territorial to the S of Woesten
Commandant 3rd line: Lieut-Colonel OC the 80^{e} Territorial.
Major of the encampment of Woesten: one Battalion Chief of the 76^{e} T^{al}.
Police guard of Woesten: (2 Sections) furnished by the 76^{e} T^{al}.

27 June

Reconnaissance of the emplacements in the morning of 27 June
Departure 19$^{\underline{H}}$30 for the Machine gun Platoon. 1er 2^{e} and 3^{e} Cies by itinerary Lion Belge Woesten Kammelbeeke; for the 4^{e} Cie by itinerary Lion Belge Paepegal (Map of Roulers).
The 1er and 2^{e} Cies and the Machine gun Platoon were in the 1st line in the segment C.
The 3^{e} Cie, counter-attack company, segment C.
The 4^{e} Cie, counter-attack company, segment D.
The 1er Cie occupied the trenches of the 1st line to the S of Segment C. On the W bank of the canal.
The Machine gun Platoon is installed facing the Het-Sas lock
The 2e Cie occupied the trenches of the 1st line to the N of the segment.
The 3e Cie occupied shelters finding itself to the E and to the W of the Yperlee, in close proximity of the communication trench found to the N of the segment and near the maison du collègue
Captain **Wéber** has command of the 1st line (3 Coys including 1 territorial).
The Battalion Chief at the Command Post, at the lightning-rod house, has command of the 1st and 2nd lines (3 Comp^{ies} of the 1er Bon de Marche d'Afrique, 4 Coys of the 79e Territorial.)
Trenches and communication trenches are in a bad state. A repair work is immediately undertaken and will continue up to the moment of the relief.
The enemy on the E bank showed great activity, his defensive works are pushed seriously, listening posts, 1st line trenches border the canal, organization of Het-Sas.
His workers are protected by grenade throwers, petards, by machine guns notably at hill 14, by snipers from positions that shoot from great distance on the reverse points, communication trenches, road crossings, etc... obstructing communications.

Losses: Wounded:

2e Cie:	8045	**Caron** Robert	chasseur 2nd class
MG Ptn:		**Claus** Albert	"
		Druvaël Jules	"
		Killed:	
2e Cie:	3704.	**Moyen** Jean	chasseur 2nd class

28 June

Losses :

1er Cie:	01530	**Niétot** Sebastien	chasseur 2nd class
	4015	**Goasguen** François	"
	6844	**Martin** Marius	" (telephonist)
	"	**Delaquerriere** Emilien	"
	5652	**Cricq** Georges	"
	3082	**Manin** Sylvain	Sergeant
		Killed:	
1er Cie	8340	**Pimont** Raymond	Chasseur 2nd class
	9131	**Lény** Laurent	"

29 June

	Losses:	Wounded:	
1er Cie		**Muguet** Antoine"	
	2889	**Michaut** Georges	"
2e Cie	9398	**Vanhoutte** Adrien	"
	04536	**Lavigne** Léonard	"
	05021	**Maronne** Henri	"
	4250	**Agnès** Claudius	"
		Killed:	
3e Cie	5179	**Prudhomme** Victor	"

30 June

Losses:

The 3e Cie underwent an intense bombardment and suffered some losses.

1er Cie		Wounded	
	3693	**Besse** Auguste	chasseur 2nd class
	5653	**Malpel** Alexandre	" 1st class
	"	**Cousin** Jules	chasseur 2nd class
	03009	**Busson** Eugène	"
	5632	**Breton** Ernest	"
	4045	**Cajol** Felix	"
X	5539	**Dubreuil** Joseph	"
	5540	**Fascelli** François	"
X	3206	**Schmitt** Michel	"
X	"	**Hervé** Louis	"
	05508	**Bernelain** André	"
	3218	**Luttenschlager** Maurice"	
2e Cie:			
	4519	**Saussure** Gabriel	"
	4591	**Bobin** Jean	Sergeant
	2814	**Thomas** Henri	chasseur 2nd class
	2684	**Binaud** Emile	"
	7052	**Crépel** Charles	"

3e Cie:

4313	**Arnoult** Raoul	chasseur 2nd class
3644	**Belaire** Joseph	Sergeant
4671	**Lladères** Louis	"
2941	**Marchand** Constant	"
4494	**Beck** Marius	chasseur 2nd class
4371	**Bonnet** Auguste	"

4e Cie:

"	**Tringue** Paul	chasseur 2nd class

Machine gun Platoon.

"	**Herle** Emile	Corporal
"	**Leplat** André	chasseur 2nd class

Killed:

3e Cie

4313	**Arnoult** Raoul	chasseur 2nd class

Part Two

War Diary

Of the 3e ~~4e~~ **Bataillon d'Infanterie Légère d'Afrique** de Marche
During the campaign against Germany
From 26 October 1914 to 1st April inclusive 1915

The present record contains 28 pages stamped and signed by us, Battalion Chief Commanding the 4e Bataillon d'Infie Légère d'Afrique.

At Camp Servière
20 August 1903
Battalion Chief
Commander.
[signed:] Diou

By dispatch nº 4509 9/11 of 2 October the Minister prescribed to study the eventuality of sending to France a Bataillon de Marche of the Infanterie Légère d'Afrique organized by taking from the 4e and 5eme Battalions.
The diverse units of the Battalion de Marche will be obtained by taking constituent detachments reduced from the best elements, and completed later by chasseurs of other units selected in a manner to constitute the Battalion with men trained rigorously, and of a high degree of morale, giving sufficient guarantees.
Under nº 61 M J of 10 October 1914 the General Commanding the Occupation Division of Tunisia made known that he addressed the following proposals:
The command of the Battalion will be exercised by Major **Dutertre** Commanding the 4e Battalion d'Afrique.
Each of the 4e and 5e Battalions d'Afrique will furnish 2 companies of 250 men obtained by taking away from each company sections constituted with their cadres of NCOs and Corporals of which the good elements alone will be conserved and completed by the good elements of the neighboring sections.
The Officers will be designated for the tour of war. The effectives will be those of the Tables of the effectives of 10 March 1914. The 4eme Battalion d'Afrique will furnish a machine gun section, the head-quarters of the bataillon de marche and will be charged with the organization of the stores.
Stores will be taken on the requisitioned Arabats currently existing at Bizerte and will have the following composition:
Combat Train:

1st Head-quarters – 4 Arabats	{to serve as {1 medical vehicle {1 food and baggage wagons {1 meat vehicle
2nd Each Coy – 3 Arabats	{to serve as {food and baggage vehicles {meat vehicle

Regimental Train

4 Arabats	{2 for food {2 for tools

Being in total 30 Arabats harnessed to 2 mules plus 2 spare mules. The proposition above will serve as a basis to study immediately in each battalion for the elements that it will be called upon to furnish.

Composition of the Corps on the day of Departure:

4 Companies and mobile Headquarters company
Companies 1 and 2 and CHR provided by the 4e Bataillon d'Afrique (1ere Cie and CHR from Kef, 2e Cie from Souk-el-Arba).
Companies 3 and 4 provided by the 5e Bataillon d'Afrique (1/2 Coy from Gafsa and 1 ½ Coys from Gabes).

Nominative Table of Officers by Company

Head Quarters

Battalion Chief **Dutertre** Commanding the Bat^{on} de Marche
Captain **Courtois** Battalion adjutant
Lieutenant **Lafargue** Quarter Master
Lieutenant **Doutreligne** Machine guns
Medical Officer 2nd class **Raynaud**
Reserve Medical Officer's Aide **Coignerai**

1ere Compagnie

Captain **Ardit**
Lieutenant **Donrault**
Lieutenant **Delon**

2eme Compagnie

Captain **Fradet**
Lieutenant **Saubies**
Lieutenant **Debat**

3eme Compagnie

Captain **Billot**
Lieutenant **Troutôt**
Lieutenant **Andru**
Lieutenant **Marchesseau**

4eme Compagnie

Captain **Fontaine**
Lieutenant **Calmet**
Lieutenant **Thuringer**

Strength in Non Commissioned Officers and rank and file

1ere Compagnie	NCOs	16	Men	237
2eme Compagnie	NCOs	16	Men	235
3eme Compagnie	NCOs	16	Men	237
4eme Compagnie	NCOs	16	Men	235
HQ Cie	NCOs	10	Men	82
	Total	73		1026

General Total: 1099

Number of Horses

Saddle Horses	13
Cart Horses	2
Mules	76
Total	91

Departure

1° Departure of the Head Quarters of the Battalion and company from Kef 26 October 6^{H}15 (railway) arrived at Tunis 26 October at 16^{H}38.
2° Departure of the company from Souk el Abra 26 October at 5^{h}15 (railway) arrived at Tunis 26 October at 11^{h}30

3° Departure of the half company from Gafsa 25 October at 21 hours (railway) arrived at Tunis 26 October at 19 hours

Embarkation

1° A Company and a half at Gabès morning 27 October on steamer "France."
2° Head Quarters and two and a half companies assembled at Tunis 29 October on the same steamer "France."

31 October

Disembarkation at Marseille 31 October at 14^H^30.
1st echelon: Head Quarters, 1ere and 2e Cies at 1^H^35'
2nd echelon: Cie H.R., 3e and 4e Cies at 2^H^
Points of passage = Avigno, Saincaize, Moulins, Vierzon, Orléans, Juvisy, Nantes, Rouen, Abbeville, Etaples, Calais.

3 November

Arrived at Dunkerque 3 November at 18^H^23

4 November

Departed Dunkerque 4 November at 12^H^
The Battalion directed itself by road in stages on Honschoote. Distance 32^km^. Arrived at Honschoote 4 November at 17^H^45. The Battalion camped at Pont-Ausserre at 2h to the west of Honschoote. The Battalion was made part of the 32e Corps d'Armée (General Humbert) 38e Division (General Muteau) groupement of Colonel Deville.

5 November

Departed Honschoote 5 November at 5 hours.
The Battalion directed itself by road on Hoogtaëde where it arrived at 8^H^. From there, it was transported by automobile trucks up to Lizerne.
Departed from Hoogtaëde at 9^H^15 arrived at Lizerne 5 November at 11^H^15
The Battalion was assembled at 300^m^ south of Lizerne and 200^m^ east of Zuydschoote, where it took a waiting position.
The 1ere and 2^e^ Cies and machine gun section brought themselves at 15^H^30 to north of Lizerne to the west of the Zuydschoote-Bixschoote-Dixmude road. The units found themselves in reserve of troops of the sector commanded by Colonel Deville. They occupied trenches to the northwest of the Lizerne-Dixmude road on the west bank of the Yser canal to Ypres.
The 3^e^ and 4^e^ Cies under the command of Captain Battalion adjutant Courtois occupied trenches to the left of the 1st ½ Battalion. The extreme left of the 2nd ½ Battalion was placed around 2^km^ to the

north of Steentade, the 4^{e} Cie in the line. The combat had been lively enough.

6 November

Losses: 4 men killed
1 NCO and 4 men wounded.

7 November

At 5^{H}45 the 1st ½ Battalion received the order to go relieve on the 1st line the battalion from Alda of the 162^{e}, close to ferme Toussaint. The ½ Battalion ceased to be commanded by Colonel Deville, and passed under the orders of Colonel Muller of the 4e Tirailleurs. The relief was completed at 8^{H}30
Losses:
1 NCO and 2 men killed
5 men wounded

8 November

The 1st ½ Battalion was relieved in the trenches by the 162e Régiment d'Inf^{ie} at 5^{H}30, the ½ Battalion left for In Het where it camped.
The 2nd ½ Battalion under the command of Captain Courtois stayed on its emplacements.

9 November

Following the order to attack, the Battalion assaulted (5^{H}30) a farm and an enemy trench in front of Kleingharburg (see documents n$^{\underline{os}}$ 1, 2, 3 and 4.
During that attack the men seized an important earthwork covered with barbed wire, while singing the Marseillaise.
The losses were important:

Captain Fontaine	killed
Captain Fradet	gravely wounded
Captain Ardit	wounded
Captain Courtois	wounded
Lieutenant Marchesseau	killed
Lieutenant Troutôt	missing presumed killed
Lieutenant Delon	gravely wounded
Lieutenant Thurninger	gravely wounded

That operation was made the object of General order N$^{\underline{o}}$ 113 of 9 November of the Division and of General order N$^{\underline{o}}$ 16 of the Detachment d'Armée de Belgique (see documents n° 5, & 6)

Thus conceived:
"The General OC the detachement d'Armée de Belgique cited to the order of the Army the 3e Bon de Marche d'Inf^{ie} Légère

d'Afrique, that gave proof in the course of the attack of 9 November of the greatest vigour and a remarkable spirit.

Signed: D'Urbal

The General OC the 32e Corps d'Armée is happy to bring General order № 16 of Mr. the General OC the D.A.B to the knowledge of the troops under his command.
He addressed anew his congratulations to the 3e Bon de Marche d'Infie Légère d'Afrique and to their Bon Chief Mr. Major Dutertre.
The Battalion remained on their positions and consolidated them during the day of the 9th and the night from the 9th to the 10th.

10 November

The 1st ½ Battalion was relieved by Tirailleurs and returned to camp at In-Het. Arrived at In-Het at 6H30

10 November

At 7H15 the ½ Battalion brought itself to the south of the windmill of Noordschoote to repulse a German counter attack that had pushed back elements of the 89e Territorial.
It took position in the trenches along the road parallel and to the west of the Yperlee.
That movement forward against the enemy offensive caused us some serious losses.
Lieutenant **Donrault** was killed.
The Battalion stayed on its positions during the days of 10 – 11 – 12 November.
On 10 November the Battalion received the order to attack the German trench along the west edge of canal at 21H30. It has to be supported

1. On the right flank by a battalion of the 162e and a battalion of the 41e
2. On its left flank by 2 ½ companies of Tirailleurs

3 companies of Zouaves took position in the trenches occupied by the Bon.
The attack succeeded but two successive enemy counter-attacks of great strength came to repulse the elements of the Battalion who retreated to their former position where they maintained themselves.
In its attack, despite orders given, the Battalion was not supported in its movement by any other troops. It went absolutely alone in the attack on the enemy trenches.
The Battalion was also not seconded by any other troops at the moment of the 2 German counter-attacks.
During the combats of 9, 10, 11, and 12 November, losses increased to:
6 NCOs and 50 men killed
12 NCOs and 197 men wounded
2 NCOs 129 men missing
Being: 8 Officers, 20 NCOs 376 men out of action (404 in total)

12 November

On 12 November in the evening the Battalion took the alert camp in the farms to the north of the Nordschoote windmill.

14 November

On 14 November in the evening the Battalion was put in general reserve at Reninghemeleu.
Losses of 14 November
3 wounded

15 November

Same emplacements

16 November

The Battalion brought itself at 3^{H}30 to the trenches of the 1st line where it relieved the 79e Régiment d'Inf^{ie} Placement of the units: 1er Cie, Machine gun section, 2e Cie, 3e Cie on the same front. The right of the 1er Cie at about 300m to the west of Maison du Passeur. The left of the 4e Cie at the burnt farm situated on the road parallel to the Yser at about 700m to the east of the Noordschoote windmill (see sketch 7)

17 November
18 November

Same emplacements. The enemy shows little activity.
Losses of the 17th
1 man killed
1 NCO and 5 men wounded
Losses of the 18th
1 man killed
6 men wounded
General Order Nº 25
G.Q.G 18 November 1914
Soldiers!
On all our fronts new and arduous battles have been entered in the books. After the check to his first troops, the enemy has called his most reputed troops to his aid.
They also have come to know the vigour of our arms. Their desperate assaults have been broken on the point of our bayonets, like the waves of the ocean against a dam of granite.
Your perseverance will continue to weary his efforts until the coming day, I hope, where we finally sortie from our trenches chasing their weakened disorganized battalions before us.

The General OC the 8e Armée
Signed: d'Urbal.

19 November

The Battalion was relieved by the 4e Zouaves, Bon Fouchard at 4^{H}30 and went to camp at the same emplacements as those occupied 14 and 15 November

20 November

Same emplacements

21 November

At 17^{H}30 the Battalion relieved the 8e Tirailleurs occupying the left sub-sector (Burnt house at the right of the 75^{e} Brigade) 2 – 3 – 4^{e} Cies and Machine gun section in the 1st line trenches. 1ere Cie in partial reserve at the Nordschoote windmill.

22 and 23 November

Same emplacements
Losses { 22 November: 4 wounded
{ 23 November: 1 killed and 2 wounded
At 17^{H}30 the Battalion was relieved by the 8^{e} Tirailleurs and camped in the farm situated on the Pipegale to Reninghe road between the In-Het cabaret and at 600m south of Renighe where it found itself in general reserve. (see sketch 8 strong points)

Battalion Order Nº 6

Order of the Division.

By virtue of the powers that were conferred to him by note of service Nº 2507 of 28 August 1914 of Mr. the General Cdr in Chief, General Bazelaire OC the 38e D.I. named sub Lieutenants to the 3e Bon de Marche d'Inf^{ie} Légère d'Afrique, to temporary title, for the duration of the war, the following NCO's:
Petit Alexis: Chief Warrant Officer to the 3e B^{on} d'Afrique (active) in replacement of Lieut. Marchesseau (killed)
Senger Eugéne: Chief Warrant Officer to the 3e B^{on} d'Afrique (active) in replacement of Lieut. Donrault (killed)
Fache Léon, Albert: Chief Warrant Officer to the 3e B^{on} d'Afrique (active)in replacement of Lieut. Troutôt (killed)
Arrighi Toussaint: Chief Warrant Officer to the 3e B^{on} d'Afrique (active) in replacement of Lieut. Thurninger (wounded unavailability 3 months)
Fournier Fernand: Warrant Officer to the 3^{e} B^{on} d'Afrique (active) in

replacement of Lieut. Delon (wounded)
These nominations will date from 23 November 1914.
Signed: de Bazelaire,

24 November

Same emplacements.

25 and 26 November

The Battalion relieved at 17H the 8e Tirailleurs occupying the left sub-sector, 1e, 3e - 4e Cies and Machine gun Section to the 1st line trenches; 2e Cie in partial reserve at the trenches of the Noordschoote windmill.
Losses: "nil"

27 November

The 1ere, 3e, 4e Cies and Machine gun Secton were relieved at 17 hours by the 8e Tirailleurs and camped in the same emplacements as those occupied on 24 and 25 November where they will be placed in general reserve.
The 2e Compagnie remains in partial reserve at the Noordschoote at the disposal of the CO of the left sub-sector.
Losses for the day of 27 November
1 killed and 5 wounded
During the day of 26 and 27 November, the enemy showed more activity. In the night of 26 and 27 our patrols met two strong German reconnaissances towards the Yperlee creek, each of 20 to 30 men which they repulsed by their fire.
During the day of the 27th from 10H to 16H30 violent enemy cannonade battering the Noordschoote windmill, surrounding farms, the command post and the trenches of the 1st and 2nd line.
The windmill and a farm were destroyed.
Following the operations orders, the construction and improvement of communication trenches, shelters, and barbed wire entanglements were actively pursued.

Order of the Battalion Nº 8

By virtue of the powers conferred to him, General Humbert, Commanding the 32e Corps d'Armée names to temporary title and for the duration of the war:
Mister Lieutenant **Calmet**, Auguste, Hippolyte, Marie Alfred, of the 3e Bon d'Afrique to the rank of Captain remaining with the said battalion
That promotion will date from 26 November 1914

General Humbert OC 32e C.A.
signed: Humbert,

29 November

On 29 November at 17H30 the Battalion relieved the 8e Tirailleurs. Same emplacements as those occupied 25 and 26 November

1st December

On 1 December the enemy artillery violently bombarded the 1st line trenches occupied by the 1ere Cie.
Losses: 2 men killed
2 NCOs wounded and 2 men
On 1 December the Battalion was relieved by the 8th Tirailleurs at 17H30 and camped at the same emplacements as those occupied on 38 and 29 November.

2 December

On 2 December the Battalion incorporated a detachment of reinforcements composed of:

5 officers:	Lieutenant	**Balme**
	-d°-	**Bresson**
	-d°-	**Mége**
	-d°-	**Battesti** (reserve)
	-d°-	**Bastide** (reserve)

2 Chief Warrant Officers
24 NCOs
25 Corporals
394 chasseurs (including 226 coming from the special groups)

3 December

Following the orders of the Colonel OC the 76e Brigade (see document 8 and 9, a detachment of volunteers at 154 effectives, 40 corporals, 20 sergeants, 1 Chief Warrant Officer Albertini, under the command of sub-Lieutenant Petit was formed by the battalion. The detachment proceeded on the 3rd in the evening to Ballivet farm.

Copy of the operations order of the 38e Division of 3 December.
A brisk attack will be made tomorrow morning on the enemy trenches to the south of Maison du Passeur.
At (4) four hours, the artillery of 75s, situated to the north of the Reninghe Noordschoote road will open slow fire on the enemy trenches to the east of Drie Grachten.
At 5H30 Infantry will open fire, slowly, adjusted on the whole front of the 1st line, from Knoche to the burnt house.
At 5H35 preparation for the attack on the objective by all the artillery of the sector and the heavy artillery, which has received instructions

to that effect.
That fire will only be opened on telephone confirmation.
At $5^{H}45$, lengthening of the artillery shoot, departure of the attack of one part on the south trenches, the other part on Maison du Passeur.
The attack will be led:
1°/ By a detachment of volunteers of the 3e Bon d'Inf Légère d'Afrique, under the orders of 2/Lieutenant Pellegrin, to which will be attached s/Lieutenant Petit and preceded by sappers of the engineers equipped with wire cutters and fascines. It will leave from the trenches of the 162e.
2°/ By a reinforcement detachment also provided by volunteers of the Bon d'Afrique, under the orders of s/Lieutenant Petit of that Battalion, followed by a section of engineers equipped with barbed wire, sand bags, fuses, heavy tools. The detachment will take along a machine gun of the 4e Zouaves.
3°/ By a detachment of 100 volunteers of the 4e Zouaves commanded by an officer of that regiment, designated by Colonel OC the 76eme Brigade.
4°/ By a detachment of 100 men of the Bon d'Afrique under the orders of an officer of that Bon.
Those last 3 detachments, leaving from the most forward trenches, will have the mission of following 300 metres from the preceding units, of flanking them, extending their action and consolidating (one tool for 2 men
All of the above detachments, on occupying the position, will pass under the orders of Captain Courtois of the 3e Bon d'Infie Légère d'Afrique.
The Bons of the 2nd line of the 4e Zouaves, the Bon of the 1er Zouaves resting to the west of Reninghe and which will be at the Moor farm at 5 hours, will make ready to be pushed forward to exploit success or intervene in a counter-attack.
In the last case, Mr. Lieutenant Colonel Eychène would take command."

Signed: de Bazelaire

The attack took place in good conditions. It succeeded. The detachment maintained itself on its positions. It was relieved on 4 December at 20 hours by the 4 companies of the Bon.
Losses: 2 killed – 2 wounded (see documents 10 and 11)

4 December

During the night of 4 to 5 December the Battalion continued the movement forward to the north begun by the detachment of volunteers.
It seized a length of trenches of about 200 metres.
During the operation, Lieutenant **Debat** was mortally wounded, Lieutenant **Lautrés** was gravely wounded.
Losses: 3 NCOs and 16 men killed.
4 NCOs and 10 men wounded

A heavy rain thoroughly drenched the ground, which rendered the whole operation very difficult.

5 December

Following the orders of the Brigade, A brisk attack on the enemy trenches on the enemy trenches to the north of Maison du Passeur, by the battalion, must take place at 15H15.
14 hours = The Battalion Chief **Dutertre**, OC the Battalion, was mortally wounded by the enemy close to Maison du Passeur, at the moment when he was giving his orders for the attack.
The Captain, Battalion adjutant Courtois took command of the Battalion
Following the order given by the 76e Brigade, the Bon attacked the enemy at 15H15.
100 metres of trenches were captured at the bayonet, by reason of mud where the men bogged down, their rifles no longer worked.
Towards 20 hours an enemy counter-attack supported by the use of large bombs and hand grenades (1) made our line retreat back to the point of departure.
The order to attack given by the Colonel OC the 76e Brigade (see no 12) could not be executed, the men being exhausted and their rifles no longer working.

Order of the Battalion № 11

Today in the attack on the German trenches, Major **Dutertre** Commanding the 3e Bon d'Infie Légère d'Afrique was killed facing the enemy.

"It was the death of the brave"
"His Battalion will avenge him"
5 December 1914
The Gen OC the 38e D.I.
Signed = de Bazelaire

The Battalion was relieved on the 5th at 22 hours by a group of 80 men taken from among the volunteers of the Corps and by 2 Coys of the 4e Zouaves. It encamps at the same emplacements as those occupied on 2 and 3 December 1914.
a/ Extract of General order nº 165 of 4 December of the Division.
I. The 38e Division attacked the left bank of the Yser last night, neighbouring Maison du Passeur. The operation, very well prepared by field artillery and heavy artillery, involved the execution of an assault of which 4 detachments of volunteers of 100 men each were present.
The 1st of these detachments commanded by s/Lieutenant Pellegrin and composed of men of the 3e Bon d'Afrique, captured the Maison du Passeur at 2H30; supported afterwards by the other detachments,

(1 (Device unknown to the men)

it pursued its advance to the north, along the canal, clearing the ground step by step, actually it still remains to clear a small length of trench: all hope that the operation can be finished tonight.
The 42[e] D.I. very happily contributed on its left to the success of the day.
The General OC the A.C. greatly congratulated the troops who took part in the battle and in particular s/Lieutenant Pellegrin and his 100 braves of the B[on] d'Afrique.
The General OC the Division wants to extend to the 3 detachments of volunteers, one of the B[on] d'Afrique and one of the 4[e] Zouaves, the complements of the CO of the Army Corps, figuring in the present order addressed to the 100 braves of the 1st detachment.
The same courage and the same energy was in fact necessary of each of those groups.
Finally, he counts on it that all the other units of the B[on] d'Afrique actually engaged, in the trenches to the north, will arrive quickly to clear it completely.

Signed = de Bazelaire

b/ General Orders № 175 of 7 December 1914 of the 32[e] C.A.
The assault of the trenches of the left bank to the north of Maison du Passeur, in the night of the 6th to 7th was executed by 135 volunteers of the B[on] d'Afrique having at their head s/Lieutenant Petit and Warrant Officer **Albertini**
Despite the explosion of 3 mines and the machine gun fire of the enemy, the assault column, leaving the left bank and the right bank at the same time, brought itself forward with a cry of "Vive la France," reaching the enemy trenches. At that moment s/Lieutenant **Petit** was gravely wounded and the detachment, decimated, had to retreat on their first position where Warrant Officer **Albertini** reformed them.
That new trait of bravery does great honour to the 3[e] B[on] d'Afrique.
The General OC the Army Corps has requested the Legion of Honour for s/Lieutenant Petit.
He awards the **Military Medal** to Warrant Officer **Albertini**.

Signed = **Humbert**,

Losses from 2 to 6 inclusive 24 killed – 90 wounded and 45 missing.

7 December

The Battalion changed camps. It proceeds to the region south of la Chapelle situated on the Oostgleteren to Renninghe road.

Order of the Battalion № 12
(Extract of Order No 439D.)

By order of the General Commander in Chief No 439D. of 24 – 11 – 14 were named; to the 3e B[on] d'Inf[ie] Légère d'Afrique
Officer of the Legion of Honour: Captain **Fradet**
Knight of the Legion of Honour: Lieutenants **Thurninger** and **Delon**
Has decorated with the Military Medal;
The Warrant Officers: **Bourbon** and **Cellier** and the Quartermaster

Sergeant **Beautenon**

General de Bazelaire OC the 38^{e} D.I.
B.O. The Chief of General Staff
signed : Illegible

8 December

The detachment of volunteers was relieved at 6 hours.
At 6 hours the B^{on} relieved a B^{on} of the 1er Zouaves in the 1st line (left sub-sector)
Day calm – on 8 December at 22 hours the B^{on} was relieved by a B^{on} of the 79e Régt Territorial.
It occupied the same encampment that it left in the morning.

9 – 10 – 11 – 12 December

Same emplacements.
On the date of 9 December the B^{on} passed to the 174e Brigade which took the emplacement occupied by the 76e Brigade.

13 December

Following the orders of the 32e Corps d'Armée, the Battalion is returned to the disposal of the 38e Division. It left its encampment on the 13th at 8 hours and brought itself in one stage by road to Vlamertinghe (by Oostgleteren) where it arrived at 13 hours. It camped in the quarters of the station.

14 December

Following Special Order nº 284 of 13 December of the 32^{e} C.A. the B^{on} left camp at 7^{H}15 and arrived at 9 hours in the area of the Chateau de Kruisstraat, where it took up a large assembly formation.
Following note nº 18 of 14 December of the 38^{e} Division the 1ere and 2^{e} Cies and Machine gun section directed themselves at 19 hours on the Chateau de Langkhof at the disposal of the Colonel OC the 76^{e} Brigade. The rest of the B^{on} halted at Kruisstraat, in reserve of the division.
In the course of a reconnaissance Lieutenant **Bresson** and 1 NCO were wounded by a shell burst.

15 December

On 15 December the 3^{e} and 4^{e} Cies left their emplacements at 9 hours and brought themselves to 300m north of Chateau Lankhof where they established themselves in an alert camp.
On 15 December at 7 hours the 1ere Cie under the command of Lieutenant Balme, participated in an attack on the German trenches, conducted by the Colonel OC the 76^{e} Brigade.
It lost in that attack:

M. Balme, wounded at the head of his company while leading the assault.
1 Sergeant and 5 men killed
14 men wounded
11 men missing
Losses of the other units "nil"
On the 15th at 17 hours the 3e Cie brought itself in partial reserve at the Command Post of the south sub-sector

16 December

On 16 December at 17 hours the 3e and 4e Cies left their emplacements and relieved the elements of the 4e Zouaves' Bon Fouchard in the 1st line in the south sub-sector, the 2e Cie already placed in the sector made part of that relief.
Captain Billot provisionally OC the Bon took command of the south sub-sector.
Losses of the days of the 16th to the 17th
1 man killed
1 NCO and 20 men wounded

Battalion Order Nº 43

General Order Nº 43

The General OC the 8e Armée cited to the order of the Army:
Lieutenant **Troutot**, Henri, Benjamin, of the 3e Bon d'Afrique
"In the combat of 9 November continued to conduct his troops in the assault despite a first wound. Was wounded gravely next morning in the entrenchments conquered last evening."
Signed : d'Urbal

17 December

Same emplacements
Losses of 17 and 18 December:
8 men killed, 33 men wounded

18 December

Same emplacements
Losses of the 18th to 19th =
1 killed and 24 wounded

19 December

Same emplacements
Losses of the 19th to 20th = 3 killed – 10 wounded
On the 19th at 18 hours the Bon was relieved by Bon Fouchard of the 4e Zouaves and went to camp in the farms situated near Chateau

Lankhof

20 December

Same emplacements
On the 20th at 17 hours following the order of the relief of the Brigade, the 4^{e} Cie was put at the disposal of Maj Caron of the 8^{e} Tirailleurs OC the south sub-sector
It was placed in sub-sector reserve,
At 18 hours the 1ere Cie also brought itself to the south sub-sector and was placed in immediate support.

21 December

Same emplacements for each of the units of the B^{on}
Losses of the 20th to 21st: 8 men wounded.

22 December

On 22 December the B^{on} relieved the elements of the 8^{e} Tirailleurs (Bon Caron) at 17 hours in the south sub sector. 2^{e} 3^{e} and 4^{e} Cies in first line.
1ere Cie in support at the Command Post. (see documents n°s 13)
Losses of 22nd to 23rd December = 7 wounded

23 December

Same emplacements. Losses of 23rd to 24th December
1 sergeant and 2 men killed
9 men wounded

24 December

Same emplacements. The 1ere Cie was placed in immediate support of the 1st line at 19 hours.
Losses of 24th to 25th:
1 sergeant and 8 men wounded. 3 men killed.
On 24 December the Battalion was attached to the 42e Division. 83e Brigade

25 December

The B^{on} was relieved at 2 hours by a battalion of the 122e Régiment d'Inf^{ie} and camped at Trois-Rois (sector reserve)
Losses: 3 wounded (by shell)

26 December

Same emplacements. Losses: 1 killed (by shell)

Major General Joffre, Commander in Chief of Army Group East, informed Mr. **Fouchard**, Battalion Chief to temporary rank with the 4e Zouaves
That by decision of 16 December 1914 he is designated to take command of the 3e Bon d'Infie Légère d'Afrique (Bon de Marche)

G.Q.G. 16 December 1914
General in Chief
Signed : J Joffre
B.O. Deputy Chief of Staff
Signed : Pellé

27 December

Following the orders of the 42e Division, the Battalion left its encampment at 16 hours and proceeded by road to Bussboom where it arrived at 20 hours.
Itinerary: Railway, Ypres Station –
Vlamerthinghe – Bussboom, distance about 12 kilometres.
The Battalion is in reserve of the army

28 December

Same emplacements.

29 December

The Battalion left its encampment at 16H30 and brought itself by road to Trois-Rois where it arrived at 20 hours.
Itinerary = Bussboom, Vlamerthinghe, Ypres station, railway, Trois-Rois.
At 22 hours the 1ere Cie relieved a Coy of the 19e Bon de Chasseurs in a wood situated to the south of Verbranden-Molen. The 2e Cie also relieved a company of the 19e Bon de Chasseurs at the same time at ferme de Blouvve-Poore, 3e and 4e Cies encamped in a farm situated at 300m to the south of Trois-Rois – Command Post of the Chief of the Trois-Rois level crossing. Machine gun section in 1st line.
On 29 December, the 3e Bon d'Afrique was attached to the 16e Corps d'Armée, 31e Division, 61e Brigade.

30 December

Same emplacements – Losses 2 wounded (MG Sec)

31 December

Same Emplacements.

1st January 1915

Same Emplacements.

2 January

At 6^{H}30 the Battalion relieved a B^{on} of the 81e Régiment d'Inf^{ie} in the 1st line trenches in the Verbranded-Molen sub-sector. 1ere, 2e, 3e Cies in first line – 4e compagnie in support immediately behind the 3rd Cie – Machine gun section same emplacement. (See document nº 14)

3 January

The machine gun section of the B^{on} placed on the front of the 96^{e} to the right of the B^{on} was put at the disposal of the Corps.
At 3^{H}30 it relieved a machine gun section on the front of the 3/81^{e}.
Losses from the 2nd to 3rd = 1 Chief Warrant Officer wounded (Bonnafous) 3 men wounded.

4 January

Same emplacements = losses from 3rd to 4th = 2 wounded.
On 4 January at 22^{H}30 the B^{on} was relieved by the 2^{e} B^{on} of the 81^{e}.
The 4^{e} Cie relieved the 10^{e}/81 in the bois de Sapins situated to the south-west of Verbranden-Molen (shelters occupied the 29 – 30 – 31 and 1st January by the 1ere Cie)
The 2^{e} and 3^{e} Cies relieved the 11^{e} and 12^{e} Cies of the 81^{e} at the Blovve Poore farm (the 3^{e} Cie occupying a farm 400 m north of Blovve Poore).
Head Quarters, 1ere Cie and Machine gun Section to Trois-Rois.

5 January

Same emplacements – 1 wounded

6 January

Same emplacements.

7 January

On 7 January at 22^{H}30 the Battalion relieved the 2^{e} B^{on} of the 81^{e} in the 1st line trenches, Verbranden-Molen sector (already occupied 2, 3 and 4 January) units and machine gun section same emplacements as the last time.
The 2^{e} B^{on} of the 81^{e} placed in reinforcement, same emplacements as those occupied by the 3^{e} B^{on} of the 81^{e} on 2, 3 and 4 January.
Losses from 7 evening to 8 morning = 2 wounded

8 January

Day of the 8th to the 9th – same emplacements.
Losses : 4 killed – 9 wounded.
The trenches were bombarded violently enough by minenwerfers.

9 January

Day from 9 in the morning to 9 in the evening, same emplacements. The Battalion Chief had the German trenches to our front battered by artillery. It reduced the minenwerfers to silence.
Losses: 2 wounded. 2 killed
On 9 January at 20^{H}30 the Battalion was relieved by the 2^{e} B^{on} of the 81^{e}. It proceeded in one stage by road to Bussboom where it encamped.
Departed from Trois-Rois at 23^{H} arrived at Bussboom on 10 January at 3^{H}30.
Itinerary = Ypres station – Vlamertinghe – Bussboom

10 and 11 January

Same emplacements.
On 11 January the Battalion incorporated a reinforcement composed of:
Captain **Dupont** (momentarily in command of cadre)
Lieutenants **Delon** and **Bornier**
4 Sergeants, 196 Corporals and chasseurs (5 corporals).
Following that incorporation the effectives of the B^{on} were brought to 17 Officers, 752 rank and file.

Names of the Officers.

	{B^{on} Chief **Fouchard** CO
	{Captain **Coutrois** Battalion adjutant
	{Lieutenant **Doutreligne** OC the MG Sec
Head-Quarters	{Lieutenant **Lafargue** Supply Officer
	{Captain **Raynaud** Chief Medical Officer
	{Lieutenant **Coignerai**, Medical Officer's aide
	{Lieutenant **Andru** OC the Coy
1ere Cie	{Lieutenant **Battesti**
	{s/Lieutenant **Delon**
	{Lieutenant **Mége** OC the Coy
2eme Cie	{Lieutenant **Bastide**
	{Lieutenant **Delon**
	{Captain **Billot**
3eme Cie	{S/Lieutenant **Arrighi**
	{Captain **Dupont**
4e Cie	{Lieutenant **Bornier**
	{s/Lieutenant **Fache**

12 January

On 12 January at 17^{H}30 the B^{on} left Bussboom and proceeded in one stage to the trenches of Verbranden-Molen where it relieved the 2^{e} B^{on} of the 81^{e} at 23 hours – 1ere 2eme 3eme Cies and machine gun

section, same emplacements as previously except that a platoon of the 3^{e} Cie occupied shelters situated along the railway, 4^{e} Cie 1 platoon at the butte de zouaves,1 platoon to the south west of the village of Verbranden-Molen.
Losses from 12 to 13 January : 2 wounded, 1 killed.

13 January

13th to 14th same emplacements – Losses: 2 killed 5 wounded.

14 January

14th to 15th same emplacements – Losses: 3 killed 6 wounded.

15 January

Day of the 15th same emplacements – Losses: 1 killed 8 wounded. The Battalion was relieved at 22^{H}30 by the 2^{e} B^{on} of the 81^{e} – after the relief the units were placed in sub-sector reserve 1ere and 4^{e} in the shelters of bois de sapins of Verbranden-Molen
2^{e} Cie at Blovve-Poore farm.
3^{e} Cie at an unnamed farm, 400m west of Blovve-Poore farm – Command Post of the Battalion Chief at Trois-Rois – C.H.R. MG Sec – Aid Post – Faubourg d'Ypres near the gas factory.

16 January

Same Emplacements – Losses 3 wounded.

17 January

Same emplacements.

18 January

On 18 January at 21 hours the B^{on} relieved the 2^{e} B^{on} of the 81^{e} in the 1st line sector of Verbranden-Molen – 1ere 2^{e} Cies Machine gun Sec same emplacements – 4^{e} Cie one platoon to the trenches on the extreme left, one platoon in the shelters situated along the railway – 3^{e} Cie one platoon at the Butte des chasseurs – 1 platoon in the shelters situated at the south edge of Verbranded-Molen.
Two sections, one of the 1ere Compagnie the other from the 2eme, were brought to the front and placed in support in the bois de sapins situated to the south of Verbranded-Molen, where they commenced construction of shelters.

19 January

19 to 20 January same emplacements.

Losses from the 19th to the 20th = 2 killed – 6 wounded.

20 January

20th to 21st same emplacements – Losses from the 21st to 22nd = 2 killed and 3 wounded

21 January

On 21 January at 20 hours the B^{on} was relieved by the 2^{e} B^{on} of the 81^{e} – after the relief the Coys proceeded singly to Ypres station where the B^{on} reformed. It proceeded afterwards to Bussboom where it encamped. Departed Ypres station at 23 hours.
Itinerary = Vlamertinghe – Bussboom. Arrived in that locality on 22 January at 2 hours.

22 – 23 – 24 January

Same emplacements.

24 January

At 16^{H}30 the Battalion left Bussboom and went to Verbranden-Molen at 21 hours to relieve the 2^{e} B^{on} of the 81ere in the 1st line.
Itinerary = Vlamertinghe, Ypres Station – Trois-Rois – Verbranden-Molen.
Losses from 24 to 25 January: 7 wounded
1ere 2^{e} Cies Machine gun section, same emplacements as previously.
3^{e} Cie, one platoon at the extreme left of the sector, one platoon in the shelters of the railway – 4^{e} Cie one platoon at the butte des chasseurs, one platoon in the shelters south east of Verbranden-Molen.

25 January

Losses from 25th to 26th: 2 killed – 1 sergeant and 4 men wounded

26 January

Losses from 26 to 27 January: 2 killed – 5 wounded.

27 January

The battalion was relieved at 21^{H}30 by the 2^{e} B^{on} of the 81^{e}, after the relief the units brought themselves in 2nd line – the 1ere and 4^{e} Cies in the shelters of the bois de sapins at Verbranden-Molen – the 2^{e} Cie at the Bovve Poore farm – the 3^{e} Cie at the unnamed farm. C.P. of the Battalion Chief at Trois-Rois. The material of the machine gun section was left in place with half the personnel . The rest of the section in shelters at the bois de sapins. The two teams relieved

themselves to permit the entire section to take some rest.
Losses of the 27th = 1 killed. 3 wounded.

28 – 29 – 30 January

Same emplacements.

Battalion Order Nº 38
General Order Nº 73.

Chasseur **Raval**, Eugène, chasseur 2nd class of the telephone team of the 3e Bon d'Afrique de Marche was cited in the order of the 8e Armée.
"Soldier of heroic courage always ready to fulfil the most perilous missions.
"Made part of a telephone team, never hesitated to go repair the lines, even under the most violent bombardment.
"Was mortally hit 15 January 1915, by a ball, in re-establishing an important telephone communication less than 200 metres from the enemy in broad daylight."
Chasseur **Ricouard**, Henri, Gustave, chasseur 2nd class of the telephone team of the 3e Bon d'Afrique de Marche.
Was cited to the order of the 8e Armée.
"Soldier without fear, always ready to do his duty. Brought back three wounded by himself to the C.P. of the Bon Chief in broad daylight in a most dangerous sector, 14 January 1915. Was gravely wounded, 15 January, in going to repair a telephone line under violent fire."

Signed: V. d'Urbal,

Battalion Order Nº 40

By Ministerial decision dated 3 January 1915 and by application of the decree of 26 August 1914,
Monsieur **Fouchard**, Battalion Chief of the 4e Régt de Zouaves, passes to the 3e Bon de Marche d'Infie Légère d'Afrique.
This transfer will date from 26 December 1914

30 January

On 30 January incorporation of:
Mr. Lieutenant Bernard
- dº Gruyer
- dº Lainé (Reserve)

Battalion Order Nº 39

Extract of the official Journal of 25 January 1915

By decree dated 22 January1915 are promoted to Captain:
The Lieutenants:
(Selection) Mr **Andru** of the 3e Bon d'Afrique

(Selection)	Mr **Mége**	- dº
(Seniority)	Mr **Balme**	- dº
(Seniority)	Mr **Bernard** of the 5e B^{on} d'Afrique	

30 January

The B^{on} relieved at 20^{H} the 2/81 in the first line trenches of Verbranden-Molen –
1ere – 2e Cies and machine gun section, same emplacements as previously
4e Cie one platoon at the extreme left of the sector one platoon in the shelters at the railway –
3eme Cie one platoon at the butte des chasseurs, 1 platoon in the shelters south east of Verbranden-Molen.
One howitzer to bomb Haazen at the extreme left of the sector, manoeuvered by a team of the B^{on}.
Losses during the night of the 30th to 31st: 5 wounded

31 January

Same emplacements.
On 31st in the evening, 2 English officers came to reconnoitre the sector of the B^{on}
Losses of the 31st to 1st February: 1 killed. 6 wounded.

1st February

Same emplacements – Losses from the 1st to the 2nd = 1 killed and 3 wounded.
Losses of the 2nd: 1 wounded
Following a German push on the front of the 342e to the right of the sector, the 3e Cie was alerted during the night of the 31st to 1st February. It did not have to intervene.

2 February

Order of the Battalion Nº 41

The General OC the 8e Armée, cited to the order of the Army:
Captain **Billot**, Marcel, Auguste of the 3e B^{tn} d'Afrique.
"Reported since the start of the campaign for his courage. Brilliantly took part in the attack of 9 November for which the Battalion was cited to the Order of the Army. On 14 January was wounded by a shell burst on the right elbow, did not want to leave his post."

Signed: d'Urbal

On 2 February at 24 hours the Battalion was relieved by an English company of the 84th Brigade.
After the relief was finished on the 3rd at 3^{H}30, the Cies proceeded singly to Ypres Porte de Lille, where the B^{on} was reformed.

3 February

Proceeded the same day to the area of Bambecque (north) in one stage by road. Itinerary = Ypres – Vlamertinghe – Poperinghe – Houtkerque . Length of the stage about 30 kilometres.
Departure from the Porte de Lille on the 3rd at 5 hours.
Arrived at Bambecque the same day at 16 hours
The companies were encamped in the farms situated between Bambecque and Kruistraat to the North of the Yser.

4 February

Same emplacements
On 4 February the Battalion incorporated a detachment of reinforcements composed of:
Captain Audibert
1 Chief Warrant Officer
4 Sergeants
10 Corporals – 186 chasseurs.
Following that incorporation the effectives of the Bon were brought to:
17 officers – 780 men

Names of the officers:

Head Quarters	{Bon Chief Fouchard CO {Captain Courtois Adj Major {Lieutenant Doutreligne OC MG Sec {Lieutenant Lafargue supply officer {Captain Raynaud Chief Medical officer {Lieut Coignerai Medical officer's aide
1ere Cie	{Captain Andru {Lieutenant Battesti {s/Lieutenant Fournier
2eme Cie	{Captain Bernard {Lieutenant Bastide
3e Cie	{Captain Billot {Lieutenant Gruyer {s/Lieutenant Arrighi
4e Cie	{CaptainAudibert {Lieutenant Lainé {s/Lieutenant Fache

On 3 February the Bon left the 16e Corps d'Armée
It was attached on that date to the 20e Corps d'Armée Head Quarters B.

5 – 6 – 7 – 8 – 9 – February

Same emplacements.

10 February

The B^{on} at effectives of 17 officers, 720 rank and file, left Bambecque at 6^{H}50 and proceeded to Warmhoudt where it embarked by bus the same day at 9 hours destined for Izel-lez-Hameau. (C.P.)
Itinerary: Bambecque – Warmhoudt – Cassel – Hazebrouk – St. Pol – Izel-lez-Hameau
Approximate distance: 85 kilometres
Disembarkation at the crossroads: St. Pol – Arras and Izel-lez-Hameau – Bethancourt at 16^{H}30
Departed from that place at 16^{H}45 – Arrived at Izel-lez-Hameau at 17^{H}45 – The Companies were billeted in the village – C.P. of the Bon Chief: Maison Bouillez.
The T.R. T.C. and machine gun section, under the orders of Lieutenant Doutreligne, left Bambecque the same day and proceeded to Izel-les Hameau where it arrived 13 February at 9 hours.
On the date of 10 February the B^{on} left the 8e Armée and was attached to the 10e Armée, 33e Corps d'Armée, 45e Division – 90e Brigade Commanded respectively by: General de Maud'huy – General Pétain – General Quiquandon – Colonel Passard.

11 and 12 February

Same emplacements

Battalion Order № 50

By decision of the General Cdr in Chief of 12 February 1915 under the № 3901:
Chief Warrant Officer Albertini of the 4e Cie and Warrant Officer Jacques of the 2e Cie were promoted to 2nd Lieutenant to temporary rank in the conditions decreed 2 January 1915.

13 February

The Battalion left Izel-lez-Hameau at 11^{H}30
It proceeded in one stage by road to the area of St. Auban where it arrived at 15 hours.
Approximate distance 16 kilometres.
The Battalion operates in sub-sector B. commanded by Lieutenant-Colonel Ancel
The 1er and 2^{e} Cies encamped at Anzin St. Aubin
The 3^{e} and 4^{e} Cies were placed in the factory of Roclincourt in support of sub-sector B. C.P. of the Bon Chief – Machine gun section and C.H.R. at St. Aubin

14 February

On 14 February at 10 hours.
a/ the 3e Cie was placed in 1st line in the west segment (Maj Montluc)
b/ the 4e Cie was placed in 1st line in the east segment (Maj Ranchet)

15 February

On 15 February at 19 hours
a) the 3e Cie was relieved by the 1ere Cie (OC the segment Maj Veau) It took the camp of the 1er Cie at Anzin St. Aubin.
b) the 4e Cie was relieved by the 2e Cie (OC the segment – Captain Courtois) It took the camp of the 2e Cie at Anzin St. Aubin

Incorporation: A detachment of reinforcements composed of: Captain Latapy – Lieutenant Bresson – 1 Sergeant-Major – 8 Sergnts 292 Chasseurs arrived at Etrun on the 15th at 3 hours.

16 February

On 16 February Lieutenant Bresson was attached to the 1ere Cie
129 rank and file were attached to the 3e and 4e Cies
The rest of the detachment encamped at Louez. The effectives of the Bon were therefore 860 rank and file.
Losses of the 14th to 15th: 3 wounded
Losses of the 15th to 16th: 1 killed 2 wounded

16 February

Same emplacements.
In the evening of 15 February 1915, Colonel Passard, OC the 90e Brigade, prescribed to Maj Fouchard to constitute a group of volunteer scouts of 100 to 150 effectives strongly led and commanded by several officers (see document nº 15)
The number of volunteers having surpassed 60 per Cie, a draw was made and the detachment was thus constituted:
Captain Audibert OC the 4e Cie Chief of the detachment.
Group of the 1ere Cie: Sergeants Lafont & Convert. 2 corporals and 30 men commanded by Chief Warrant Officer Chauveau.
Group of the 2e Cie: Sergeants Poiret and Durand 2 Corporals and 30 men Commanded by Chief Warrant Officer Thô.
Group of the 3e Cie: Sergeants Viala and Géromini. 2 corporals and 40 men commanded by s/Lieutenant Arrighi
Group of the 4e Cie: Sergeants Paoli and Nal. 2 corporals and 40 men, commanded by Warrant Officer Chambaud

17 February

In the night of 16 to 17 February the detachment was assembled at the factory of Roclincourt:
The groups of the 3e and 4e coming from the camp of Anzin St.

Aubert, those of the 1e and 2e Cies having been relieved from the trenches of the east and west segments where their Coys held garrison since the evening of the 15th.
The departure formation had to take place in the communication trench to the right and to the left of the sunken road close to the French 1st line: Group of the 3e Cie and 4e Cie on the right – Group of the 1e and 2e Cie on the left.
The men had entrenching tools in their belts. They brought 2 sandbags, provisioning of cartridges was brought to 200, they had 2 days rations in their haversacks.
Departed on the 17th at 3H30 in the morning.
At the sand pit, the petards were missing, Captain Audibert certified later that an NCO of the engineers responded to him that he had no more of them.
At 5H30 the troops were placed ready to bound.
At 6H10 the explosion took place, the attack was launched immediately; Officers NCOs in the lead.
Group Arrighi passed the craters, ran the Germans who resisted through and pushed with bayonet into the sunken road, but the enemy was well provisioned with petards, he began to pepper the assailants.
A machine gun opened fire; the losses began to be serious.
Thanks to the elan of the men the offensive was pursued nevertheless, s/Lieutenant Arrighi continued up to mid-way to the 3rd line, Warrant Officer Chambaud pushed into the right communication trench, Chief Warrant Officer Thô won the 2nd line trenches on the left.
It was at that moment that Captain Audibert was wounded (7H30); Chief Warrant Officer Chauveau had been some time previously, Thô therefor took command of the 2 groups on the left.
It was now necessary to think of consolidating, the defensive passages accumulated in the sunken road and numerous petards thrown by the enemy breaking all offensive.
The groups actively employed themselves there despite an intense bombardment, some barriers were organized, some elements of trenches established.
10 hours = the enemy was completely recovered, despite his serious losses.
He counter-attacked, but he was put to a stop by violent musketry fire and above all by bombs Germans abandoned on the conquered ground.
<u>Noon</u> = Thanks to the barrier, the machine gun fire is less deadly. Fortunately, because the effectives were reduced by half. A new counter-attack at the start of the afternoon was again repulsed by means of German bombs in our possession.
14 hours = 2nd Lieutenant Arrighi was killed by a ball in the middle of the forehead, Warrant Officer Chambaud took command of the groups of the 3e and 4e Cies.
At the end of the day the groupe franc was relieved by the 3e and 4e Cies of the Bon and by Zouaves of the 11e Cie, they had lost by that

time 2/3 of their effectives.

17 February

On the 17th from 10 hours in the morning the Lieutenant-Colonel Commanding sector B. reporting bloody resistance by the enemy and his ardent desire to retake the lost trenches at all costs, prescribed to the Bon Chief to bring up the 2 companies in camp at Anzin St. Aubin 3e and 4e Cies in reserve at Roclincourt factory. Commander Fouchard gave orders to those units to get underway and proceed in small groups to the indicated points.
The movement was without loss despite an intense artillery bombardment between Arras and Roclincourt.
At 13 hours the 3e Cie received the order to bring itself in support in the east large smoke stack; at 13H30 the 4e Cie brought itself into the covered road that goes from Roclincourt to the east large smoke stack.

17 February

From 15 hours the 3e Cie was ready to reinforce the 1st line at the craters of the sunken road. It began to suffer heavy losses, caused by minenwerfers and above all by the petards which the Germans possessed in incredible supply.
Towards 16H30 Battalion adjutant Captain Courtois received command of the 3e and 4e Cies from Lieut-Colonel Ancel with orders to counter-attack in the 2nd German line to push our success up to the Lille highway.
Captain Courtois must put the 3e Cie in the lead, arm them with petards, make the advance by detachments of grenadiers etc…
That officer proceeded to the command post of the line of fire – post E1 – but the communication trenches were so encumbered and the confusion so great that hours were needed to get the units in order.
Captain Courtois estimated that he would gain time by placing the 4e Cie in the lead leaving the 3e Cie towards the craters
The petards were lacking, or rather the parties of men bringing them could not get forward.
Finally at the precise moment when the 4e Cie prepared itself for the assault, it was itself counter-attacked by the enemy, but the chasseurs were prompt with their riposte; a certain number of Germans were beaten on the parapet, many fell between the trenches of the German 3rd and 2nd line, others fled by the communication trench of the sunken road.
We noted that the Zouaves of the 11e Cie readied an effective support to the 3e Cie of the Bon, which had suffered the most from the counter attack.
Toward 20 hours the incident was over, the 4e Cie finished placing itself on the left of the 3e Cie and those 2 units employed themselves quickly and very actively in reversing the trenches of the German 2nd line, installing battlements there and using bombs taken from the

enemy.
During the night two other counter attacks took place, of which the most lively, that of 4 Hrs in the morning was preceded by an intense bombardment
Our men were by no means shaken by an arduous enough day, succeeded by a night without sleep.

18 February

On 18 February from 6^H in the morning the Bon Chief prescribed to the survivors of the groupe franc to go reinforce their respective units.
At 7 hours he received command of the line of fire from Lieut-Colonel Ancel with orders to hold at all costs. He would be able make call to the 3 segment COs to accomplish his mission. Maj Fouchard noted the obstinate resistance by the 3^e and 4^e Cies, but also the considerable losses they had already suffered.
Numerous cadavers were strewn about the trenches. The situation was serious, the 4^e Cie on the left was particularly threatened.
On the enemy side the supply of petards, in minenwerfer bombs was prodigious. The 2nd line trenches had become untenable on his left part. Already 2nd Lieutenant Fache had withdrawn his men little by little towards the 1st German line, but without permitting a single enemy to push into the 2nd line.
At 9 hours the 4^e Cie received a platoon of reinforcements from the 5^e Cie of the 3^e bis Zouaves.
Towards 10 hours, a German counter-attack produced itself again; at the 3^e Cie two strong explosions were produced in the crater where Lieut. Gruyer and his forty survivors had obstinately held at all costs under a hail of petards and an unbreathable atmosphere. Nearly all his braves fell on their backs, struck dead or insensible; only Lieut. Gruyer who found himself at the entrance of the crater and Warrant Officer Ballou, already wounded 2 times, and who had not wanted to leave his post in combat, escaped the explosion. Some moments later Lieut. Gruyer and Warrant Officer Ballou presented themselves to the Bon Chief and said to him simply ("we are the only ones left of the 3^e Cie")
At the same time other explosions caused by mines, or by bombs, were produced in the German 2nd line trenches and more to the left, causing fewer losses as nearly all were evacuated.
It was in that interval that Captain Dufest of the 45^e Division Headquarters presented himself to the C.P. of the line of fire, he assisted in aborting that counter-attack. He also assisted in sending a new reinforcement directed towards the left of our line.
The artillery readied for us at that moment very effective assistance: a Lieutenant observer had come to the C.P. of the line of fire to better report on the points that needed to be battered at all costs.
There was therefore , two hours of respite in the middle of that terrible day that permitted the placement of the 2^e Cie of the B^on d'Afrique, withdrawn from the front of the east segment, without

encumbrance into the 1st line between the 3e and 4e Cies. It was also during that respite that the Bon Chief called his 1ere Cie from reserve, relieved in the night of the 17th to 18th, from the front of the west segment.

18 February

Thus the entire Bon was grouped for the normal counter-attack of the afternoon.
He needed a few of them who were not exhausted!
From 14H30 the German bombardment resumed. Pieces of all calibres raged on that corner of ground, the machine guns mowed us coming at once from the northwest – from the north, and from the south east. It was only after a half hour of furious bombardment that the counter-attack was launched in the form of a hail of bombs and petards. It is no exaggeration to say that 500 minenwerfer shots were fired that afternoon by the Germans between the sunken road and the Lille highway.
The attitude of the men was admirable, stoic while enduring the bombardment, they dressed themselves for the riposte as soon as the enemy infantry advanced, if they had had enough petards, they would have hurled themselves on their adversaries. They contented themselves with shooting them.
At 15H30 Maj Allouchery of the Tirailleurs arrived at the C.P. of Maj Fouchard, at the time that the counter-attack began to slacken.
At 16 hours rifle shots and cannon shots more rare. Two companies of Tirailleurs arrived as reinforcements, the German counter-attack was going to be reduced to impotence from now on.
A new attempt was made nevertheless from 18 to 19 hours, but much less violent, the chasseurs of the Bon were thus honoured to give Zouaves and Tirailleurs, their comrades in arms, an example of resistance to the last.
At 20 hours the German 1st line trenches were evacuated by orders after having been mined.
At 23 hours, those who remained of the 2e 3e & 4e Cies returned after relieved to the factory of Roclincourt.
Of the 646 men available for the trenches after the situation of the parade of 16-2-15 there remained no more than 233 men as of the 19th.
345 were passed to the Refuge for the Wounded at the factory of Roclincourt.
In summary, the 1ere Cie did not have to go into action
The losses were distributed in the following fashion between the 1er 2e 3e 4e Cies
1ere Cie : 24 killed, wounded or missing (including 1 Chief Warrant Officer and 2 Sergeants wounded) That company only provided the group of volunteers.
2eme Cie: 54 killed, wounded, or missing (including Captain Bernard wounded not evacuated; 3 sergeants wounded)
3e Cie: 167 Killed, wounded or missing (including s/Lieutenant Arrighi

killed, 2 Sergts killed, Lieutenant Gruyer wounded not evacuated, 1 WO wounded, 4 sergeants wounded including 1 not evacuated) more than 80% losses.

4eme Cie 139 killed, wounded or missing (including 3 sergeants killed, Captain Audibert wounded, Lt Laine and 2nd Lieut Fache not evacuated, 1 Warrant Officer wounded not evacuated, 4 sergeants wounded.

That is in total 382 killed, wounded or missing out of 646 that is to say more than 60% losses

In view of such figures, the Chief of the Corps, does he not have the right to conclude, that on that day, his men would have died to the last, rather than cede the ground that they had so valiantly conquered.

Seen and transmitted by Lieutenant Colonel Ancel OC s/sector B.

"The conduct of the 3e Bon de Marche d'Infie Légère d'Afrique has been heroic and and merits to be cited in the order of the Army."

"Commander Fouchard, its Chief who had exercised Command of the occupation troops of the conquered trenches from 7H30 to 15H30 on the 18th, who had known how to inspire in his officers as well as his men the sentiments of true heroes also merits to be cited in the order of the Army.

Captain Latapy took command of the 4e Cie.

19 February

At 19 hours the companies left Roclincourt and proceeded individually to Hermaville where they encamped

The machine gun section remained in their emplacements.

20 February

The Battalion incorporated the 2nd portion of the reinforcement detachment that is 172 men.

After that incorporation the composition of the Bon is as follows:

Names of Officers.

Headquarters	{Battalion Chief **Fouchard** CO
	{Captain **Courtois** Battalion adjutant
	{Lieutenant **Doutreligne** OC Machine gun Sec
	{Lieutenant **Lafargue** supply officer
	{Captain **Reynaud** Chief Medical Officer
	{Lieutenant **Coignerai** Medical Officer's Aide
1ere Cie	{Captain **Andru**
	{Lieutenant **Battesti**
	{Lieutenant **Bresson**
	{s/Lieutenant **Fournier**
2e Cie	{Captain **Bernard**
	{Lieutenant **Bastide**
	{s/Lieutenant **Jacques**
	{Captain **Billot**

3eme Cie {Lieutenant **Gruyer**
{s/Lieutenant **Albertini**
{Captain **Latapy**
4e Cie {Lieutenant **Lainé**
{s/Lieutenant **Fache**

Troops
1ere Compagnie.....................133

20 February

1ere Compagnie.................	133
2eme Compagnie.................	144
3e Compagnie..................	145
4e Compagnie..................	140
Cie Hors Rang....................	111

21 and 22 February

Same emplacements – Losses of 22 February:
1 killed. 2 wounded (MG Sec).

23 February

Conforming to General order Nº 209 of 21 February of the Division, the 45e Don was relieved from the front by the 19e Division and was placed in Army reserve.
The Battalion left Hermaville at 10 Hrs and proceeded to Fosseux by Lattre, where it arrived at 13H30
The T.R. is encamped at Izel-lez-Hameau.

24 February

Same emplacements
The team of the machine gun section, still in the 1st line was relieved by a section of the 19e Division, on 24 February at 1 hour (less material left in place)
The entire section rejoined the Battalion at Fosseux where it arrived at 13 hours.

25 February

The material of the machine gun section was returned to the disposal of the corps. The material was picked up at Roclincourt by the personnel of the machine gun section of the Battalion.

26 February

The Battalion left Fosseux at 11H30 and proceeded in one stage to Beaufort where it encamped (distance about 7 kilometres). Arrived at Beaufort at 13H30.

The T.R. stayed at Izel-lez-Hameau.

27 – 28 February

Same emplacements.

1st 2, 3, 4, 5 and 6 March

Same emplacements.

7 March

Same emplacements.

Extract of Order No 655 D.

Mr Audibert Joseph, Captain,
Is named to the Order of the Legion of Honour at the rank of Knight.
"On 17 February 1915, commanding the group of volunteer scouts of the Bon, was charged with capturing with his 150 men the elements of the German first and 2nd line trenches and superbly launched his troops after having distributed them in a judicious fashion. Gravely wounded in the course of the assault did not leave the conquered trenches up to the point of collapsing."
The Military Medal is conferred to soldiers including the following names:
Thô Philippe, Chief Warrant Officer of the 3e Bon d'Afrique
"On 17 February 1915, chief of the volunteer scouts of his Coy, threw himself into the assault on the 1st and 2nd line German trenches to the north of Roclincourt. Took command of the groups of the 1er and 2e Cies, the captain commanding the detachment having been wounded. Obstinately resisted German counter-attacks. Himself wounded, did not want to leave the conquered trenches before the relief of his troops."
Chambaud Joseph, Warrant Officer of the 3e Bon de Marche d'Infie Légère d'Afrique.
"on 17 February 1915, chief of the volunteer scouts of his company, dashed to the assault of the German 1st and 2nd line trenches to the north of Roclincourt. Took command of the groups of the 3e and 4e Cies, 2nd Lieutenant Arrighi having been killed in the assault, and organized the conquered ground defensively with much intelligence and energy. On 18 February gave new proof of the most beautiful military qualities. Obstinately resisted all German counter-attacks."
Convert, Joseph, Jules Sergeant
"On 17 February 1915, at the head of the volunteer scouts of his company, fell upon the enemy trenches north of Roclincourt. Pursued the assault up to the German 2nd line. Wounded, continued to exhort his men, refused to let himself be evacuated, has not ceased since the start of the campaign to give proof of a superb valour and bravado."

Bertrand Raymond, Emile chasseur 2nd cl.
"Superb bravery and bravado in the combats of 17 & 18 February. Runner for Captain Audibert, seemed to be larger than life near that officer, when he was wounded. Was seen revolver in hand, determined to blow the brains out of anyone who would have wavered. Volunteered for the most perilous missions, in the course of 2 harsh battles to the north of Roclincourt."

Extract of Order № 666.D

The Military Medal is conferred to soldiers whose names follow:
Ballou Pierre, Warrant Officer.
"Gave proof of heroic courage in the course of the days of 17 and 18 February. Wounded on 17 February, bandaged himself in place and continued to fight.
Wounded more gravely on the 18th only looked after himself on the formal order of his Coy Commander, then rejoined the front soon after. Offered himself to the Bon Chief to guide the reinforcement Coys and placed the sections at the most threatened points in the conquered trenches."
Bernard Eugène, sergeant.
"Elite NCO. Distinguished himself in the attacks of 9 November and was gravely wounded there. In the battles of 17 and 18 February, gave proof of admirable courage. Knew how to communicate to his men his obstinate will to hold under a furious bombardment. Gravely wounded in the course of the action."
Casanova A. M. Sergeant.
"Elite NCO. Distinguished himself in the attacks of 9 November for which he was cited to the Order of the Army. Was gravely wounded there. In the battles of 17 and 18 February made proof of admirable courage. Knew how to communicate his stubborn will to hold on under furious bombardment to his men. Gravely wounded in the course of the action."
Lafont, F. R. Sergeant.
"Drew attention to himself in a particular fashion on 17 February in an assault on the trenches. Absolutely remarkable section chief. Vigorously insisted on being accepted among the volunteers as chief of a half-section. Launched himself to the head of the most brave up to the 2nd enemy line. Wounded very gravely in the course of the assault.
Praud G. C. Corporal.
"Bravery, so bright in an earlier battle, that the General OC the Army Corps declared in front of the Bon that he would have a medal in hand if he had come forward as a candidate. Wounded gravely enough, returned to the front scarcely recovered, presented himself as a volunteer for the capture of the 1st and 2nd line on 17 February. Showed heroic courage there. Wounded grievously in the course of the action."

Order of the Xeme Armée N° 53.

General Maud'huy OC the 10e Armée cited to the Order of the Army: The 3eme Bataillon de Marche d'Inf[ie] Légère d'Afrique.

In the coup de main attempted 18 February, against the German lines, the 3e Bon de Marche d'Inf[ie] Légère d'Afrique gave proof of the most energetic conduct under its chief, Maj Fouchard, of the greatest bravery, suffering, without producing a movement of weakness, the repeated counter attacks and a particularly deadly fire."

Battalion Chief Fouchard OC the 3e Bon de Marche d'Inf[ie] Légère d'Afrique.

"Conducted with the greatest energy an attack against the German trenches, knew how, though under very violent fire, to conserve the conquered trenches during the time necessary for their destruction."

Lieutenant Gruyer.

"Knew how to communicate his tenacious will to resist to his men on conquered ground against German counter-attacks. Lightly wounded by an explosion that carried away the last of his men, soon reported to his Bon Chief to continue to make himself useful on the front."

2nd Lieutenant Arrighi.

"Gave an example of magnificent courage to his troops, in an assault on German trenches. Knew how to organize the conquered ground to resist the furious counter-attacks of the adversary. Died gloriously hit by a ball in the middle of the forehead."

2nd Lieutenant Fache.

"His captain and his Lieutenant out of action, took command of the 4e Cie in difficult circumstances. Knew how to keep his men in the conquered trenches despite a frightful bombardment. Wounded seriously enough, never wanted to abandon his post in combat."

Reserve chasseur Jamin

"Mortally wounded in throwing himself into the German trenches, had the energy to climb up to the parapet to continue to give fire on the escaping enemies."

7 March

Chasseurs Pingot Jean and Beaujeau Alfred,

"Gave proof since the start of the campaign of remarkable energy and courage."

Presented themselves as volunteers for all the perilous missions."

Sergeants Poiret and Duvaud.

"Rushed to the head of their men on the German trenches. Reached the 2nd line from which they chased the enemy with bayonet. Were gravely wounded in the course of the action."

Corporal Hubert.

" Gave proof of the greatest courage in the assault of the German trenches. Fell mortally hit in charging with bayonet."

Chasseur Teisseire Charles

"Was everywhere supplying the 1st line with petards at the most critical moments. During one counter-attack, camped himself in the open, bayonet fixed, at the entrance of a communication trench ready to strike the first man who would have retreated.

Sergeant Viala

"Fell gloriously in the assault on German trenches at the head of his men.

Sergeant Machefert

"Struck dead while heroically resisting with a handful of men in trenches conquered from the Germans."

Chasseur 1st class Lemée Edouard

"Runner for the Bon Chief, risked his life several times to bring urgent orders. Wounded in the head, instead of looking after himself to bandage himself, offered to go, under a hail of bullets to find amadou[1] to light the petards."

Chasseur Charles.

"After showing himself to have an exemplary bravery in combat, earned the admiration of all at the aid post by encouraging his comrades even though he himself came to have his left hand completely blown off by a bomb."

Sergeant Duvivier

"Gave proof, in the course of several battles, of a remarkable courage and tenacity, was gravely wounded in repulsing a German counter-attack."

Sergeant Nal.

"Rushed on the German trenches at the head of his men. Reached the second line, from which he chased the enemy with bayonet. Was gravely wounded in the course of the action."

Sergeant Griselle

"Struck dead while resisting with a handful of men in trenches conquered from the Germans."

Sergeant Laliou

"Struck dead while resisting with a handful of men in trenches conquered from the Germans."

Chasseur Odet

"Drew attention to himself by his courage since the start of the campaign. Hit by a shell burst in the left arm, did not want to leave the trenches to go bandage himself."

Sergeant Daude.

"Struck dead while resisting with a handful of men in trenches conquered from the Germans."

Sergeant Paoli

"NCO of remarkable valour and sang-froid. Energetically led his troops up to the German 2nd line. Gravely wounded in the course of the action, succumbed to his wounds."

[1 The diarist is probably referring to "amadou chimique," which was a slow match of cotton cord infused with a flammable chemical. The word comes from the amadou tree fungus that is used for tinder.]

7 March

Chasseur Bock.
"Number 1 position on a gun in a machine gun section, gave proof since the start of the campaign of exemplary courage. Was killed at his gun in supporting a counter-attack under violent enemy fire."
In addition 1 officer and 6 rank and file have been cited to the Order of the 33e Corps d'Armée
1 officer and 19 rank and file have been cited to the Order of the 45e Division
And 27 rank and file have been cited to the Order of the 90e Brigade
Review of the Battalion on the occasion of its citation to the Order of the Army.
Afternoon – Battalion Feast

8 & 9 March

Same emplacements.

9 March

The Battalion left the 33e Corps d'Armée and was attached to the 10e C.A. Remained at Beaufort in Army reserve.

10 and 11 March

Same emplacements.

12 March

Following the order of the 45e Division № 8442 of 11 March the Bon left Beaufort at 10H30 and proceeded to Wanquetin. Distance 9 kilometres. Arrived at Wanquetin at 12H30. The Bon occupies part of the village.

13 March

Same emplacements.

14 & 15 March

Same emplacements.

15 March

Constitution of a Machine gun Platoon
Official Report of the formation of a Machine gun platoon of the 3e Bon d'Afrique de Marche.
In the year Nineteen Hundred and Fifteen, We, Hannedouche, Junior Military Intendant 2nd class of the Quartier Général of the E.N.E of the

10e Corps d'Armée,
In view of notes 9287 of 30 January and 3821 of 16 February 1915 of the G.Q.G.
Have, in the presence of Mr. the Bon Chief Fouchard, delegated by Mr. the General Commanding the 10e C.A.
Conforming to the prescriptions of the 1st art. of instructions of 20 March 1906, enacted the following operations in view of the constitution of a machine gun platoon of the 3^{e} B^{on} d'Afrique de Marche

Inspection of strength

The results of the inspection of strength passed by us, are consigned to the tables hereafter:

A) Table, nominative, by rank, of officers with indication of those who must form the cadre of the platoon.

Names and First Names	Rank and Employment	Fixation to the table of the War Establishment	Strength Present	Observations
Mr. Doutreligne Clément	Lieutenant Ptn Chief	1	1	

B) Composition of the cadre and establishment of the platoon.

Designation of Ranks	Employment	Fixation to the table of the War Establishment	Strength Present	Observations
NCOS	Section	2	2	[1] The mules
(Sergeants	Chief	1	1	were taken
-do-	Clerk	4	4	from the
(Sergeants)	Gun Chief	8	8	strength of
Corporals	Gunners	8	8	the C.H.R.
Chasseurs	Loaders	8	8	
	Loader's aides	2	2	
	Range Finders	2	2	
	Armourers	2	2	
Corporal	Runners/	1	1	
Chasseurs	Orderlies	8	8	
	Quarter-master	1	1	
Corporal Chasseurs	Ammunition numbers	30	30	
	T.R. NCO Drivers Mules	30	30[1]	

15 March

After the constitution of that platoon the composition of the B[on] was the following:

	{B[on] Chief Fouchard CO
Head-	{Captain Battalion adjutant Courtois
	{Lieutenant Lafargue Supply officer
Quarters	{Captain Reynaud Chief Medical Officer
	{Lieutenant Coignerai Medical Officer's aide
	{Captain Andru
	{Lieutenant Bresson
1ere Cie	{Lieutenant Battesti
	{s/Lieutenant Fournier
	{Captain Bernard
2e Cie	{Lieutenant Bastide
	{s/Lieutenant Jacques
	{Captain Billot
3e Cie	{Lieutenant Gruyer
	{s/Lieutenant Albertini
	{Captain Latapy
4e Cie	{Lieutenant Lainé
	{s/Lieutenant Fache
Machingun Ptn:	Lieutenant Doutreligne

16 March

Incorporation of a reinforcement detachment composed of: 2 Sergeant-Majors – 18 Sergeants 187 rank and file.
Following that incorporation the effectives of the battalion were brought to 19 officers, 873 rank and file.

1ere Cie:	180	
2e Cie:	179	
3e Cie:	179	} 873 rank and file
4e Cie:	176	
C.H.R.:	82	
MG Ptn:	77	

17, 18, 19, 20, 21 March

Same emplacements

22 March

Same Emplacements
Incorporation of a reinforcement detachment composed of: 1 officer: Mr. Marizés:
5 Sergeants 86 rank and file plus 63 rank and file who overstayed leave from last reinforcement.
Following that incorporation, the effectives of the Battalion were brought to 20 officers, 1027 rank and file

	Officers	Troops
1ere Cie	4	216
2e Cie	3	217
3e Cie	3	213
4e Cie	3	218
C.H.R.	5	86
MG Ptn	$2^{(1)}$	77
Totals	20	1027

(1) added Mr. Marizés s/Lieutenant

23, 24, 25, 26 March

Same emplacements

26 March

Following note n° 9192 of 26 March of the 45e Division the 1er and 3e B^{ons} d'Afrique de Marche were attached organically to the 45e Division as of 26 March. However those corps remained at the disposal of the General OC the 10^{e} C.A. to be employed alternately on the front in conditions that permitted them to be withdrawn rapidly. The two B^{ons} d'Afrique de Marche will remain at the disposal of the General OC the 45^{e} Division and will not be embarked.

27 March

Same emplacements.

28 March

Following the orders of the 19^{e} Division of 28 March, the Battalion left Wanquetin at 17 hours and proceeded on foot in one stage to Roclincourt by Montenescourt, Gouves, Duisans, Louez – Anzin St Aubin – St Catherine – approximate distance 18 kilometers.
Arrived at Roclincourt at 23 hours. The T.R. stayed provisionally at Wanquetin – the T.C. encamped at Anzin-St Aubin.
The B^{on} relieved the 1er B^{on} d'Afrique de Marche in the sector of Roclincourt segment "Chanteler." CO of the Sector Colonel Sausselier of the 48e Régiment d'Inf^{ie} – OC the segment Maj Fouchard OC the B^{on} (see document n° 16)
The 1ere Cie – Platoon Gruyer of the 3e Cie and a section of the Machine gun platoon (Lt Doutreligne) are in the 1st line – 2e Cie in 2nd line (support) 2e Peloton of the 3e Cie – 4e Cie and 2^{e} section of the machine guns in reserve at south part of Roclincourt
C.P of the Battalion Chief south edge of Roclincourt
A telephone network connects the Platoon and Coy of the 1st line as well as the Coy of the 2nd line with the C.P. Bon Chief C.P. connects with the C.P. of the CO of the sector.
To the left of the segment 48^{e} d'Inf^{ie}, to the right the 47^{e} d'Inf^{ie}.
Relief finished on 29 March at 2^{H}30

29 March

The 1ere Cie was relieved by the 2e Cie, Platoon Gruyer was relieved by platoon Albertini (3e Cie)
The 4e Cie relieved the 2e Cie in the line
Reserve at Roclincourt – 1e Cie – Platoon Gruyer 3e Cie one section of Machine guns (Lieutenant Doutreline relieved by section Lt Marizis.
Relief commenced at 18H30 finished at 20H30
Losses: 2 wounded

30 March

The 4e Cie relieved the 2e Cie in the first line.
The 1ere Cie relieved the 4e Cie in the 2nd line. Platoon Gruyer of the 3e Cie relieved Platoon Albertini – Machine gun section Doutreligne relieved section Marizis. In reserve at Roclincourt: 2e Cie Platoon Albertini, Machine gun section Marizis.
Losses: 2 wounded.

31 March

The T.R. left Wanquetin and went to camp at Hermaville.

Nominative STATE of Officers, NCOs and soldiers killed, wounded, made prisoner or missing in the battle of 6 to November to 8 November 1914 inclusive

NAMES	RANKS	KILLED	WOUNDED	PRISONNER	MISSING	HORSES KILLED OR LOST	OBSERVATIONS
Corey Paul	2nd cl		1				
André	2nd cl		1				
Wailly Alfed	2nd cl	1					
Guillois Emile	Sergt	1					
Andrieux	2nd cl	1					
Lecante	2nd cl	1					
Torre	Sergt		1				
Mol	1st cl		1				
Couvreux	2nd cl	1					
Mederkorm		1					
Saugnat		1					
Lahaye		1					
Gilet		1					
Pinard			1				
TO REPORT		9	5				

31 March

The 1ere Cie relieved the 4^{e} Cie in the first line
The 2^{e} Cie relieved the 1ere Cie in the 2nd line. Platoon Albertini relieved Platoon Gruyer in the 1st line. Machine gun section Marizis relieved Machine gun section Doutreligne.
Relief finished at 20^{H}30
Losses: 1 killed – 1 wounded

1st April

The 2^{e} Cie relieved the 1^{e} Cie in the 1st line. The 4^{e} Cie relieved the 2^{e} Cie in the 2nd line.
Platoon Gruyer relieved platoon Albertini in the 1st line. Mg Sec Doutreligne relieved section Marizis.
In reserve at Roclincourt: 1ere Cie – Platoon Albertini – Mg Sec Marizis.
The erection of defensive accessories – hedgehogs, rests, were actively pursued. Towards 20^{H}50 the sound of barbed wire cut by snips was heard in front of the Coy on the right. A reconnaissance patrol sent out saw nothing.
Towards 23^{H} a sapper reported having heard a sound below him in the sap of the left listening post. A listening team of the engineers was immediately organized.
At 0^{H}45, at 1^{H} and at 2^{H} our 75s hit the German trenches towards the Chanteeler salient.
Losses: 1 man wounded

War Diary

Of the **3eme Bataillon** de Marche d'Inf[ie] Légère d'Afrique

During the campaign against Germany
From 2 April 1915 to 5 September 1916.

The present record contains fifty-two pages stamped and signed by our Battalion Chief Commanding the 3e Bataillon de Marche d'Inf Légère d'Afrique.

To the Armies on 2 April 1915
Battalion Chief Ardit CO

2 April 1915

The 4e Cie relieved the 2e Cie in the first line, the 1er Cie relieved the 4e Cie in the second line. Platoon Gruyer was relieved by Platoon Albertini. Machine gun section Marizis relieved Machine gun section Doutreligne
In reserve at Roclincourt: 2^{e} Cie, Platoon Gruyer, Mg Sec Doutreligne, relief finished at 20^{H}30.
Losses: 2 men killed and 8 wounded.

3 April

The 1ere Cie relieved the 4^{e} Cie in the first line the 2^{e} Cie relieved the 1ere Cie in the second line, Platoon Gruyer relieved platoon Albertini. Mg section Doutreligne relieved MG section Marizis.
In reserve at Roclincourt 4^{e} Cie P^{on} Albertini MG Section Marizis
Relief finished at 22 hours. Losses 3 wounded

4 April

Conforming to the relief order of 4 April of the 19^{e} Division the Battalion was relieved around 21 hours by the 1er B^{on} d'Afrique de Marche.
The units directed themselves singly on Wanquetin where they were reformed.
Arrival at Wanquetin of the last company relieved (1ere) on 5 April at 5 hours
The Battalion encamped at Wanquetin in the same emplacements as those left on 28 March
Losses = 2 killed. 3 wounded

5 April

A detachment of reinforcements composed of:
One Captain: Mr. Ardit
Five NCOs, 86 men.
Arrived at Wanquetin on 4 April, were incorporated.
After that incorporation, the strength of the Battalion was distributed as follows:

5 April

1er Cie	227	rank and file
2^{e} Cie	227	d^{o}
3^{e} Cie	239	d^{o}
4^{e} Cie	250	d^{o}
C.H.R	90	d^{o}
MG Ptn	77	d^{o}

That is 1110 rank and file in total

Mr. Captain Ardit was promoted to Adjutant Major and took command of the C.H.R. as of 6 April in replacement of Captain Courtois

6 April

Mr. s/Lieutenant Marizis transferred to the automobile service (decision of 20 January 1915)

7 April

Following order No 2374e of 7 April of the 10e C.A. the Battalion left Wanquetin at 15 hours by bus, and proceeded to Frévent, strength transported 17 officers 1026 men.
The T.R. left Hermaville at 12 hours. The T.C. and the animals left Wanquetin at 12^{H}15
The two echelons also directed themselves on Frévent
Arrival at Frévent

1. Of the Battalion at 17^{H}30
2. Of the T.C. at 18^{H}15
3. Of the T.R. at 21^{H}

The Battalion encamped at Frévent

8 April

The Battalion left Frévent by railway at 8^{H}8'
Strength and material transported
19 officers – 1110 rank and file
110 animals – 30 vehicles
Rations drawn before departure:
2 days disembarkation rations
1 day railway rations
Itinerary: St Pol, Lillers, Hazebrouck, Esquelbecq.
Arrived at Esquelbecq at 13^{H}20. The Battalion disembarked and reformed close to the station.
Following order N° 9724 of April of the 45^{e} Division, the Battalion proceeded to Cinq Rues where it encamped. Departed Esquelbecq at 15 hours arrived in camp at 17 hours

9 April

Same emplacements

10 April

Following order N° 313 of 9 April of the 45^{e} Division, the Battalion left its camp at Cinq Rues at 7 h^{rs} and proceeded in one stage by road to Proven, approximate distance 24 kilometres
Itinerary: Esquelbec, Wormoudt – Herzeele – Hautkerque – Proven.
Arrived at Proven at 15 hours
The Battalion encamped in the farms situated in the area south of Proven.

11 April

Same emplacements.

12 April

Following order N° 396 of 10 April 1915 of the 45^{e} Division, the Battalion left Proven at 7^{H} and proceeded in one stage by road to Woesten.
Approximate distance 17 kilometres. Arrived at Woesten at 12 hours.
The B^{on} encamped in the farms situated in the area north west of Woesten.
The T.R. encamped at Eykhoek.

13 – 14 – 15 – 16 April

Same emplacements.

17 April

Conforming to the order of the Groupement d'Elverdinge of 17 April, the Battalion left Woesten at 14^{H}30 to relieve the 1er Battalion d'Afrique in the 1st line in the Langemark sector. Arrived at Boesinghe at 16^{H}30.
The Battalion took an assembly formation at the south west edge of the village.
A long halt was made there untill 19 hours.
The companies proceeded to Langemarck at 19^{H}35 in the following order – 2^{e} Cie at 19^{H}35 MG Ptn 19^{H}45 – 3^{e} Cie 19^{H}55 – 4^{e} Cie 20^{H}5 1ere Cie 20^{H}15 – Itinerary railway from Boesinghe to Langemarck – the 2^{e} Cie occupies half the segment (right part) the 3^{e} Cie occupies half the segment (left part)
MG Ptn, one section in 1st line – one section in alert camp at Langemarck
1^{e} Cie at the Chateau – 4^{e} Cie west edge of the village
C.P. east edge – relief finished at 22 hours.

18 April

Same emplacements. Losses from 18th to 19th – 3 killed 10 wounded

19 April

The 1ere and 4^{e} Cies relieved the 2^{e} and 3^{e} Cies respectively around 20^{H}30.
Relief finished at 22 H^{rs}
Losses from 19th to 20th = 6 men wounded.

20 April

Same emplacements. Losses of the 20th to 21st – 2 men killed and 11 wounded.

21 April

The Battalion was relieved around 21 hours by the 1er Bataillon d'Afrique de Marche.
Relief finished at 23 hours.
The Battalion proceeded after the relief into the region comprised between Elverdinghe and Woesten where it encamped. Losses of the 21st to 22nd 2 wounded.

22 April 1915

At 16^{H}30 a violent enemy cannonade on the Steenstraat and Ypres front with asphyxiating shells
At 18 hours the Battalion was alerted and put at the disposal of the 87^{e} D^{on} T^{le}. At 21^{H}45 the B^{on} brought itself to Zuidschoote. Order of March 2^{e} – 3^{e} – 4^{e} – 1ere Cies MG Ptn C.H.R. Medical Sec T.C.
At 23^{H}40' the B^{on} assembled itself in double column to the south of the road from the Zuidschoote windmill to Steenstraat – 2^{e} and 3^{e} Cies in the lead – 1er and 4^{e} Cies from left 400m interval and distance between each unit. Mg Ptn in the shelter behind the houses of the windmill. The B^{on} is in reserve of Colonel Descrienne OC a Brigade of the 87^{e} D^{on} T^{le}.

23 April

At 2^{H}40 the Battalion received the order from Colonel Descrienne to "launch and attack in depth on Steenstraat – one B^{on} of the 76^{e} T^{al} holds Het-Sas. 1 Bon of the 80^{e} T^{al} attacks Steenstraat coming from Lizerne" (note nº 17)
At 2^{H}40 the Captain Battalion adjutant Ardit received from Maj Fouchard the following order: "The B^{on} came to receive the order to launch an attack in depth at 3^{H}45 on Steenstraat. One battalion of the 76^{e} holds Het-Sas – one B^{on} of the 80^{e} attacks Steenstraat coming from Lizerne.
"Take command of the 2^{e} and 3^{e} Cies, bring them from their actual emplacements straight towards the east, on the highway, that is to say for the 3^{e} Cie directly on Het-Sas. Once on the highway take as first objective the farm – as second objective the bank of the canal north north-east of that farm. The 4^{e} Cie will support your movement towards the south also bringing itself on the farm.

23 April

The 1ere Cie will form echelon behind and to the left. The Bon Chief will march with the 1ere Cie.

@ 3^{H}45 the artillery must batter the canal from Steenstraat up to 500m to the south.
"Take advantage of that moment to throw yourselves resolutely on the canal straight forward and prolong yourself as far as possible on Steenstraat.
At 2^{H}50 Captain Latapy OC the 4^{e} Cie received from Bon Chief Fouchard the following order.
"The B^{on} has the order to launch an attack in depth on Steenstraat at 3^{H}15. The Captain Battalion adjutant taking command of the two Coys in the lead 2^{e} and 3^{e} Cies, direct them straight to the east on the highway then take as first objective the farm at 800m to the south of Steenstraat.
"Bring yourselves also towards that farm in echelon, behind the 2^{e} Cie at 200m. The MG Ptn marches with you. It is tasked with installing itself in that farm, and to batter the canal while protecting our right flank. The 1ere Cie in reserve will itself be in echelon behind and to the left of you.
Your mission is to cooperate with the attack in depth on the bank of the canal and Steenstraat – by prolonging the movement of the 2^{e} and 3^{e} Cies further north. The French artillery will make a preparatory fire at 3^{H}15."
At 3^{H}5' Lieutenant Doutreligne OC the Machine gun Platoon, received the following order
"Leave to the left of the 4^{e} Cie. Your mission is to install yourself at the farm. First objective of that Coy is to cooperate with an attack in depth that we are going to launch on Steenstraat and the bank of the canal further east by battering that entire canal with your fire, in particular take under fire any machine guns that may appear on the bank of that canal to your right flank."
At 3^{H}25 the 2^{e} and 3^{e} Cies were stopped on the Lizerne – Boesinghe road by Germans entrenched at 80 metres to the east of that road in our works at the bridgehead of Steenstraat Het-Sas. The Coys deployed themselves along the west embankment – the 1ere Cie brought itself to the left.
The left is 200m to the south of Lizerne.
The musketry fire of the Germans was very violent – our losses where heavy.
At 3^{H}45 the Germans, by their cries, drew attention to our line which ceased fire – on our entire front Germans left their trenches and by their gestures declared to want to surrender. But a German officer cried "Rendez-vous," from another part whistle blasts came from their trenches, some columns advanced themselves towards the first line. The movement on their part had been made to make our fire cease and to try to advance on our left where a gap existed of 300 metres at least with the Territorials holding Lizerne. A heavy fire on our part put a stop to that feint. The entire Battalion was deployed except Section Battesti of the 1ere Cie still in reserve at the C.P. of the Bon Chief (ferme brûlée)
All day the B^{on} organized the embankment of the road – its right (3e Cie) was connected with the 76e Territorial – its left could not put

itself in contact with the 80e which held Lizerne! Despite the insistent demand of Bon Chief Fouchard to Colonel Descrienne to make the 80e support on our left.
At 20 hours Lieutenant Battesti with his section came to prolong the left of the Bon and to take command of the 1ere Compagnie in replacement of Captain Andru, killed in the morning.
Section Poli of the 3e Cie in reserve at the C.P.

24 April

The battle continues in the same emplacements. At 21 hours a platoon of the 3e bis Zouaves was put at the disposal of the Bon. That platoon stayed at the C.P. in reserve – one section in the farm the other section in a waiting position between the 1st line and section Poli, facing Lizerne ready to counter-attack.
The 4e Cie placed itself facing Lizerne which came to be occupied by the enemy. 2 machine gun pieces took the same position. Those last inflicted bloody losses on the enemy.

25 April

Same emplacements. The battle continues. Our artillery crushed the first line and the enemy rear works.
At 20 hours Section Poli rejoined its company
Section Albertini of the 3e Cie came to the C.P. in reserve. The platoon of Zouaves relieved the 1ere Cie which came into reserve at the C.P.

26 April

Some German elements leaving Lizerne advanced on Zuidschoot and brought the rear of the battalion under fire.
At 15H a patrol leaving the C.P. made contact with Zouaves attacking Lizerne.
At 17H a section of the 2e Cie under the orders of Chief Warrant Officer Sebastiani left the C.P. and directed itself on the German elements placed to the west of Lizerne. That section suffered heavy losses including Chief Warrant Officer Sebastiani wounded and was stopped. At 19H Section Dupuy of the 1e Cie reinforced section Sebastiani. Those two sections cleared the ground up to 100 metres from the Lizerne-Boesinghe road – then reinforced by a section of the 1e Cie under the orders of Lieutenant Gruyer and s/Lieutenant Fournier, brought itself on the west embankment of that road and connected itself on the right with the Bon to the left with the Zouaves who occupied a part of Lizerne. The embankment was immediately organized by the two sections and by a platoon of the 80e Territorial which came to prolong the two sections on the left.
At 22 hours the 4e Cie under the orders of Capt Battalion adjutant Ardit created trenches at 100m behind the embankment thus occupied.

At 20H section Albertini rejoined the 3e Cie in the 1st line.

Nominative STATE of Officers, NCOs and soldiers killed, wounded, made prisoner or missing in the battle of 30 April 1915

NAMES	RANKS	Killed	Wounded	Prisoner	Missing	Horses Killed or Lost	OBSERVATIONS
Clairet Henri	Sergeant-Major	1					
Pierre Edouard	Corporal		1				
Colindre Marcel	2nd cl		1				
Hebrant Ferdinand			1				
Honorez André			1				
Kops Paul			1				
Dijoud Emile			1				
Astié Benoit			1				
Cozzi Jacques			1				
Revesche Henri			1				
Crepelliere Henri			1				
To Report:		1	10				

27 April

Same emplacements. The battle continues effectively supported by our artillery which continues to crush the enemy trenches.
At 22 hours the Bon and the Ptn of Zouaves were relieved by the 268e. Relief finished on the 28th at 2 Hrs

28 April

The Companies assembled themselves at 3 hours near a farm situated 800m south south-east of Wampbeck
They proceeded at 3H15 by Elverdinghe near milestone 23 on the Elverdinghe-Woesten road and made a halt for a meal until 7 hours.
At 7 Hrs the companies proceeded into their encampments (farms situated between Elverdinghe and Woesten) at 7H45 the Bon received the order to make ready to take arms at 11 hours. A 13H20 the alert was lifted – the Bon is the reserve of the forward zone.

29 April

Same emplacements
The losses suffered by the B^on^ during the battles from 23 to 28 April inclusive are summarized thus.

__Killed__	
Captain Andru	23 April
Captain Latapy	__d^o^ __
NCOs	10
Chasseurs	75
Horses	1
__Wounded__	
Lieutenant Doutreligne	23 April
Lieutenant Bresson	__d^o^ __
NCOs	19
Chasseurs	219
__Missing__	
Men	22
That is in total:	five officers
	345 rank and file

30 April

Lieutenant Gruyer took command of the 1ere Cie as of 26 April.
Captain Ardit took command of the 4e Cie on 25 April
s/Lieutenant Fournier took command of the MG Ptn as of 30 April
The Battalion was alerted at 1H. The 2e and 3e Cies brought themselves to the north edge of Elverdinghe
At 10H45 enemy 77 artillery killed a sergeant-major and wounded 10 men of the 3e Cie

1st May

At 1H30 the companies brought themselves singly – 100m distance – to the Zwaanhof farm.
Order of march detachmt 1er Bon d'Afrique 3e – 4e – 1e – 2e – MG Ptn
Itinerary = Elverdinghe – Chapelle de Notre Dame
The 1er Baton d'Afrique at a strength of 130 men under the command of Lieutenant Lefébre was joined to the 3e de Marche
At 4H30 the Bon was reformed as follows on the east bank of the Yser canal and immediately to the south of Zwanof farm – the Coys echeloned in depth in the shelter of the bend in the bank.
Detachmt of the 1er Bon d'Afrique – 3e 4e 1ere 2e Cies MG Ptn.
Following the General order nº 13 of 1st May the 3e bis Zouaves and the 3e Bon d'Afrique (reinforced by elements of the 1er Bon d'Afrique) were charged with launching and attack in the direction of

[The online journal omits the remainder until 5 May 1915]

Nominative STATE of Officers, NCOs and soldiers killed, wounded, made prisoner or missing in the battle of 5 to 9 May 1915

5 - 9 May							
NAMES	RANKS	Killed	Wounded	Prisoner	Missing	Horses Killed or Lost	OBSERVATIONS
Donard François	2nd cl		1				
Stanchina Eugène			1				
Lasalle Louis		1					
Poulet Marius			1				
Mouille Victor			1				
Dufour Louis			1				
Girre Eugène			1				
Hatty Louis			1				
Chambaudu Alfred		1					
Brigaud Raymond		1					
Gorignon J M	Sergt		1				
Lavieville Jules	1st cl		1				
Ithier Emile			1				
Thant Camille			1				
Chapel Antoine			1				
Canone René			1				
Narbonne			1				
Clerc Joseph			1				
Ripamonte Antoine			1				
Scoazec Corentin			1				
Benazet Henri			1				
Le Sech Louis			1				
Taurelle Louis			1				
Tiaffay Gaston			1				
Pelletier Jean			1				
Kerruel Raoul	Cpl		1				
Point Laurent	sergt		1				
Thevance Louis			1				
Marchal Georges			1				
To Report:		3	26				
M. Ardit	Capt		1				

5 May

At 19^{H}30 the B^{on} proceeded to the south of the Zwaanhof farm on the east bank of the canal and occupied shelters there and communication trenches in the following order:
1 platoon of the 2^{e} Cie in the communication trench leaving from Zwaanhof farm and directing itself on the 1st line. To the south of the farm – 1 platoon of the 2^{e} Cie – 3^{e} Cie – 1er B^{on} d'Afrique – 4^{e} Cie 1^{e} Cie MG Ptn. 1 machine gun piece attached to a piece from the 2^{e} bis Zouaves established itself on the west bank of the canal about 300m south of Boesinghe. (railway bridge)

6 May

At 23 hours the B^{on} relieved Bon Armand of the 2^{e} bis Zouaves in the first line sector B to the north of Zwaanhof. The units placed themselves in the following order, from right to left –
2^{e} Cie – 3^{e} Cie 1er B^{on} d'Afrique (hangar) 4^{e} Cie (its left on the canal) 1ere Cie in support less Platoon Battesti placed between 1er B^{on} d'Afrique and 3^{e} Cie one machine gun at the hangar and one piece on the front of the 4^{e} Cie.
Wounded: 1 NCO and 4 men.

7 May

Same emplacements.
Losses from 6 to 7 May
7 men wounded. 2 killed

8 May

Same emplacements
Losses from 7 to 8 May.
1 NCO and 5 men wounded

9 May

Same emplacements.
Conforming to Order n° 18 of the 45^{e} Division and attack order n° 39 of 8 May of the 90^{e} Brigade, a group of 40 volunteers and the 1er Cie forming a column of assault – objective, the German salient east part – facing the hangars
Bon Demetz of the 2^{e} Zouaves constituted 2 assault coys, objective the German trenches situated to the north of the hangar 2 coys in reserve along the canal.
Two coys of the 3^{e} B^{on} d'Afrique (2^{e} and 3^{e}) will be ready at the 1st signal to launch themselves on the German trenches – at 12^{H} all troops having to participate in the attack are to be ready. At 14 hours the assault will be given, but on the order of the Colonel OC the 90^{e} Brigade.

The preparation made by the artillery having been insufficient – another preparation was made from 15H40 to 16H10. The results obtained were no better, by reason of the trees masking the enemy trenches. A 3rd preparation was made from 17H15 to 17H25, the fire having become dangerous to our troops, it was suspended on the order of Bon Chief Demetz OC the attacking troops.
The projected attack did not take place.
Losses from 8 to 9 May
Captain Ardit lightly wounded
8 men wounded.

10 May

The Battalion was relieved by the 3e Bon of the 3e at 3 hours – after relief it proceeded into the region comprised between Elverdinghe and Woesten where it encamped.

Nominative STATE of Officers, NCOs and soldiers killed, wounded, made prisoner or missing in the battle of 11 to 12 May 1915

NAMES	RANKS	Killed	Wounded	Prisoner	Missing	Horses Killed or Lost	OBSERVATIONS
M. Battesti	Lieut	1					
M. Bastide	"	1					
Fidelin Henri	Cpl	1					
Chéroux Henri	2nd cl		1				
To Report:		3	1				

Order of the Battalion № 98

Extract of the General Order of the 9e Corps d'Armée dated 5 May 1915

The Military Medal has been conferred to the soldier whose name follows:
Sebastiani Dominique Chief Warrant Officer of the 3e Bon de Marche d'Inffie Légère d'Afrique.
"Already reported in the battles of 9 and 10 November and 15 December. Came anew to show his beautiful qualities of courage and sang-froid in the course of the battles of 23 and 26 April and received two grave wounds."

11 May

Same emplacements.
A German bombardment on Woesten at 14 hours killed Lieutenant Battesti and Lieutenant Bastide.
Captain Ardit rejoined the B^on^ at 12 in the morning.
As of 11 may the B^on^ was composed in the following fashion:

	Officers
	{B^on^ Chief Fouchard OC
Head	{Captain Lafargue supplies
Quarters	{Chief Medical Officer Raynaud
	{Medical Officer's aide Coignerai
1er Cie	: Lieutenant Gruyer
2e Cie	: Captain Bernard
3e Cie	{Captain Billot
	{s/Lieutenant Albertini
4e Cie	{Captain Ardit
	{Lieutenant Lainé
MG Ptn:	s/Lieutenant Fournier

	Troops NCOs		Men	Total
1ere Cie	11		97	108
2e Cie	7		107	117
3e Cie	11		103	114
4e Cie	10		95	105
C.H.R.	11		73	84
MG Ptn	3		54	57
Animals:	94	Total =		582

12 May

Same emplacements. 1 man killed and 1 wounded

13 May

Battalion order n° 108
<u>Extract of Général Order no 869 D. of the Grand Quartier General dated 5 May 1915</u>
By virtue of the powers conferred to him by Ministerial Decision nº 12285 H of 8 August 1914. The General Commander in Chief awards, on the date of 5 May 1915, to the order of the Legion of Honour, the following promotions and nominations.
Knight
Mister <u>Balme</u> E. E. Captain of the 3e Bon de Marche d'Inf^le^ Légère d'Afrique.
"Officer of great merit and the most beautiful bravery. Had heroic conduct in bringing himself to the assault of German trenches on 15 December 1914. Gravely wounded, right arm was amputated."

At the Grand Quartier General
5 May 1915
The General Commander in Chief.
Signed: J. Joffre

13 May

Following Order n° 1200 of 13 May 1915 of the 45ᵉ Don, Maj Fouchard replaces Mr. Lieutenant Colonel Levêque in the left sub-sector of the 45ᵉ Dᵒⁿ. Assumed duties at 19 hours.
Captain Ardit assumed the function of Battalion adjutant and took provisional command of the Battalion during the period of the special duty of Commander Fouchard
By decision nº 1155 of 12 May 1915 of the 45ᵉ Division, Lieutenant Mattei , Maestracci , Pierre, Louis was attached to the 3ᵉ Bᵒⁿ d'Afrique de Marche as Coy CO.
Following the relief order no 211 of 12 May 1915 of the 91st Brigade the Bᵒⁿ left camp at 19ᴴ30 and replaced the Bᵒⁿ of the 1ᵉʳ Tirailleurs in their emplacements of sub-sector B of the left trenches of Vannebeck.
The units were placed in the following order
1ᵉ 2ᵉ – 1ᵉʳ Bᵒⁿ d'Afrique – 3ᵉ 4ᵉ MG Ptn
T.C. – Two machine gun pieces were established against aircraft.
Relief finished at 20ᴴ30

14 – 15 – 16 May

Same emplacements
Losses during the day of 16 May:
1 NCO and 3 men wounded –
The Battalion Chief was relieved at 21 hours by Lieutenant Colonel Bourgeois in command of sub-sector B.
At 19ᴴ30 conforming to order nº 149p.c. of 16 May of the 45ᵉ Division, the Bᵒⁿ brought itself into the trenches (2nd line) to the S.E. of the Ypres railway at Boesinghe in reserve at the disposal of General Codet. The Bᵒⁿ chief put himself at the disposal of General Codet.

17 May

At 2 hours the Bᵒⁿ left its emplacements and brought itself (documents n° <u>18 & 19</u>
1°/ 2 Coys detachment of the 1ᵉʳ Bᵒⁿ d'Afrique east bank of the canal, left of the ridge of Zwaanhof farm under the command of Captain Battalion adjutant Ardit
3ᵉ & 4ᵉ Cᶦᵉˢ and MG Ptn, west bank of the canal, the right at the ridge of the Zwaanhof footbridge, where the C.P. of the Bᵒⁿ Chief is found. Troops placed at 3ᴴ15. (see document n° 1
At 6ᴴ Captain Battalion adjutant Ardit received the following order from Maj Fouchard: "Bring yourself immediately with 3 units placed

under our orders to the right of Bon Ayme of the 2^{e} Zouaves to proceed with him to attack hill 14. Bon Ayme is the one going north descending the east slope of the canal. Establish contact with him and launch your offensive movement methodically by sub-units. (Order given in execution of document n° 20)

By reason of the troops massed in the trenches and communication trenches the 3 units of Capt. Ardit were only definitively in place at 16 hours (see documents 21 & 22)

8 hours = The Bon Chief gave (in exec of documents n° 23) the order to the 3^{e} and 4^{e} Cies to bring themselves on the east bank of the canal.

By reason of the troops massed on that bank, only Platoon Albertini of the 3^{e} Cie arrived at the place indicated at 15 hours. For lack of space the 2^{e} peloton of the 3^{e} Cie and the 4^{e} Cie stayed in their emplacements.

From 14^{H}30 to 16^{H}15 the 1st line of sub-sector A, the east & west banks of the canal were violently bombarded by German artillery (105 & 150)

At 17 hours the Bon Chief brought himself on the east bank of the canal at 200 m north of Zwaanhof farm – At 20^{H} the 2^{e} Peloton of the 3^{e} Cie brought itself on the east bank of the canal.

During the night from 17 to 18 May, no movement was made by the units of the corps, who organized (in 1st line 1ere Cie, 2^{e} Cie and detachmt 1er B^{on} d'Afrique) their positions (document n° 24)

6 hours order was given to the 1^{e} 2^{e} Cies and detach^{mt} 1^{e} B^{on} d'Afrique to take the following emplacements (document n° 25)

1ere Cie and detachment 1er B^{on} d'Afrique on the west side of the canal, the head on the ridge of the Zwaanhof footbridge, the left supporting itself (towards the south) at the pontoon bridge.

2^{e} Cie on the east side of the canal to the north of Zwaanhof farm.

At 8^{H} the movement was finished except for the 2^{e} Cie which only left its emplacement at 18 hours and came to place itself on the left of the 1ere Cie at 19 hours, conforming to special order n° 1689 of 18 May of the Groupement, the Battalion left its emplacements and proceeded into segment C of sub-sector B. where it relieved Bon de Fabris of the 1re Tirailleurs.

The Companies were placed in the following order:

3^{e} Cie – 4^{e} Cie and one section of the 1er B^{on} d'Afrique in 1st line (3^{e} at left – 4^{e} at right with the 1er B^{on})

One section of machine guns at the railway bridge the 3rd piece at the disposal of the OC segment D.

In 2nd line (support)

1ere Cie at right, 2^{e} Cie at left.

Relief finished at 20^{H}30

The losses suffered during the days of 17 to 18 May are summarized thus:

Killed = 9 men

Wounded = 1 NCO – 28 men.

19 May

Same emplacements.
Losses of the 19th to 20th = 2 men wounded

Order of the Battalion Nº 112.

Extract of Order No 903 D. of the G.Q.G. dated 13 May 1915.

Mr. Billot M. A. Captain of the 3e Bon de Marche d'Infie Légère d'Afrique, has been named into the order of the Legion of Honour at the rank of Officer:
"Officer of great value, cited to the Order of the Army on 30 January 1915. In the attack of German troops, on 23 April, took the most judicious dispositions on the right wing of the Bon. Maintained the offensive under terrible machine gun fire, then remarkably organized the conquered position."
Mr. Doutreligne Clement, Lieutenant of the 3e Bon de Marche d'Infie Légère d'Afrique,
Has been named into the Order of the Legion of Honour at the rank of: Knight;
"Commanding the Machine gun Platoon of the Battalion, gave proof since the start of the campaign of the most beautiful military qualities, courage, dash, constant activity of spirit, remarkable tactical sense. Obtained from his machine gunners complete devotion, a superb spirit, and excellent shooting. On 23 April by installing a machine gun that blocked all breakout from a village, received a grave wound in the face that entailed the loss of his left eye."
The Military Medal has been conferred to the soldiers whose names follow:
Napias Jean Nº Mle 3392, Sergeant of the 3e Bataillon de Marche d'Infie Légère d'Afrique
"Old NCO, having a profound sense of duty. Of remarkable courage and spirit. In the battle of 23 April, carried his men under the fire of German machine guns to bring them forward. Reached the position first. Was gravely wounded in the arm in the course of the action."
Casabianca Marc, Nº Mle 6735
Sergeant of the 3e Bataillon de Marche d'Infie Légère d'Afrique
"On the front since the Battalion entered the campaign; had always showed an exemplary courage and remarkable energy that he knew how to communicate to his men. Already distinguished himself in the battles of 9 and 10 November and of 15 December.
Came to be reported again on 23 April in leading his men forward despite intense enemy machine gun fire. Was gravely in the right arm at the head of his chasseurs."
Felpin Albert, Sergeant of the 3e Bataillon de Marche d'Infie Légère

d'Afrique.
"Chief of a machine gun section of courage and sang-froid above all praise; on 23 April did not cease to inflict bloody losses on the Germans. Was wounded at his piece which he only abandoned after being relieved by a new team."

At the G.Q.G. 13 May 1915
Signed: J. Joffre

Order of the Battalion Nº 113.

Extract of the Official Journal of the French Republic of 27 April 1915 (page 2619)

The Minister of War,

In view of the ordinance of 13 August 1914, decrees:
Unique Article: Are inscribed on a special table of the Military Medal, dating from 10 April 1915, the soldiers whose names follow:
Deligny E. L. chief Warrant Officer of the 3e Bataillon de Marche d'Infie Légère d'Afrique.
"Very meriting NCO , having a beautiful calling for service. Came to the front with a detachment of reinforcements on 22 January. Numerous years of service and previous campaigns."

At G.Q.G. 28 April
Lieutenant Colonel Chief of the Office of Personnel
signed: illegible

Order of the Battalion Nº 114.

Extract of Order Nº 903 D of the G.Q.G. dated 13 May 1915.
The Military Medal has been conferred on the Soldiers whose names follow:
Falco Nº Mle 5941 chasseur 2nd class of the 3e Bataillon de Marche d'Infie Légère d'Afrique.
"Very good soldier, had always had very good conduct during his time with the Battalion. Brilliantly comported himself on 9 November, in the course of a night attack on German trenches. Was wounded in the course of the action."
Casbonne Joseph, Chasseur 2nd class of the 3e Bataillon de Marche d'Infie Légère d'Afrique.
"Very good soldier with superb courage. Always gave proof of zeal and discipline. Conducted himself very well in the battle of 9 November 1914, in the course of which he was wounded."

At G.Q.G. 13 May 1915.
Signed: J. Joffre,

20 May

Around 20^{H}30, the 2e Cie relieved the 3e Cie
The 1^{e} Cie relieved the 4^{e} Cie
The 3^{e} and 4^{e} Cies occupy the support trenches.
Relief was finished at 22 hours
Losses of 20 to 21 May:
Killed: 1 man
Wounded: Captain Bernard
5 men.

21 May

Conforming to the order of relief of the 90e Brigade of 21 May, the sector of the B^{on} extends itself and comprises the bridge of the Boesinghe-Pilkem road. Around 20^{H}30, the 3e Cie brought itself to segment D, and relieved Bon Teyssère of the 3e Zouaves.
The 3rd machine gun piece of the B^{on} and a piece from the 1er Tirailleurs guard the bridge of the road. The 4e Cie is alone in support.
All the elements of the 1er B^{on} d'Afrique are at segment D with the 3e Cie.
Losses from 21 to 22 May:
Killed = 1 man
Wounded = 9 men

22 May

Same emplacements
19 hours = The Bon Chief proceeded to Chateau Boesinghe where he established his C.P.
Losses of 22 May
Killed 1 NCO, 2 men
Wounded = 4 men

Order of the Battalion Nº 118

Extract of General Order Nº 8
The General Commanding the Detachment d'Armée de Belgique, cited to the Order of the Army:
Captain Bernard Maurice Jean of the 3e Bataillon de Marche d'Inf^{ie} Légère d'Afrique
"On 23 April, in the attack of German troops, knew to push forward the march of his company despite violent machine gun fire, then solidly organized the conquered position."
Captain Ardit Albert, of the 3e Bataillon de Marche d'Inf^{ie} Légère d'Afrique:
"Remarkable Company Commander, very beautiful conduct in the battle of 9 November. Wounded, returned to the front scarcely healed. Having received command of two companies at the head

of the Battalion at the battle of 23 April, kept them on the offensive despite terrible machine gun fire and contributed strongly to the occupation of the enemy position."

Captain Andru Georges Emile of the 3e Bataillon de Marche d'Inf^{ie} Légère d'Afrique,

"Officer of high value. Distinguished himself in all the affairs in which the 3e Bon de Marche d'Inf^{ie} Légère d'Afrique took part. Killed gloriously on 23 April in carrying his company to the assault."

Captain Latapy Maurice of the 3e Bataillon de Marche d'Inf^{ie} Légère d'Afrique.

"Took command of a company of the 3e Bon de Marche d'Inf^{ie} Légère d'Afrique in the midst of combat on 18 February; contributed by his tenacity to the success of the day

Wounded mortally, at the head of his company in the course of the battle of 23 April."

Lieutenant Bresson Pierre, of the 3e Bataillon de Marche d'Inf^{ie} Légère d'Afrique.

"In the course of the battle of 23 April, having taken command of the 1ere Compagnie, after the death of the Captain, knew how to keep his troops on the march forward despite terrible machine gun fire. Was gravely wounded in the course of the action."

2nd Lieutenant Fache Albert, Francois of the 3e Bataillon de Marche d'Inf^{ie} Légère d'Afrique.

"Heroic soldier, inspiring in his men deep admiration and obtaining prodigious bravery from them. Already cited to the Order of the Army. Wounded mortally on 23 April in giving example to all."

Chasseur 2nd class Jacquemin Emile N^{o} M^{le} 6383 of the 3e Bataillon de Marche d'Inf^{ie} Légère d'Afrique.

"Stretcher bearer with heroic courage, particularly distinguished himself in the course of 23, 24, 25 and 26 April. Despite a first wound, continued his service and fell gloriously in the first line while bringing back a wounded man."

---

23 May

Same emplacements. At 13^{H} and at 15 hours violent bombardment near the C.P. (105 and 150)

Captain Lavalée was attached to the Corps (1ere Cie)

Losses of the 23rd: killed 2 men. Wounded 16 men

24 May

2^{H}45 violent fusillade and intense cannonade on the right – direction Verlorenhoek.

Losses of 24 May: 1 man killed and 5 wounded.

25 May

Same emplacements. Losses: 3 men wounded.

Order of the Battalion № 119.

Extract of General Order № 9 dated 21 May 1915

The General Commanding the Detachement d'Armée de Belgique, cited to the Order of the Army:
Mister Battesti Pierre (R) Lieutenant of the 3e Bataillon de Marche d'Infie Légère d'Afrique.
"Reserve Officer, of high value having made proof under fire for 6 months, of the most superb qualities of endurance of spirit and command. Was killed by a shell burst on 11 May 1915, in the course of a particularly perilous reconnaissance.
Mister Bastide Rossel (R) Lieutenant of the 3e Bataillon de Marche d'Infie Légère d'Afrique.
"Reserve officer of high value, whose appointment was instantly requested as recompense for his superb calling to service in war. Cited on 5 May to the Order of the Army for beautiful conduct under fire. Was killed by a shell burst on 11 May 1915, in the course of a particularly perilous reconnaissance."

Nominative STATE of Officers, NCOs and soldiers killed, wounded, made prisoner or missing in the battle of 19 to 26 May 1915

NAMES	RANKS	Killed	Wounded	Prisoner	Missing	Horses Killed or Lost	OBSERVATIONS
Charpentier Ferdinand	2nd cl		1				
Dache Marius	Cpl		1				
Bontemps Pierre	2nd cl		1				
Daoudal Amédré			1				
Toussaint Charles			1				
Menut François			1				
Germain Fernaud	Cpl		1				
Michel René	2nd cl		1				
Allaux louis			1				
Morel Jean			1				
Compagnie Auguste			1				
Caignard Charles			1				
Thô Don César	sergt		1				
Petit Ernest	2nd cl	1					

Rogue André			1				
Allier François			1				
Simon J.B.		1					
Vinart Georges		1					
Manquat Louis			1				
Stephan Joseph			1				
Broutta Kléber			1				
Carbone Paul			1				
Matignon Louis			1				
Journet Auguste			1				
Galetti Sampierro		1					
Aussy Paul			1				
Barbreu Gaston			1				
Malvoisin			1				
To Report:		5	23				
Musso Auguste	2nd cl		1				
Gallet Stephane			1				
Benteux Georges			1				
Bounet Georges			1				
Laposse Noël			1				
Traval Pierre			1				
Lehied Jacob			1				
Mathieu Jules			1				
Diot Marcel			1				
Jouanie Aimi			1				
Lebourg Marcel			1				
Lebraire Marcel		1					
André Abel	Cpl		1				
Renaud Marcel	2nd cl	1					
Ducreux Jean	1st cl		1				
Richard Louis			1				
Arnaud Désiré			1				
Jarry Emile							
To Report:		7	39				
			46				

26 May

Conforming to the order of relief N° 25 of 24 May of the 45e Division and special Order N° 42 of the 90e Brigade of 26 May, the B^{on} was relieved around 21^{H}30 by the 3e B^{on} of the 9e Zouaves (Maj Petitot) after relief it proceeded into the area north east of the Chapelle N.D. where it encamped
(Reserve of the 90^e Brigade)

27 May

Same emplacements.

28 May

Conforming to General Order N° 26 of 26 May of the 45^e Division, the B^{on} left the area north east of the Chapelle at 2 hours and proceeded on foot into the area comprised between Eykhoek-St Sixte where it encamped. Arrived in encampment at 6 hours.
The 90e Brigade is in Divisional reserve.

Order of the Battalion N° 126

Extract of Order 939 D of the G.Q.G. dated 23 May 1915

The Military Medal has been conferred to the Soldier whose name follows:
Jeandin E. L. N° M^{le} 3890, Warrant Officer of the 3e Bataillon de Marche d'Inf^{ie} Légère d'Afrique
NCO of the greatest merit. Attitude under fire superb. Came again to distinguish himself on 7 May making a perilous reconnaissance of the ground where his company had to attack. Was gravely wounded. (Warrant Officer Jeandin will have the right to the Croix de Guerre with palm.)

At the G.Q.G.
signed: J. Joffre,
23 May 1915

29 May

A detachment of reinforcements composed of :

	{M.M.	Herbelin
3 Captains	{	Duran
	{	Vigouroux
1 Lieutenant	: Mr.	Arrighi
2 s/Lieutenants	{M.M.	Chiappa
	{	Roux

1 Chief Warrant Officer – 1 Warrant Officer – 1 sergeant-major –

14 sergeants
21 corporals – 494 chasseurs, arrived at the T.R. at Crombecke, were incorporated.
After incorporation the Battalion was thus constituted by taking into account some transfers and promotions within the Corps.

	Officers:	
	{Commander Fouchard	
	{Captain Adj Major Ardit	
Head-Quarters	{Captain Duran	supernumerary
	{Captain Lavallée	-d^{o}
	{Captain Lafargue	Quartermaster
	{s/Lieutenant Fournier	Deputy Chief of Corps
1ere Cie	{Captain Vigouroux	
	{Lieutenant Mattei Maestracci	
	{Captain Bernard	
2eme Cie	{Lieutenant Guidicci	
	{s/Lieutenant Chiappa	
3e Cie	(Captain Billot	
	{s/Lieutenant Albertini	
	{Captain Herbelin	
4e Cie	{Lieutenant Arrighi	
	{Lieutenant Lainé	
MG Ptn	{Lieutenant Gruyer	
	{s/Lieutenant Roux	
Medical Sec	{Medical Officer 2nd cl Reynaud	
	{Medical Officer's aide 1st cl Coignerai	

	Troops.
1ere Cie :	220 rank and file
2e Cie :	225 -d^{o}
3e Cie :	218 -d^{o}
4e Cie :	221 -d^{o}
C.H.R. :	82 -d^{o}
MG Ptn:	53 -d^{o}

{20 officers
That is in total {1019 rank and file.
Conforming to Order N° 2685 of 29 May of the 45^{e} Division, the B^{on} was alerted at 20 hours.

30 May

At 9^{H}30, the 90^{e} Brigade made known that the B^{on} ceased to be at alert.

31 May

Same emplacements.

Appendices

Appendix A

Extracts of laws relevant to *Sections d'Exclus* and recruitment of the *Infanterie Légère d'Afrique* as of 1913

Law of 21 March 1905 on the Recruitment of the Army

FIRST ARTICLE.
All Frenchmen must do personal military service.
ART. 2.
Military service is equal for all. Except in the case of physical incapacity, it implies no dispensation.
It lasts twenty-five years and is accomplished according to the mode determined by the present Law.[1]
ART. 4.
(Modified by the laws of 11 April 1910 and 30 March 1912)
Are excluded from the army, but put, either for their term of active service, or in case of mobilization, at the disposition of the departments of War and the Colonies following the allotment which will be enacted by decree rendered on the proposition of the interested ministries:

1) Individuals who have been condemned to a corporal or infamous punishment;
2) Those who have been condemned to a correctional punishment of two years of imprisonment and above, have been, in addition, by application of article 42 of the penal code, struck with interdiction of all or some of the exercise of their civic, civil, or family rights;
3) Exiled collectively or individually;
4) Individuals condemned abroad for a crime or offence punished by a French penal law of a corporal, infamous punishment or of two years at least of imprisonment, after statement, by the correctional tribunal of the interested civil domicile, of the regularity and legality of the condemnation.

During the duration of their active period after their return home in the circumstances cited by article 47, and in case of call to service after mobilization, the excluded are put under the dispositions governing the soldiers of the active army, reserves, the territorial army and its reserve …

1 The so-called "three years law" of 7 August 1913 brought length of service to 28 years; 3 in the active army, 11 in the reserves, 7 in the territorial army, and 7 in the territorial reserve.

ART. 5.

(Modified by the laws of 11 April 1910 and 30 March 1912)

Individuals known culpable of crimes and condemned only to imprisonment by application of articles 67, 68 and 463 of the penal code;

Those who have had a correctional condemnation of six months of imprisonment at least, either for injury or voluntary assault, by application of articles 309 and 311 of the penal code, or for violence towards children, cited by article 312, paragraph 6 and following of the same code, or for rebellion;

Those who have had a correctional condemnation of one month of imprisonment at least for public indecency, for theft, fraud, breach of trust or moral offences cited by article 334 of the penal code;

Those who have been condemned correctionally for pimping, offence cited by article 2 of the law of 3 April 1903, no matter what the duration of punishment;

Those who have been the object of two or more condemnations of which the total duration is of three months at least, for one or more of the offences specified in line 2 of the present article;

Those who have been the object of two or more condemnations, of which the total duration is of three months at least for one or more of the offences cited by articles 269 to 276[2] inclusively of the penal code;

Those who have been the object of two or more condemnations of which the total duration is of three months at least, for the offence of stealing food cited by article 401 of the penal code;

Those who have been the object of two or more condemnations no matter what the duration for one or more of the offences specified in line 3 of the present article;

Are incorporated in the battalions of the African Light Infantry, except for contrary decision of the Minister of War after inquest into their conduct since leaving prison.

Those individuals who, at the moment when their class is called find themselves detained, for those same faults, in a penitentiary establishment, will be incorporated in the said battalions at the expiration of their punishment, to accomplish their term of service prescribed by the present law.

ART. 6.

(Modified by the law of 11 April 1910)

No soldier can be sent to the battalions of African Light Infantry by simple ministerial decision, except in the case envisaged by article 93.

The dispositions of articles 4 and 5 above are not applicable to individuals condemned for political acts or in connection to political acts.

In case of appeal, it will be judged by the civil tribunal of the place of residence, conforming to article 28 below.

Those individuals will follow the departure of the first class called after the expiration of their punishment.

All soldiers with a correctional condemnation before their incorporation of a punishment of less than three months for an offence specified in the second paragraph of article 5 can, in case of grave misconduct, after a minimum delay of three months since their incorporation, be sent to a battalion of African Light Infantry. Sending him is to be proposed by the commander of

---

2 Articles 269 to 276 of the penal code cited offences of vagrancy and begging.

the army corps on the advice of a disciplinary council and pronounced by the Minister of War.

After the same delay and following the rules specified in the preceding paragraph, those who by faults reiterated against military regulations or by bad conduct bringing harm to discipline and constituting a break in the moral value of the body of troops in which they are part, can be sent to special sections which will be organized in replacement of the disciplinary companies by a decree of the President of the Republic.

Men incorporated by virtue of the present article and the preceding article into the battalions of African Light Infantry, or in special sections, who are remarked upon in the face of the enemy, who have accomplished an act of courage or devotion, and those have kept regular conduct, during six months in the special sections, and during one year in the battalions of African Light Infantry, can be returned to a body of troops of ordinary service, to continue their service there, by decision of the Minister of War, rendered on the proposition of their Commanding Officer.

ART. 50.

(Modified by the law of 11 April 1910)

All Frenchmen or naturalized Frenchmen, as is said in articles 11 and 12 of the present law, as well as young men who must be inscribed on the tables of the conscription register or who are authorized by law to serve in the French army, can be admitted to contract a voluntary engagement in the active army, in the following conditions.

The engaged volunteer must:

1) If he enters into the metropolitan troops, be eighteen years of age;

If he enters into the colonial troops, be eighteen years of age and contract an engagement of which the length is such that he is able to sojourn two years in the colonies from the moment when he will reach twenty-one years of age. That last disposition is not applicable to young men residing in the colonies or a protectorate country where the engagee will be stationed in their colony or protectorate country;

2) Be neither married nor widowed with children;
3) Have no condemnations falling under the stroke of article 5 of the present law. Nevertheless, men incorporated in the battalions of African Light Infantry can contract re-engagements renewable one year in the conditions of article 54 of the present law;
4) Enjoy his civil rights;
5) Be of good character and morals

ART. 93.

(Modified by the law of 11 April 1910)

Article 5, paragraph 5 of article 6, the last paragraph of article 41 and line 3 paragraph 2 of article 50, do not apply to men having benefited from the law of 26 March 1891, at least if they have not been condemned for pimping.

In case of grave misconduct during their presence under the flag, men called or engaged as per the paragraphs above can, on the proposition of their Commanding Officer and by ministerial decision, be sent to battalions of the African Light Infantry.

Appendix B

Identified Fatal Casualties of the *1er Bataillon de Marche d'Infanterie Légère d'Afrique*, November 1914 to May 1915

Surname	Name	Department of Birth	Date of Birth	Died	class	Rank
Rossé	Louis Xavier	90-Terretoire de Belfort	Jan-5-1885	21/11/1914	?	2nd class
Secondi	Jacques Antoine	20-Corse	Jan-28-1889	22/11/1914	1909	2nd class
Carré	Etienne Marcel	75-Paris	Mar-2-1891	26/11/1914	1911	1st class
Marochin	Gustave Edouard	72-Sarthe	Jan-16-1891	26/11/1914	1912	2nd class
Créon	François	33-Gironde	Oct-5-1891	26/11/1914	1911	1st class
Descollaz	Jean Marie Henri	69-Rhone	Oct-21-1891	27/11/1914	1911	2nd class
Demortier	Pierre	92-Hauts-de-Seine	Jan-12-1891	29/11/1914	1911	1st class
Lacour	Alexandre Alphonse	78-Yvelines	Oct-5-1891	29/11/1914	1912	2nd class
Montaz	Jean François	42-Loire	Feb-9-1891	29/11/1914	1911	2nd class
Pouilly	Joseph Louis Auguste	62-Pas-de-Calais	Feb-13-1891	29/11/1914	1911	2nd class
Lagache	Charles	75-Paris	Mar-25-1891	29/11/1914	1911	2nd class
Lanchez	Jean	29-Finstere	Jan-20-1891	29/11/1914	1911	2nd class
Sicre	Henri Silvestre Louis	66-Pyrenees-Orientale	Jul-10-1893	29/11/1914	1913	Corporal
Laffont	Léon François	30-Gard	Sep-17-1891	29/11/1914	1911	Corporal
Gradeler	Paul Eugène	88-Voges	Jun-20-1887	29/11/1914	1907	Sergeant
Legrand		Unknown	Unknown	29/11/1914	n/a	2nd class
Lecotten	Laurent	Unknown	Unknown	29/11/1914	n/a	2nd class
Bertheaux		Unknown	Unknown	29/11/1914	n/a	2nd class
Pujat		Unknown	Unknown	29/11/1914	n/a	2nd class
Camps	Marius Michel	Algeria	Apr-16-1891	30/11/1914	1911	2nd class
Pointel	Victor Julien	76-Seine Maritime	Jun-21-1891	30/11/1914	1911	2nd class
Passereaux	Alexandre	75-Paris	Jun-1-1892	01/12/1914	1912	2nd class
Aubert	Marcel René	75-Paris	Jul-18-1891	02/12/1914	1911	Corporal

Lindsal	Louis Lucien	75-Paris	Jun-3-1893	02/12/1914	1913	Corporal
Petitjean	Arthur Léon	52-Haute-Marne	Jul-29-1891	02/12/1914	1911	2nd class
Hérambourg	Gaston Alphonse	76-Seine Maritime	May-18-1891	03/12/1914	1911	2nd class
Roux	Barthelemi Jean	13-Bouches-de-Rhone	Nov-10-1891	03/12/1914	1911	2nd class
Gorenflot	Paul Aristide	60-Oise	May-5-1891	03/12/1914	1911	2nd class
Marchal	Julien Edouard Alphonse	54-Meurthe-et-Moselle	Oct-13-1891	05/12/1914	1911	2nd class
Girard	Louis Edmond Alfred	76-Seine Maritime	Dec-22-1891	07/12/1914	1911	2nd class
Diamiano		Unknown	Unknown	07/12/1914	n/a	2nd class
Noury		Unknown	Unknown	07/12/1914	n/a	1st class
Aubert	Felix Paul	13-Bouches-de-Rhone	Apr-16-1892	11/12/1914	1912	Corporal
Lepoutre	Jean Baptiste	59-Nord	Mar-6-1891	13/12/1914	1911	2nd class
Bourdat	Adrien	26-Drome	Nov-11-1893	20/12/1914	1913	Corporal
Mouton	Unknown	Unknown	Unknown	23/12/1914		2nd class
Dubois	Ferdinand	42-Loire	sep-11-1891	26/12/1914	1911	2nd class
Orchampt	Marie François Xavier Joseph	70-Haute-Saone	Nov-29-1887	26/12/1914	1907	Sergeant-Major
Vincelot	Abel Aimé	86-Vienne	Feb-12-1888	30/12/1914	1908	Sergeant
Provost	Celestin	75-Paris	Dec-27-1887	15/01/1915	1907	Bugler
Beretti	Antoine Marie	20-Corse	Feb-23-1891	15/01/1915	1911	Sergeant
Pinault	George Etienne Joseph Marie	35-Ille-et-Vilaine	May-5-1893	15/01/1915	1913	2nd class
Charpentier	Julien Eugène Edouard	14-Calvados	Jun-11-1891	15/01/1915	1911	2nd class
Goy	Henri	75-Paris	Aug-15-1890	15/01/1915	1910	2nd class
Rouxel	Ernest	Unknown	Unknown	15/01/1915		2nd class
Voissard	Jean	Unknown	Unknown	15/01/1915		2nd class
Chardonnet	Louis	63-Puy-de-Dome	Dec-26-1891	16/01/1915	1911	2nd class
Blondeau	Eugène Raoul Jean Baptiste	25-Doubs	Jun-12-1890	17/01/1915	1910	Sergeant
Leloup	Arthur Elovie Désiré	61-Orne	Sep-12-1886	20/01/1915	1906	2nd class
Nicolini	Alfred Gustave	90-Terretoire de Belfort	Aug-2-1889	20/01/1915	1910	2nd class
Potot	Henry	21-Cote-d'Or	May-14-1877	20/01/1915	1897	Captain
Jeannot	Armand Jean Baptiste	29-Finstere	Jan-10-1887	20/01/1915	1907	Corporal
Drouard	Prosper	75-Paris	May-8-1890	20/01/1915	1910	Sergeant
Berthomet	François	16-Charente	Oct-5-1887	20/01/1915	1907	Sergeant-Major

Gasté	Théophille	Unknown	Unknown	20/01/1915	n/a	2nd class
Patry	Ernest	Unknown	Unknown	20/01/1915	n/a	2nd class
Herbet	Gabriel	78-Yvelines	Feb-23-1890	20/01/1915	1910	2nd class
Papaïx	Fernand Jules	81-Tarn	Dec-26-1890	21/01/1915	1901	Corporal
Constant	Maurice Gaston	75-Paris	Feb-5-1895	21/01/1915	1913	2nd class
Vinet	François	44-Loire Atlantique	Jul-01-1890	22/01/1915	1910	2nd class
Flambeaux	Louis	75-Paris	Jan-25-1891	22/01/1915	1911	2nd class
Oguer	Felix	29-Finstere	Jul-11-1890	23/01/1915	1910	1st class
Renaudier	Auguste	Unknown	Unknown	23/01/1915	n/a	Sergeant
Faget	Louis	75-Paris	Apr-2-1892	04/02/1915	1912	2nd class
Servoise	Emile Désiré	51-Marne	Apr-2-1893	08/02/1915	1913	2nd class
Dubois	Marcel Léon	41-Loir-et-Cher	Nov-21-1889	13/02/1915	1909	2nd class
Abeillon	Auguste	07-Ardeche	Sep-23-1886	17/02/1915	1906	2nd class
Michée	Benjamin Ludovic	76-Seine Maritime	Sep-26-1885	17/02/1915	1905	Sergeant
Cauvin	Alfred Alexandre	27-Eure	Jan-28-1892	17/02/1915	1912	2nd class
Bursin	Eugène Aime	71-Saone-et-Loire	Dec-9-1891	17/02/1915	1911	2nd class
Finet	Camille	38-Isere	Mar-17-1892	17/02/1915	1912	2nd class
Montreynaud	Joseph	07-Ardeche	Jan-7-1894	17/02/1915	1914	2nd class
Jacques	Clément Philibert Louis	28-Eure-et-Loir	Nov-22-1891	18/02/1915	1911	2nd class
Druant	Grullmann	Unknown	Unknown	18/02/1915		2nd class
Bouffay	Marcel Edouard Georges	61-Orne	Dec-27-1892	20/02/1915	1912	2nd class
Herce	Edmond Eugène Alexandre	72-Sarthe	Jul-27-1890	27/02/1915	1910	2nd class
Hudenou	Ernest	Unknown	Unknown	01/03/1915	n/a	2nd class
Toulza	Albert	75-Paris	Aug-9-1877	24/03/1915	1897	2nd class
Paulain		Unknown	Unknown	05/04/1915	n/a	2nd class
Carrot	Petrus Antoine	43-Haute-Loire	Jun-30-1893	14/04/1915	1913	2nd class
Ivorra	Mariano	Unknown	Unknown	14/04/1915	n/a	2nd class
Kerrirzin	Stanislas Marie	22-Cotes d'Armor	Dec-21-1891	15/04/1915	1911	2nd class
Delporte	Léon Henri	75-Paris	May-18-1892	16/04/1915	1912	Corporal
Terrier	Joseph Georges Gaston	33-Gironde	Oct-19-1880	17/04/1915	1900	Chief Warrant
Brazier	Emile Henri	02-Aisne	Apr-2-1891	21/04/1915	1911	2nd class
Chaffraix	François Alfred	09-Ariege	Jan-23-1882	22/04/1915	1902	2nd class
Ernst	Lucien Henry Pierre Marceau	Tahiti	Apr-18-1887	22/04/1915	1907	Lieutenant

Malherbe	Gustave Edmond Edouard	80-Somme	Aug-8-1891	22/04/1915	1911	2nd class
Goudalle	Eugène Godefroy Paul	62-Pas-de-Calais	Jan-9-1894	22/04/1915	1914	2nd class
Mars	Achille Pierre Auguste	59-Nord	Nov-18-1891	23/04/1915	1911	2nd class
Duthe	Emile Henri	62-Pas-de-Calais	Apr-17-1892	06/05/1915	1912	2nd class
Calvat	François (Francis) Elisée	05-Hautes-Alpes	Jan-8-1878	07/05/1915	1898	2nd class
Rochee	Auguste Charles Marie	40-Landes	Nov-11-1886	17/05/1915	1906	2nd class
Guichard	Léon Paul Gaston	75-Paris	Jun-15-1892	17/05/1915	1912	2nd class
Moyen	Jean	19-Correze	Apr-2-1879	27/06/1915	1899	2nd class
Pimont	Raymond Henri Albert	76-Seine Maritime	Jan-23-1894	28/06/1915	1914	2nd class
Leny	Laurent Raymond Louis	61-Orne	Jun-18-1894	28/06/1915	1914	2nd class
Prudhomme	Victor Désiré	75-Paris	Jun-21-1892	29/06/1915	1912	2nd class
Arnoult	Raoul Armand	51-Marne	Dec-4-1893	30/06/1915	1913	2nd class
Deconihout	Ernest Constant	76-Seine Maritime	Sep-16-1883	01/09/1915	1903	Sergeant
Sauvage	Alfred	02-Aisne	Dec-21-1881	16/05/1916	1901	Captain

Source: Memoires des Hommes, http://www.memoiredeshommes.sga.defense.gouv.fr

Appendix C

Chart showing the organization of the Battalions of the African Light Infantry

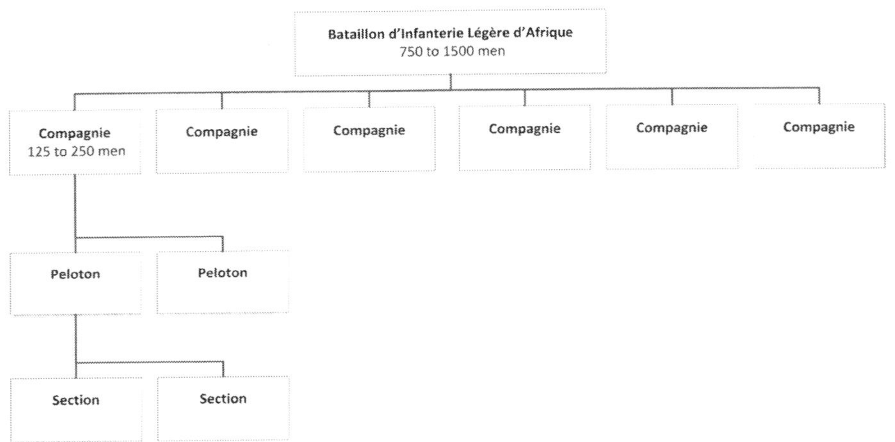

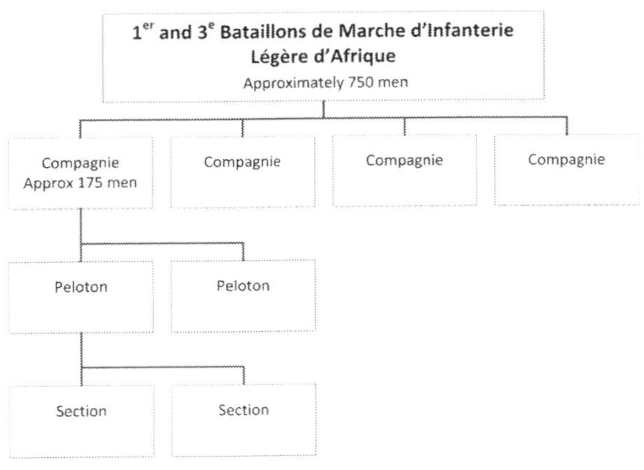

Appendix D

Chart showing the relationship of the African Light Infantry to the disciplinary system of the French army

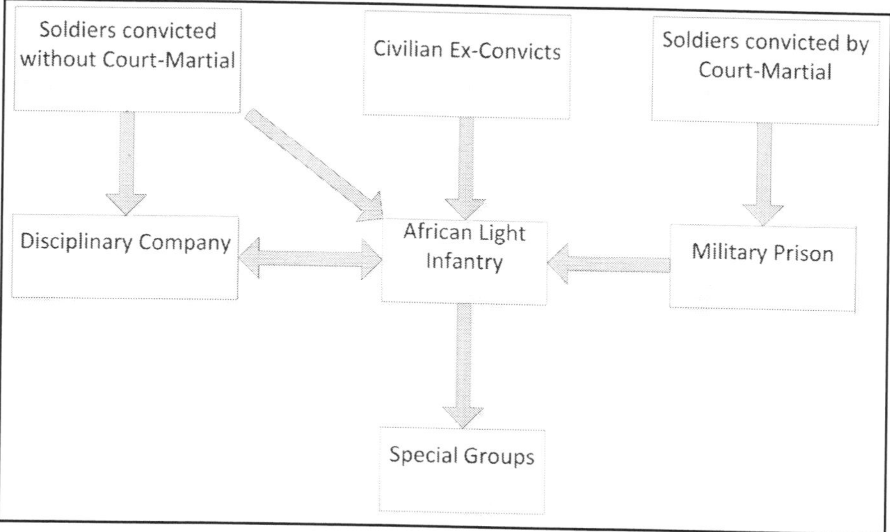

Acknowledgements

Any work of this kind is a collaborative effort and there are many people I would like to acknowledge and thank for their contributions.

First I must wholeheartedly thank several French government agencies for making this work possible. In 2008 the War Diaries of French formations of the First World War were made available online as scanned images. The *Secrétariat général pour l'administration* (SGA), the *Direction de la mémoire, du patrimoine et des archives* (DPMA), the *Service historique de la défense* (SHD) and the *Mémoire des Hommes* website deserve to be acknowledged for the magnificent job they have done of making the history of the French army in the First World War accessible. Scanned images of the original diaries were accessed on the *Mémoire des Hommes* website at the following addresses:

For the *1er Bataillon de Marche d'Infanterie Légère d'Afrique*:

http://www.memoiredeshommes.sga.defense.gouv.fr/jmo/img-viewer/26_N_859_001/viewer.html

For the *3e Bataillon de Marche d'Infanterie Légère d'Afrique*:

http://www.memoiredeshommes.sga.defense.gouv.fr/jmo/img-viewer/26_N_860_003/viewer.html

http://www.memoiredeshommes.sga.defense.gouv.fr/jmo/img-viewer/26_N_860_004/viewer.html

Additionally, the *Bibliothèque nationale de France* offers exceptional reproduction and online services that permitted access to books and images that would have been very difficult to obtain otherwise.

Special thanks go to Dominiek Dendoovan and the documentation centre staff at the In Flanders Fields Museum in Ypres, Belgium. Thank you all for helping to make my visit a productive and enjoyable one! Dominiek graciously responded to all of my queries and offered many valuable insights.

I would also like to thank historians Anthony Clayton, Tim Cook, Clare Dale, Julian Putkowski and Ian Radforth for their insights, support and encouragement. This series was years in the making and their words of encouragement helped sustain me through the effort. Clare Dale deserves special thanks for the proofreading services she provided. Her expertise gave this book a far more professional quality than I could ever have achieved by myself, of course all shortcomings in this work are entirely my own.

I have been privileged to be part of a superb historical re-enacting group, the recreated King's Royal Regiment of New York, which researches the loyalist experience of the American War of Independence and portrays those difficult times for the public. Having a network of friends and professionals who are all superb military historians is beyond value. Many of my friends in the King's Royal Yorkers offered valuable feedback and deserve to be singled out, namely Matt Liness, Reg James, Steven Sandford, Rob Stewart and Gavin Watt. I have many good friends in other re-enacting units as well. Christian Cameron, Douglas Cubinson, Dana Bogdanski and Jevon Garret all offered advice and assistance. About a decade ago, Jevon and I were enjoying an afternoon under the shade of a tree at an historical re-enactment, discussing the Second Battle of Ypres. Jevon's reaction to my description of the retreat of the *45e Division Algérienne* made me stop and think. Why did I assume that they had simply fled in panic? Perhaps there was more to the story. I had to admit that I was simply re-iterating what I had read without questioning it. A seed was planted that day, though it would be years before I began to actively pursue the idea.

The staff of the Western Front Association, of which I am a member, also provided assistance.

And of course, I could never have done any of this without the love and support of my family. My father, mother, my mother-in-law, my brothers Stephen and Daniel and my sister Sarah always offer their enthusiastic encouragement. My lovely and talented wife, Kathy, not only gave me the support at home to put in the long hours needed to complete this project, but she also provided insightful critique, worked closely with me to format this book for print and designed the cover. My daughter, Flora, always assured me that this book was going to turn out great. This is my first work in print, and I dedicate it to her, my first child.

Abbreviations

A.C.	Artillerie de Campagne (Field Artillery)
A.D.	Artillerie Divisionale (Divisional Artillery)
BILA	Bataillon d'Infanterie Légère d'Afrique (Battalion of African Light Infantry)
BMILA	Bataillon de Marche d'Infanterie Légère d'Afrique (Field Battalion of African Light Infantry)
B.O.	By Order of
Bon	Bataillon (Battalion)
C.A.	Corps d'Armée (Army Corps)
Capt	Captain
Cie, Coy	Compagnie (Company)
C.H.R.	Compagnie Hors Rang (Head Quarters Company)
CO	Commanding Officer
C.P.	Command Post
CVAD	Convoi Administrative (Administrative Convoy)
D.A.B.	Détachment d'Armée Belgique (Detachment of the Belgian Army; a French formation that reinforced the Belgians)
D.I.	Division d'Infanterie (Infantry Division)
Div, Don	Division
D.I.T., D.T.	Division d'Infanterie Territoriale (Territorial Infantry Division)
D°	Ditto
D.R.	Division de Réserve (Reserve Division)
HQ	Head Quarters
JMO	Journal de Marche et Operations (War Diary)
Lieut	Lieutenant
MG	Machine gun
M^in A. M^or	Médecin Aide Major (Senior Medical Officer's Aide)
N° M^le	Numéro Matriculaire (Service Number)
OC	Officer Commanding
P.C.	Pour Copie (Certified True Copy)
Pon, Ptn	Peloton (Platoon)
Régt	Régiment (Regiment)
Sec	Section
S.H.R	Section Hors Rang (Head Quarters Section)
S/Lieutenant	Sous-Lieutenant (Second Lieutenant)
Tal, Tle	Territorial, Territoriale (Territorial)
T.C.	Train de Combat (Combat Baggage)
Teurs	Tirailleurs
T.R.	Train Régimentaire (Regimental Baggage)

Bibliography

Anonymous. *Historique du 1er Bataillon d'Infanterie Légère d'Afrique*. Paris: Berger-Levrault, 1919.

Anonymous. *Historique du 1er Bataillon d'Infanterie Légère d'Afrique*. Paris: Henri Charles-Lavauzelle, 1920.

Anonymous. *Historique Succinct du 2e Bataillon d'Infanterie Légère d'Afrique*. Casablanca: G. Mercié, 1920.

Anonymous. *Historique du 3e Bataillon d'Infanterie Légère d'Afrique*. Paris: Henri Charles-Lavauzelle, 1920.

Anonymous. *Historique du 3e Bataillon d'Infanterie Légère d'Afrique*. Paris: Imprimerie Adm. & Militaire A. Mauguin, 1920.

Anonymous. *Historiques du 3e Bataillon de Marche et du 4e Bataillon*. Paris: Henri Charles-Lavauzelle, 1920.

Anonymous. "Les Bataillons d'Afrique et leur Organisation Actuelle." *Journal des Sciences Militaires*, Tome 18 (1903), 408-423.

Ben Mahmoud, Feriel. *Bat' d'Af, La Légende des Mauvais Garçons*. Paris: Mengès, 2005.

Bou-Saïd, Captain. *Livre d'Honneur du 2e Bataillon d'Infanterie Légère d'Afrique*. Paris: Librairie Militaire de L. Baudoin et Cie., 1887.

Clayton, Anthony. *France, Soldiers and Africa*. London: Brassey's Defence Publishers, 1988.

—— *Paths of Glory*. New York: Cassel, 2003.

Camus, Antoine. *Les Bohêmes du Drapeau*. Paris: P. Brunet, 1863.

Combe, Louis, Dr. *Le Soldat d'Afrique – 1, Le Soldat du Bataillon d'Afrique, Le Soldat des Compagnies de discipline, Le Détenue des Prisons, Pénitenciers et Ateliers de Travaux Publics*. Paris: Henri Charles-Lavauzelle, 1912.

Commandant Ordioni. *La Réorganisation des Bataillons d'Infanterie Légère d'Afrique*. Paris: Librairie Militaire R. Chapelot et Cie., 1911.

Crépin, Annie. *Histoire de la Conscription*. Paris: Gallimard, 2009.

Dimier, Joseph. *Un Regulier Chez les Joyeux*. Paris: Bernard Grasset, 1928.

Doré, Francis. *Albert Londres N'A Rien Vu*. Paris: Eugène Figuière, 1930.

Dufour, Pierre. *Les Bat' d'Af', Les Zéphyrs et les Joyeux (1831 – 1972)*. Paris: Pygmalion, 2004.

Garros, Louis. *Historama hors serie No 10 – Les Africains*. Saint-Ouen: Chaix-Desfosses-Neogravure, 1970.

Jude, Dr. R. *Les Dégénérés dans les Bataillons d'Afrique*. Vannes: B. Le Beau, 1907.

Kalifa, Dominique. *Biribi, Les Bagnes Coloniaux de l'Armée Française*. Paris:

Perrin, 2009.
Londres, Albert. *Dante N'Avait Rien Vu*. 1924; Reprint, Paris: Arlea, 2010.
Mac Orlan, Pierre. *Le Bataillon de la Mauvaise chance, Un civil chez les "Joyeux."* Paris: Les Éditions de France, 1933.
Mangin, Charles, Lieutenant-Colonel. *La Force Noire*. Paris: Librairie Hachette et Cie., 1911.
Naudin, Bernard. "Biribi." *L'Assiette au Beurre*, 5 August 1905, p. 289-304.
Nicholson, G. W. L., Colonel. *Canadian Expeditionary Force, 1914-1919, The Official History of the Canadian Army in the First World War*. Ottawa: Queen's Printer, 1964.
Salle, Muriel. «Corps rebelles. Les tatouages des soldats des Bataillons d'Afrique dans la collection Lacassagne (1874-1924)», *Clio. Histoire, Femmes et Sociétés*, 2010, n° 26 : «Clôtures», p. 145-154.
War Office, General Staff. *Handbook of the French Army, 1914*. 1914; Reprint, Nashville: The Battery Press, 1995.

Legislation:
Code de justice militaire pour l'armée de terre (9 juin 1857), Annexes, formules, modèles et dispositions diverse. Paris: Henri Charles-Lavauzelle, 1908.
Recueil des textes législatifs en vigueur à ce jour : 21 mars 1905, 14 juillet 1906, 10 juillet 1907, 14 avril 1908, 11 avril 1910, 13 mars 1912, 6 décembre 1912 et 7 août 1913, concernant le service militaire (Recrutement de l'armée). Toulouse: Imprimerie Régionale, 1913.
Duvergier, J. B. *Code Pénal, Annoté, edition de 1832*. Paris: A. Guyot et Scribe, 1833.
Ministère de la Marine. Direction militaire des services de la flotte. Service du personnel militaire de la flotte (Bureau des équipages de la flotte). *Loi du 21 mars 1905 sur le recrutement de l'armée, modifiée par les lois des 14 avril 1906, 16 juillet 1906,10 juillet 1907, 14 avril 1908, 25 mars 1909, 22 mai 1909, 11 avril 1910, 13 mars 1912 et 30 mars 1912.* Paris: Imprimerie Nationale, 1912.

Personal Memoirs:
Attia, Nicole. *Jo Attia, mon père*. Paris: Gallimard, 1974.
Deschaume, Paul F. *Un Ch'ti chez les Joyeux, de Lille à Tataouine*. Versailles: TdB Éditions, 2008.
Taravo, Joël. *Les Derniers Joyeux, "Bat' d'Af" 1960*. Paris: La Jeune Parque, 1968.

Fictional Works:
Armandy, André. *Les Réprouves*. Paris: Librairie Alphonse Lamerre, 1930
Blanc, Julien. *Joyeux Fais ton Fourbi*. 1948; Reprint, Paris: Finitude, 2012.
Bruant, Aristide. *Aux Bat' d'Af'*. Paris: Editions Jules Tallandier, 1910.
Darien, Georges. *Biribi*. Paris: Albert Savine, 1890.
Mac Orlan, Pierre. *Le Bataillonnaire*. 1931; Reprint, Paris: Gallimard, 1989.

Internet sites:
http://www.memoiredeshommes.sga.defense.gouv.fr/

About the Author

Allan Lougheed is a graduate of the University of Toronto with degrees in History and Literary Studies. He is a former Master Bombardier in the 7th (Toronto) Regiment, Royal Canadian Artillery, of the Canadian Armed Forces Reserve. Allan is an independent researcher with a life-long passion for military history.

Coming soon:

Too Many Heroes, Volume 2: The Translated War Diaries of the *1er Régiment de Marche de Tirailleurs Algérienne*, From Mobilization to 2nd Ypres.

Two battalions of Algerian *Tirailleurs* were holding the front line at Ypres on 22 April 1915, when the first chlorine attack decimated their ranks and forced them to retreat. Despite the shock of what had just occurred, the *Tirailleurs* who were still capable of fighting fell in on the left of the Canadian lines and did what they could. Reduced to just a single battalion in the aftermath of the chlorine attack, the *1er Tirailleurs* participated in poorly planned counter-attacks that yielded no meaningful results. Since the outbreak of war, atrocious casualties and a scarcity of reinforcements had already forced their amalgamation with other regiments twice prior to the Second Battle of Ypres. In June 1915 they were amalgamated again with the *7e Zouaves* to become the *3e Régiment Mixte de Zouaves et Tirailleurs.*

More than any other solders at 2nd Ypres, it is the *Tirailleurs* that have been the target of criticism for retreating. What is forgotten in the discussion of those men, is that they were well-trained professional soldiers and highly respected within the French army. They had been sent to the Ypres Salient along with the *45e Division* to reinforce the sector with a capable, aggressive fighting formation. Tirailleurs were regarded as the conquering heroes of the French North African empire. They had always fought with distinction, in Africa, Crimea, and during the Franco-Prussian War. Like every regiment of the French army, the *1er Tirailleurs* suffered greatly from the disastrous tactics of August 1914. As a regiment, the *1er Tirailleurs* were only as good as the Officers commanding them, and like every regiment, they had to learn a whole new way of fighting. Yet the lessons they had learned could hardly have prepared them for what they would face at Ypres.

Made in the USA
Charleston, SC
17 October 2012